Inside West Virginia

Public Policy Perspectives
for the 21st Century

Inside West Virginia

Public Policy Perspectives
for the 21st Century

Bruce Keith and Ronald Althouse, Editors

West Virginia University Press

Morgantown, WV

1999

West Virginia University Press, Morgantown 26506
© 1999
All rights reserved. First edition 1999
Printed in the United States of America

Inside West Virginia: public policy perspectives for the 21st century
/ {edited by} Bruce Keith, Ronald Althouse.
Morgantown, WV: West Virginia University Press, 1999.

Library of Congress Catalog Card Number: 99-65572

ISBN 0-937058-50-5 [paperback]

Table of Contents

Appendix: West Virginia Social Indicators Survey:
  Methodology and Questionnaires

List of Tables

Table

Figure

Foreword

Legislative policies that seek to enhance economic opportunities for West Virginians must necessarily address how the state's residents are likely to react, given the context of their various social conditions. To this end, *Inside West Virginia* builds upon the macro-economic perspective previously published by Dilger and Witt (1993) with an emphasis on the various ways individuals manage their daily lives. Written with state legislators, policy planners, and research analysts in mind, the book offers a detailed examination of how public policies may succeed or fail based on West Virginians' abilities to actually realize social and economic opportunities from various social policies given the context of their varying circumstances.

Moreover, and as evidenced throughout this book, researchers located at land-grant colleges and universities are uniquely positioned to assist public agencies in the collection of data that can inform state legislators and policy planners in the design of legislative initiatives intended to benefit the public in specific ways. The book shows that cooperation among government and university centers is more likely to produce desired outcomes when the legislative process is based on research of the public that is attentive to their existing needs.

Acknowledgements

This book would not have been possible without the commitment and dedication of many people throughout the state of West Virginia. First and foremost, save for the endorsement of the West Virginia Survey Research Center by Dr. Gerald E. Lang, Provost and Vice President for Academic Affairs and Research at West Virginia University, the omnibus West Virginia Social Indicators Survey (WVSIS) would most certainly not have materialized. In his previous capacity as the Dean of the Eberly College of Arts and Sciences at WVU, Dr. Lang was instrumental in underwriting the Center's mission and research activities. His successors, Dr. Rudy Almasy and Dr. M. Duane Nellis, continued to encourage the Center's growth and financial self-reliance. Moreover, Dr. Nancy Lohmann and Dr. Richard Bajura were instrumental to the Center through their support of its mission to assist public agencies in collecting data and inform policy planners. In addition, Dr. Ruth Jackson, who recognized the usefulness of *Inside West Virginia* as a resource for understanding the relationship between public opinion and public policy, assisted us in the text's initial development and editorial revision. Finally, we are indebted to Patrick Conner and Tony Michael of the WVU Press and Kathy Hyman of the WVU Graphic Services who offered us encouragement and thoughtful guidance in bringing the text to fruition.

We are also grateful to those persons who have contributed to this book as authors, each of whom met their deadlines, patiently complied with our editorial suggestions and awaited the book's publication through various revisions. Insofar as the authors' contributions reflect their participation in the omnibus survey conducted by the Center, many holding positions as policy analysts throughout the state, they have forged an active and indelible relationship between one land-grant university and its state government for service to and the benefit of West Virginians

We willingly acknowledge our reliance on the Center's Research Associates, who have worked many long and hard hours during their tenure with us, and especially to those Graduate Research Assistants who swiftly found strong reasons for their deep dedication to "doing" good research. Their assistance was, without question, essential to the culmination of research presented throughout this text. In particular, we are grateful to Lee Beaumont, Bill Tolbert, Donna Spencer, Laura Carter, Jenny Sundra, Beth Taylor, Beverly Elswick, James Noonan, Christa Foster, Mike Wadsworth, Joe Stankovich, Lynn Spencer, Belinda Weimer, Kitty Townsend, Susan Derk, Yuling Li, and Gary Rezek. A special note of thanks is also extended to Barbara Reiprich for her untiring administrative support of the Center's projects and her willingness to overlook our shortfalls.

Author Profiles

Ronald Althouse is professor of sociology, chairperson of the Department of Sociology and Anthropology, and director of the Survey Research Center at West Virginia University, Morgantown, WV 26506-6321; e-mail: u0d28@wvnvm.wvnet.edu. His research has focused on workers' risk and workers' health, statewide health care delivery, and assessment of rural health systems. He has extensive research and consulting experience in the mining industry, including mine rescue and recovery, mine management processes, safety, and miner health. His NIOSH published study of occupational stress among underground coal miners remains the only research monograph on psycho-social aspects of miners work relations and conditions in the United States. More recently, Dr. Althouse has contributed to the literature on athletic participation, and is committed to efforts focused on social justice in sports. As Director of the University's Survey Research Center, he has consulted on an array of statewide problems and university projects, covering issues as diverse as the well-being of West Virginia's children, citizen expression of environmental risk, and changes in the court's responsibility for dealing with child abuse and neglect.

Mary McPhail Gray is associate director of cooperative extension and professor of human development and family studies at Colorado State University, 1 Adm. Building, CSU, Ft. Collins, CO. 880523-4040; e-mail: mgray@coop.ext.colostate.edu. In this position she is responsible for all state programs in Family Life, Youth Development, Natural Resources, Community Development, and Agriculture. She supervises campus faculty in five colleges: Natural Resources, Agriculture, Applied Human Sciences, Engineering, and Veterinary Medicine who develop programs for the state of Colorado. She is also responsible for evaluation of programs across the state.

Rory Fraser is an assistant professor in the Division of Forestry at West Virginia University, Morgantown, WV 26506-6125; e-mail: fraser@wvu.edu. His scholarly interests include forest policy, forest based economic development and global forestry issues. He has written on forestry policies, forest dependency and the forest industry.

Steve Hollenhorst is associate professor in the Division of Forestry at West Virginia University, Morgantown, WV 26506-6125, 304-293-3721, shollenh@wvu.edu. He is also Program Coordinator of the Recreation, Parks, and Tourism Resources Program at WVU. His scholarly interests include public land policy, environmental attitudes, and wilderness and protected areas management. He has also written extensively about the high risk and extreme sports phenomenon in American culture.

Alan Collins is associate professor in the Division of Resource Management at West Virginia University, Morgantown, WV 26506-6108; e-mail: acollins@wvu.edu. He serves as ndergraduate Coordinator for the Agricultural and Resource Economics Program at WVU. His research interests include environmental issues related to water resources, recycling of solid and agricultural wastes, and the use of pesticides on fruit orchards. He has written over 40 professional publications, many as a part of multidisciplinary efforts.

Renate Pore is a health policy analyst with the office of the vice-chancellor for health sciences of the University System of West Virginia in Charleston, 1018 Kanawha Blvd. East, Suite 1100, Charleston, WV 25301-2827; e-mail: pore@scusco.wvnet.edu. She works with higher education, state agencies, and community groups on health care policy issues related to insurance coverage and children's health. She is the project director of the W.K. Kellogg-funded West Virginia community Voices Project to improve health care access for under-served people.

Daniel M. Christy, M.P.A. is Director of the State Health Statistics Center, WV State Health Department, 1411 Virginia St., Room 142, Charleston, WV 25301; e-mail: danchristy@wvdhhr.org. Prior to 1996, he worked in various capacities within state public health planning, including, community health promotion, health reform information management planning, interagency data systems coordination, Healthy People 2000 planning, and health survey research activities. Prior to 1989, Mr. Christy served as the state drug control and violent crime program specialist, and worked for nearly a decade in community development activities including parks and recreation, fairgrounds management, county government, and hospital public relations and marketing.

Bruce Keith is assistant dean for academic assessment and associate professor of sociology at the United States Military Academy, Office of the Dean (MADN-AAD), West Point, NY 10996; e-mail: zb9599@exmail.usma.edu. His areas of specialization include the sociology of science with an emphasis on institutional status and graduates' career patterns and educational administration with a focus on student learning outcomes and institutional quality. Previously, he served as a member of the faculty at West Virginia University where he was instrumental in directing the development of the West Virginia Social Indicators Survey.

Josh Masnick Kim is a visiting assistant professor in the Department of Sociology and Anthropology at West Virginia University, Morgantown, WV 26506-6321. He received his Ph.D. from Brown University in 1999. Dr. Kim is married and is the father of two young children.

Sally Ward Maggard is National Program Leader-Rural Sociology, Economic and Community Systems, CSREES, U.S. Department of Agriculture; e-mail: u0c97@wvnvm.wvnet.edu. She is also currently serving as the editor of the Journal of Appalachian Studies. Her research centers on economic and social development of lagging regions, including the Central Appalachian and Hungarian coal fields. She has published on economic restructuring, labor organizing, social protest, public education, and the intersections of class, gender, and race. She has held research fellowships and grants from the Pro Kultura Foundation of Hungary, American Association of University Women, Business and Professional Women's Research Foundation, Mellon Foundation, Rockefeller Foundation, and Kentucky Foundation for Women. She is currently on leave from West Virginia University where she is associate professor of sociology, adjunct associate professor of history, a faculty research associate at the Regional Research Institute, and Women's Studies Faculty Associate.

F. Carson Menken is an assistant professor of sociology in the Department of Sociology and Anthropology at West Virginia University, West Virginia University, Morgantown, WV 26506-6326; e-mail: fmencken@wvu.edu. His research focuses on the spatial aspects of economic growth and development. Much of Dr. Mencken's research is conducted on the Appalachian region. His related research articles can be found in *The Sociological Quarterly, Sociological Focus, The Journal of Appalachian Studies,* and *Growth and Change.*

Chapter 1

The Role of Social Research in Public Policy Administration: Linking Land-Grant Universities to State Policy Initiatives

Bruce Keith and Ronald Althouse

While an important dimension of social well-being is economic opportunity, the purpose of this book is to balance the macro-economic perspective of West Virginia, as in the seminal study by Dilger and Witt (1993), with an emphasis on the various ways individuals manage their lives within existing social conditions. Implicit in this book is the realization that all persons do not share common experiences, but that personal concerns often reflect varying social circumstances. Public policies that are ideologically grounded operate under a set of assumptions about how society functions. Yet frequently absent from such policies is a critical examination of how subsequent implementation may differentially affect the social and economic opportunities of persons within the policy domain. Consequently, legislative policies that attempt to create opportunities for economic progress must address both macro-economic concerns and remain attentive to the manner in which individuals from various social conditions are likely to be affected by implementation.

This challenge in the formulation of public policy is evident in the following illustration. A policy aimed at assisting households with dependents through tax relief is unlikely to address the daily child care needs of working women with dependent children. Many women with dependent children earn an income insufficient to place them above the poverty line and must often choose between work and child care. Similarly, the structural dimension of work is likely to produce differential effects on families based on the type of work undertaken (White and Keith 1995), ethnic characteristics of the persons involved (Rexroat 1995), and changes in the availability of occupations within a particular market sector (Johnson and Booth 1988).

These factors underscore the important relationship that should be continuously nurtured between centers of social research located at land-grant universities and various governmental agencies within their respective states. Instead of operating in a separate sphere from that of government, land-grant universities are uniquely positioned to assist public agencies in the collection of data that are of use, ultimately, to residents of the state.

The results of such research can inform state legislators and policy planners with the type of empirical detail necessary to carefully craft legislative initiatives intended to benefit the public in specific ways. This type of cooperation is more likely to produce desired outcomes because the legislative process is based on research of the public and is attentive to their current needs.

Central to this study is a focus on the health and well-being of West Virginians as experienced through their daily lives. Specific needs that are examined include health care, physical activity, child care, environmental protection, economic opportunities, and informal economic activity. Each of the book's chapters focuses on a specific aspect of social and economic well-being using data collected through the West Virginia Social Indicators Survey: an annual omnibus study assessing the quality of life in West Virginia. Each chapter highlights a specific social issue with a discussion of existing public policy and policy initiatives that could improve the lives of West Virginians. This study approaches the quality of life issue in this manner because of the interconnected nature of physical and human infrastructure. While a highly productive workforce, clearly desired in West Virginia, requires healthy individuals and a resolution of dependent care concerns (Dilger and Witt 1993), attention should also be directed toward the varying social conditions within which these macro-social outcomes can be realized. As the state of West Virginia moves into the twenty-first century, there is a critical need to develop an economic vision that incorporates a solid understanding of the quality of life and health conditions currently experienced by all West Virginians. Public policy initiatives that account for the intersection of micro-level human needs with macro-level concerns are more likely to create direct paths toward that vision.

In a previous research study, Dilger and Witt (1993) argued that both government and private investment in the physical and human infrastructures of West Virginia were necessary in order for the state to become regionally competitive in economic investment and growth. They suggested that the state adopt an economic development strategy formulated by the 1992 Commission on the Future of the South based on a set of ten general recommendations. To this end, effective implementation of all ten recommendations will require a needs assessment of the state's population to understand the economic, health, education, and familial concerns of various segments of the population as they pertain to policy initiatives. The present inquiry, in building on the work of Dilger and Witt (1993), argues that specific policy recommendations must account for differential needs and experiences in order to produce desired outcomes. For example, upgrading education and training programs will aid in the improvement of the state's overall economic condition only if residents from all social and regional strata are able to overcome the diverse health, familial, and economic obstacles that currently characterize the social structure of the state.

Strategies for Assessing the Needs of West Virginians

Several design strategies are available to researchers to identify social needs and concerns of a population. Those likely to yield the most accurate data will rely on individuals from various regions throughout the state to report their concerns or needs and to quantitatively document these concerns and needs. In that respect, while community focus groups or local studies may provide insights into the concerns voiced by persons in localities throughout the state, the primary disadvantage of that research strategy is the inability of researchers to draw generalizations about regional or state populations or to meaningfully compare findings from one locality to that of others.

As an alternative research approach, the telephone survey is based on a random sample of a state's population. While telephone surveys are quite expensive in comparison with other methodological approaches, they generally produce results that are more valid across respondents, the results of which are generalizable to specific populations within known margins of error (Dillman 1978; Lavrakas 1993; Warwick and Lininger 1975). Consequently, a balance between telephone surveys and personal interviews with local groups is generally advisable for an accurate assessment of a state's social needs.

Social indicator studies incorporate the strengths of the telephone research design with a focus on monitoring the well-being of residents in a particular population. The underlying objective of such studies is to investigate social concerns and present the findings to policy planners and government officials in an effort to solve prevalent social problems. Social indicator studies also provide a single base of data comparable over time and across regions to assist government officials in making more informed decisions about perplexing social issues.

The West Virginia Social Indicators Survey

The West Virginia Social Indicators Survey (WVSIS), on which this book is based, is designed to meet the diverse needs of researchers at public agencies and policy planners within the state of West Virginia. The survey annually gathers current information about the social and economic conditions of West Virginians and monitors changes in the quality of their lives over time. This survey is quite similar to several other state and national public opinion surveys that are routinely used to gather information about public perceptions, quality of life, and economic conditions of people residing within their respective regions.

The WVSIS is administered by staff at West Virginia University's Survey Research Center with a detailed technical methodology report written annually to explain the manner in which data were collected during a given year (see Keith 1993, 1994; Keith, Carter, and Townsend 1995; Keith, Carter, and Farmer 1996; Foster and Wadsworth 1997). The instrument and design selection for the WVSIS is structured to accommodate the needs of various researchers. Initially, a set of "core" questions was developed with the intention of repeating these questions in subsequent years, thereby providing a longitudinal basis of comparison. These core items, asked of all respondents annually, include demographic information on households and individuals as well as indicators on economic and political participation, residential mobility, and community satisfaction. Selected items provide information of most use to policy planners at the state and local levels and provide maximum comparability with other state and national social indicator data. A detailed description of the survey's methodology is presented in Appendix A; copies of the questionnaires from 1993 to 1997 are included in Appendix B through F.

Each year, a random sample of the state's population is drawn for the WVSIS and consists of non-institutionalized persons residing in West Virginia who live in households with telephones during the survey period. Persons under 18 years of age, persons in custodial institutions, transient visitors to the state, and persons without telephones are excluded from the sampling frame. One drawback to this design is that the sampling frame does not represent the characteristics of persons without telephones, commonly the least affluent members of the state. But recent evidence suggests that at least 90 percent of the state's population have one or more telephones (Charleston Gazette 1994). In drawing a random sample of telephone numbers, the WVSIS employs a Random Digit Dialing (RDD) technique (for more information see, Lavrakas 1993; Waksberg 1978). This technique has been carefully evaluated for its validity and found to produce results of comparable quality and representativeness to conventional sampling procedures but at a significantly lower cost (Groves 1989; Groves and Kahn 1979; Sudman 1983).

Since the WVSIS is intended to be representative of both households and individuals, care is taken to ensure that each person in the household has a known and equal probability of selection. To alleviate sampling errors associated with interviews of persons who initially answer the telephone, respondent selection techniques are employed (Kish 1965; Lavrakas 1993) that select the designated respondent from among all eligible persons in the household. If the designated respondent is not available for the interview at the time of the initial contact, an alternative time is scheduled and a return call is made.

Outline and Scope of the Study

This book is composed of two general sections. Part I examines the social circumstances of West Virginians' and the management of their daily lives, with a focus on health, physical well-being, and dependent care of family members. Part II examines economic structures and individual opportunities in West Virginia during the 1990s. The text has been organized in this manner to address social concerns of most importance throughout the state. Within these categories, the authors define specific problems that necessitate the need for better understanding of effective implementation of economic policies within the state.

The first section consists of three chapters. One of the chapters examines social concerns related to the daily care of dependent family members while two others focus on health related issues among West Virginians. In Chapter 2, Keith and Gray offer policy recommendations intended to reduce declines in worker productivity that are attributable to child care needs. In Chapter 3, Wright addresses preventative health care through an examination of West Virginians' daily physical activity and exercise routines and barriers to such activity. In Chapter 4, Christi and Pore examine the extent to which West Virginians have access to health insurance and identify areas where potential problems persist among households in the state. Actively involved in the legislative bills that are considered by the West Virginia Legislature on health reform, their analysis is tied directly to policy initiatives and concerns regarding health care.

Part II examines the micro-economic trends and needs of West Virginians in light of proposed macro-economic policies. In Chapter 5, Kim and Mencken analyze changes in economic trends and employment opportunities among West Virginians during the 1990s. By concentrating on economic and residential mobility patterns based on the self-reports of individuals in the state, they have been able to offer recommendations from both economic and social perspectives. In Chapter 6, Mencken and Maggard examine informal economic activity among West Virginians, particularly focusing on households' participation in and reliance on informal labor markets. Such markets include agriculture, hunting, and barter economies and may represent an economic sector that has largely been overlooked among policy decision-makers within the state. In Chapter 7, Fraser, Hollenhorst, and Collins examine West Virginians' environmental concerns and their faith in government as an instrument for insuring that environmental protections are equitably distributed across society. Their discovery of a unique form of environmentalism in West Virginia, in which concern and activism are highest among the state's poor, rural, female, and elderly, is contrary to most literature on the subject and offers important policy implications for managing economic needs with environmental concerns.

The common theme connecting these chapters throughout the book is the focus on public policy initiatives in relation to micro-level social issues. Given the large scope of legislative policy concerns and space limitations of research reports, only a few policy areas deserving of attention could be examined in this study. Nonetheless, important insights are offered to social researchers who are interested in improving the understanding of the needs and concerns of West Virginians and to policy planners who must translate these concerns into effective public policy. Throughout this book, the primary objective has been to bring together researchers and public policy planners in an effort to examine how the development and implementation of statewide policies can be improved through detailed understandings of the diverse experiences of individuals throughout the state.

Ultimately, the challenge for researchers and policy decision makers alike is to transform the findings of public opinion research into legislative policies that will benefit all West Virginians regardless of their social circumstances. In this manner, the land-grant university, and other research agencies, may be an instrument of considerable importance to state administrators in their efforts to fully understand the relative impact various social conditions may have on public policy legislation intended to enhance economic progress throughout the state of West Virginia. Our hope is that this text represents only the first of many such collaborative efforts between university personnel and state policy analysts, undertaken for the sole purpose of benefitting West Virginians through the creation of public policies that represent their social diversity and unique circumstances.

References

Charleston Gazette. 1994. "1 out of 10 W.Va. homes lack phone, survey shows." Thursday, 18 August. p. 5A.

Dilger, Robert Jay and Tom Stuart Witt. 1993. *West Virginia in the 1990s: Opportunities for Economic Progress.* Morgantown: West Virgina University Press.

Dillman, Don A. 1978. *Mail and Telephone Surveys: The Total Design Method.* New York: Wiley and Sons.

Foster, Christa and Michael Wadsworth. 1997 *The 1996 WVSIS Methodology Report: Sample Design, Questionnaire, and Technical Forms.* Morgantown, WV: West Virginia University Survey Research Center.

Groves, Robert M. 1989. *Survey Errors and Survey Costs.* New York: Wiley and Sons.

Groves, Robert and Robert L. Kahn. 1979. *Surveys by Telephone: A National Comparison with Personal Interviews.* New York: Academic Press.

Johnson, David R. and Alan Booth. 1988. "Rural Economic Decline and Marital Quality: A Panel Study of Farm Marriages. *Family Relations.* 39:159–165.

Keith, Bruce. 1993. *The 1992 WVSIS Methodology Report: Sample Design, Questionnaire, and Technical Forms.* Morgantown, WV: West Virginia University Survey Research Center.

______. 1994. *The 1993 WVSIS Methodology Report: Sample Design, Questionnaire, and Technical Forms.* Morgantown, WV: West Virginia University Survey Research Center.

Keith, Bruce, Laura Carter, and Kitty Townsend. 1995. *The 1994 WVSIS Methodology Report: Sample Design, Questionnaire, and Technical Forms.* Morgantown, WV: West Virginia University Survey Research Center.

Keith, Bruce, Laura Carter, and Karen Farmer. 1995. *The 1995 WVSIS Methodology Report: Sample Design, Questionnaire, and Technical Forms.* Morgantown, WV: West Virginia University Survey Research Center.

Kish, Leslie. 1965. *Survey Sampling.* New York: Wiley and Sons.

Lavrakas, Paul. 1993. *Telephone Survey Methods: Sampling, Selection, and Supervision.* Newbury Park: Sage.

Rexroat, Cynthia. 1995. "Race and Marital Status Differences in the Labor Force Behavior of Female Family Heads: The Effect of Household Structure.", in Gary L. Bowen and Joe F. Pittman (eds.), The Work *and Family Interface: Toward A Contextual Effects Perspective.* Minneapolis: National Council on Family Relations.

Sudman, Seymour. 1983. "Applied Sampling.", in Peter H. Rossi, James D. Wright, and Andy B. Anderson (eds.), *Handbook of Survey Research.* San Diego: Academic Press.

Waksberg, Joseph. 1978. "Sampling Methods for Random Digit Dialing." *Journal of the American Statistical Association.* 73:40–46.

Warwick, Donald P. and Charles A. Lininger. 1975. *The Sample Survey: Theory and Practice.* New York: McGraw-Hill.

White, Lynn and Bruce Keith. 1995. "The Effect of Shift Work and the Quality and Stability of Marital Relations.", in Gary L. Bowen and Joe F. Pittman (eds.), The Work *and Family Interface: Toward A Contextual Effects Perspective.* Minneapolis: National Council on Family Relations.

Chapter 2

The Prevalence of Child Care Needs Among West Virginia Households

Bruce Keith and Mary McPhail Gray

Abstract

Quality child care is a social problem because of its widespread effects on children, households, businesses, and communities. This chapter documents the demand for such care in West Virginia and argues for a multidimensional solution to ensure that child care provisions are accessible, affordable, flexible, and of high quality. Five public policy recommendations, which follow from the discussion of the analysis, emphasize the importance of governmental regulation of child care providers, job flexibility plans, employer provided care facilities, paid maternity leave, and the creation of cooperative child care facilities.

Introduction

This chapter examines the prevalence of child care needs among West Virginia households and offers recommendations to assist policy planners in breaking down barriers that may impede access. In order to be of use to persons involved in child care assessment and policy planning within the state, this chapter is organized around three key areas: potential demand, current status of child care, and the relation of child care to income levels. The first section of the chapter estimates the potential demand for child care in West Virginia and identifies the number and percentage of households at risk, (i.e., the percentage of the state's population requiring some form of child care during 1993). The second section examines child care needs and arrangements for households with children under twelve years of age. Issues addressed include characteristics of child care providers, location of child care arrangements, and distance from child's home and parents' place of employment. Also examined is the proximity of the care provider's location to the child's school and mode of transportation used to transport the child to this location. The third section presents an overview of child care needs among various income levels, focusing particularly on households of single parents.

Child Care as a Social and Institutional Problem: National Trends

In recent years, demand for child care has increased dramatically throughout the United States. Part of this greater demand is undoubtedly due to the increased levels of female employment where the percentage of labor force participation among women with children under six years of age jumped 54 percent between 1975 and 1994. In 1975, 39 percent of women with pre-school children were employed; this figure reached 60 percent by 1994 (Gormley 1995).

In economic terms, increased demand creates a need for new markets that is often satisfied by enterprising entrepreneurs. Unfortunately, in the case of child care, an economic paradox arises such that those who would most benefit from the expansion of quality centers are generally the least likely to be able to afford them. This trend occurs because the lower limit of the fertility interval containing the most productive child bearing ages is located precisely during those years when average annual income levels are predictably at their lowest. Consequently, responsibilities associated with child care, employment, and citizenship become competitive rather than complimentary, thus producing a problem that extends far beyond the individual. In effect, the child care problem in America dramatically impacts employers, governmental regulatory agencies, and communities.

In her 1989 presidential address to the American Demographic Association, Harriet Presser, a noted sociologist, outlined how child care affects many different facets of social life. In particular, she identified the following concerns:

- A large majority of children are placed in care arrangements for extended intervals of time.
- Access to quality care is restrictive because the child care industry is characterized by extremely low wages (child care workers are the second lowest paid workers in the US after controlling for education and expenses).
- Turnover in child care facilities is very high, producing low stability in the daily routines of children who utilize these centers.
- Parents lose work time in order to care for children who are either sick, and cannot be placed with their regular provider, or because they are distracted on the job due to genuine concerns over their childrens' well-being.

- Quality child care, when it is available, is often prohibitively expensive for parents of young children. Researchers have defined quality as care with low child/staff ratios, small groups, and well-trained and educated providers.
- Parents of young children often have difficulty balancing the responsibilities of citizenship with parenthood. The resulting decisions to spend time with children produces less involvement with parents' respective communities, creating a widening gulf between family and society.

These circumstances present governments (both in their capacities as regulatory agencies and policy planners), businesses, and communities with a set of challenges directed toward the well-being of children; in fact, the children represent our very future. In this regard, child care represents a multi-dimensional problem, socially and institutionally, that must collectively involve representatives from both the private and public sectors if viable solutions are to be advanced. Literature is replete with evidence that the physical and intellectual development of our children requires a nurturing, stable environment that is both stimulating and interactive (see, e.g., Belsky's (1991) discussion and extensive bibliography). The fundamental question that arises is, who will pay for basic quality care provisions that protect the well-being of children?

One could argue from a conservative business perspective that such care is entirely the responsibility of parents who choose to enter the workforce instead of dividing the division of labor between domestic and economic work. After all, why should businesses and government pay for something that is beyond their purview? Critics of this perspective contend that the notion of work is quite gendered historically and that the culture of women's work is characterized most notably by employment that varies by social class position and ethnic background (Amott and Matthaei 1991; Ferree 1991), that women have always worked, in many cases double-shifts (Hochschild 1989), that women's work benefits the economy and labor supply (Ferree 1991; Skold 1988), and that the real problem is not so much female labor force participation but structural impediments to accessibility of quality child care (Presser 1989; Skold 1988).

The reality is that provision of quality child care benefits children, parents, employers, and communities alike. Children benefit through the maintenance of an environment that is supportive of growth. Parents benefit through enhanced access to care and flexibility of job schedules that allow their households to meet basic economic needs. Businesses benefit as a result of an increased labor pool and higher worker productivity. Governments become the regulatory bodies that must ensure child care providers actually offer the requisite care. If quality child care is to become both accessible and affordable, much like a basic education, all of these groups must pay. For the population of West Virginia, the underlying questions must certainly involve issues of demand and types of providers.

Data and Analysis

Data employed in this study are derived from the 1993 West Virginia Social Indicator Survey (Keith 1993). Issues concerning collection of these data, including sampling design, respondent selection, and representatives of the survey, are cited in Appendix A. Variables used in this analysis are represented by 24 items included on the questionnaire (see Appendix F, questions 103–126), that requested information on each household's need for and use of child care arrangements. These questions were asked of respondents only if the household contained children twelve years of age and younger. A total of 506 of the 1,882 households interviewed reported the presence of one or more children twelve years of age or younger (27 percent).

This analysis will be presented in three sections; these include the potential demand for child care in West Virginia, existing child care arrangements, and variations in care income level and single-parent status. A discussion of the results will follow from the analysis, leading to a set of policy recommendations.

The potential demand for child care in West Virginia.

According to the 1990 U.S. decennial Census of West Virginia, 129,438 persons less than six years of age comprise seven percent of the total state population of 1,793,477 as shown in Table 1 below. Findings from the 1994 WVSIS found that 276 households, or 15 percent of the sample of 1,882 households, contained one or more children below the age of six. Inferring these findings to the state population translates into approximately 103,284 out of the 688,557 households in West Virginia that contain children in this age category. Sixty percent of the households with children below the age of six in the survey reported using some type of child care. Generalizing to the state-wide population, approximately 61,970 of the 103,284 households with children below age six rely on some type of child care arrangement.

The 1990 U.S. Census revealed that 172,582 persons between the ages of six and twelve account for ten percent of the state's total population. Findings from the 1994 WVSIS indicate that 346 households, or 18 percent of the WVSIS sample, contain children between ages six and twelve. Generalizing these findings to the state population produces an estimate of

123,940 households in West Virginia containing one or more children within this interval. The WVSIS revealed that 42 percent of households with children between the ages of six and twelve report the use of some type of child care arrangement. Applying this percentage to the state population produces an estimate of 52,055 of the 123,940 households with children in this age category that would need to rely on child care.

Table 2-1:
Age Distributions for Children By States Bordering West Virginia

Location	Number/Percentage of Children Under Six	Number/Percentage of Children Six to Twelve
West Virginia	129,438 (7.2%)	172,582 (10.0%)
Kentucky	302,844 (8.2%)	381,727 (10.4%)
Maryland	427,274 (8.9%)	447,014 (9.4%)
Ohio	945,545 (8.7%)	1,107,410 (10.2%)
Pennsylvania	956,721 (8.1%)	1,092,388 (9.2%)
Virginia	530,531 (8.6%)	582,311 (9.4%)

Some overlap obviously exists between the 103,284 estimated households with children under age six and the 123,940 households estimated to contain children between the ages of six and twelve. The WVSIS revealed that 116 of the 622 households containing children within these two age intervals have two or more children that are both less than six years of age and six to twelve years old, a 19 percent overlap. Using this estimate to generalize to the state population, we find that approximately 43,173 of the 227,224 households with children in either age group contain them for both age intervals. Hence, approximately 184,051 total households in West Virginia contain an estimated 280,615 children twelve years of age or younger. This represents an average of 1.53 children under 13 years of age in these households.

Table 2 presents information from the WVSIS on the proportion of child care usage in West Virginia broken down by the age of child. The proportion of households using child care is greater for those with children under six than that of households with children six to twelve years of age, at 60 and 42 percent respectively. The WVSIS finds that the two to three year age group contains the highest percentage of households using a care provider at 64 percent, and that the ten–twelve year age group is the lowest at 39 percent. The average number of different providers giving care to children is found to range between 1 and 20 for children under six, with the largest mean reported for children under two at 2.83 different providers. The mean number of care providers steadily declines for each age group until the ten-twelve year age group, which increases to 2.35 providers. The fifth column in Table 2 reveals that over one-quarter, and in many instances nearly one-third, of all households using child care have relied on three or more care providers. The final column in Table 2 reveals that a very small percentage of households actually use the services of a care provider who is registered by the state of West Virginia. Twenty percent of households with children under age six and maintaining a child care provider report that this person is registered by the state. This figure further decreases for households with children age six to twelve with 16 percent of them indicating the provider is registered. Households with children under two, at 9 percent, are least likely to use such a person while households with children ages four-five, at 29 percent, are most likely to rely on a registered provider. The percentage of households employing a registered child care specialist steadily increases from the under age two category to the four to five age category, after which it declines rather dramatically leveling off around 12 percent.

Table 2-2:
Proportion of Child Care Usage in West Virginia by Age of Child

Age of child	Proportion of households using a care provider	Average number of providers	Range in number of providers	Percentage with 3 or more providers	Percentage of providers registered by state
Under 2	56% (58/104)	2.83	(1 - 20)	31%	9% (5/58)
2 - 3	64% (73/114)	2.27	(1 - 12)	29%	21% (15/73)
4 - 5	61% (77/127)	2.11	(1 - 9)	29%	29% (22/77)
6 - 7	44% (52/118)	2.03	(1 - 8)	27%	14% (7/52)
8 - 9	46% (56/122)	1.93	(1 - 8)	23%	14% (8/56)
10 - 12	39% (76/195)	2.35	(1 - 21)	30%	12% (9/76)

Child Care Arrangements.

Child care is typically required due to employment patterns of one or both parents. This is certainly true among households with child care needs in West Virginia. Table 3 below shows that for all age categories, over two-thirds of all child care needs result from parental employment patterns. For children under age six, 73 percent of all households with child care needs reported that child care provisions were necessary due to parental employment.

Table 2-3:
Child Care Needs Due to Parental Employment

Age of child	Child care needed due to parental employment	Both parents working	Only father employed	Only mother employed	Number of cases
Under 2	66% (38/58)	79% (30)	11% (4)	8% (3/38)	38
2 - 3	77% (56/73)	79% (44)	12% (7)	9% (5/56)	56
4 - 5	75% (58/77)	74% (43)	14% (8)	12% (7/58)	58
6 - 7	62% (32/52)	76% (25)	6% (2)	18% (6/33)	33
8 - 9	70% (39/56)	64% (25)	15% (6)	21% (8/39)	39
10 - 12	67% (51/76)	61% (31)	14% (7)	25% (13/51)	51

Sixty-seven percent of households containing children ages six to twelve and requiring care provisions reported that this need arises due to parental employment. In most cases, child care is required because both parents work, but a noticeable proportion of care is needed when either the father or mother is employed. For children under six years of age, 11 percent of the households require child care due to parental employment, and only the mother is employed. This figure increases to 22 percent for households with children six to twelve years of age. While the number of cases is quite small in the "only mother employed" category, the data reveal that most of these women are single working mothers. As such, 11–25 percent of all households that require child care due to parental employment do so because they are headed by women with dependent children.

A considerable proportion of child care is provided within a relatively short distance of the father's or mother's workplace. Over half of all child care arrangements occur within ten miles of the father's workplace, for both children under six and those between the ages of six and twelve. As shown in Table 4, similar patterns are found across age categories, with 20 percent of all care arrangements taking place 25 or more miles from the father's workplace.

Table 2-4:
Number of Miles from Father's Workplace

Miles from Home	Age of Child					
	Under 2	2 – 3	4 – 5	6 –7	8 – 9	10 – 12
Less than one	3% (1)	8% (4)	4% (2)	4% (1)	6% (2)	3% (1)
1-5	38% (13)	29% (15)	34% (18)	44% (12)	29% (9)	37% (14)
6-10	29% (10)	19% (10)	28% (15)	33% (9)	13% (4)	21% (8)
11-19	15% (5)	21% (11)	17% (9)	15% (4)	26% (8)	18% (7)
Greater than 20	6% (2)	15% (8)	8% (4)	4% (1)	13% (4)	13% (5)
Missing Data	9% (3)	6% (3)	9% (5)	— (0)	13% (4)	8% (3)

A comparison of employment patterns of men and women suggest that women work in closer proximity to the location of their child's care provider than their male counterparts. Table 5 reveals that nearly three-quarters (72%) of all employed women with child care arrangements are within ten miles of the providers location, a 32 percent increase over their male counterparts. This is true regardless of the child's age category. In addition, only 14 percent of all employed women with dependent children work farther than 25 miles away from their child care provider's location as compared to 20 percent of the men, resulting in an increase of 43 percent.

When asked whether the respondent or his/her spouse, where applicable, had ever left a job because of child care, 13 percent of households with children present twelve years of age or younger answered in the affirmative. Table 6 suggests that households with older children (ages 2–12) were more likely to answer yes to this question, but such difficulties could have occurred at a much earlier period in time. What is clear from Table 6 is that employers in West Virginia are not likely to provide any information about child care to employees who are parents of dependent children. When information is provided, it is much likely to be about existing places rather than offering a benefits package or providing a child care center at

Table 2-5:
Number of Miles from Mother's Workplace

Miles from Home	Age of Child					
	Under 2	2 – 3	4 – 5	6 –7	8 – 9	10 – 12
Less than one	3% (1)	2% (1)	4% (2)	10% (3)	3% (1)	9% (4)
1-5	66% (23)	58% (28)	42% (21)	37% (11)	31% (10)	34% (15)
6-10	14% (5)	21% (10)	26% (13)	27% (8)	34% (11)	36% (16)
11-19	6% (2)	4% (2)	16% (8)	20% (6)	19% (6)	12% (5)
Greater than 20	— (0)	13% (6)	6% (3)	6% (2)	10% (3)	7% (3)
Missing Data	11% (4)	2% (1)	6% (3)	— (0)	3% (2)	2% (1)

the workplace. Employers are even less likely to give some type of financial aid to offset some of the costs associated with the child care needs of their employees. Those that do offer financial assistance are much more likely to provide pre-tax spending options over vouchers or sliding scale arrangements.

The majority of child care is provided by relatives and friends both for children below the ages of six and between the ages of six and twelve. A much smaller percentage of households with children in either age-inter-

Table 2-6:
Job Difficulties and Employer Assistance

Age of child	Left job due to child care difficulties	Child care information provided by employer	Financial aid given by employer
Under 2	5% (3/58)	9% (5/58)	5% (3/58)
2 - 3	14% (10/73)	9% (6/67)	4% (3/67)
4 - 5	10% (8/77)	8% (6/75)	8% (6/75)
6 - 7	17% (9/52)	4% (2/48)	2% (1/48)
8 - 9	11% (6/56)	7% (4/56)	4% (2/56)
10 - 12	16% (12/76)	7% (5/72)	3% (2/72)

val is likely to rely on professional child care providers. Table 7 below examines the question of who actually provides care by age breakdowns. Overall, 76 percent of households with children under six who rely on a care arrangement turn to relatives and friends. This figure increases to 82 percent for children between the ages of six and twelve. Breaking down the primary care provider by the six categories associated with age of the child reveals that relatives and friends are the first choice in over 70 percent of households, regardless of a child's age. However, the use of professional care givers is highest for children below the age of six and is most pronounced among households containing children in the two to three and four to five age groups. Fourteen (14) and 21 percent of these households were found to use professional care givers respectively. Professionals are employed less often for children above the age of six.

Table 2-7:
Who Provides Care?: Primary Care Provider by Age of Child

Primary Care Provider	Age of Child					
	Under 2	2 – 3	4 – 5	6 –7	8 – 9	10 – 12
Relative	62% (36)	47% (34)	54% (42)	58% (30)	66% (37)	68% (52)
Friend	17% (10)	26% (19)	17% (13)	23% (12)	14% (8)	17% (13)
In-House Sitter	8% (5)	7% (5)	8% (6)	6% (3)	9% (5)	3% (2)
Professional	10% (6)	14% (10)	21% (16)	8% (4)	7% (4)	7% (5)
Other, Unspecified	3% (2)	4% (3)	— (0)	2% (1)	2% (1)	1% (1)
Missing Data	2% (2)	— (0)	— (0)	4% (2)	2% (1)	4% (3)

For households that have children either under six years of age or between six and twelve, the children are more likely to be cared for in someone else's home, with 53.5 percent and 62.3 percent of households reporting this trend respectively. Also noteworthy is the finding that children ages six to twelve are less than half as likely to be cared for in a child care facility than are children under six years of age.

A detailed age breakdown of the location of care is addressed in Table 8 below. Over 50 percent of child care is given in a home other than the child's; 52 percent of all households containing children under six and 61 percent containing children ages six to twelve, placing them in such an arrangement. This coincides with the findings reported in Table 7 where a large proportion of care is provided by relatives and friends of the families. As seen in Table 8, the child's home is more likely to be the location where care is administered for children below the age of two. Older children are frequently cared for in someone else's home. Toddlers and pre-school age children are the ones most often found in child care facilities, with 14 and 18 percent respectively of households containing children in these age groups relying on centers.

Table 2-8:
Where is Care Provided?: Location of Care by Age of Child

Primary Care Location	Age of Child					
	Under 2	2 – 3	4 – 5	6 –7	8 – 9	10 – 12
Child's Home	43% (25)	31% (23)	33% (25)	30% (16)	27% (15)	34% (26)
Someone Else's Home	48% (28)	55% (40)	49% (38)	60% (31)	70% (39)	59% (45)
Child Care Facility	9% (5)	14% (10)	18% (14)	10% (5)	3% (2)	3% (2)
Other Place, Unspecified	— (0)	— (0)	— (0)	— (0)	— (0)	4% (3)

Many children are placed with a child care provider for less than ten hours per week, especially children between the ages of six and twelve, with 73.9 percent of this age group being placed with a provider between one and ten hours per week. The hours children are left in child care arrangements varies depending on the age of the child. The majority of children under six years of age remain with their providers over ten hours per week. Fifty-seven (57) percent of these children spend more than ten hours with their providers weekly, and 23 percent spend over 31 hours with their providers per week.

Table 9 breaks down the number of hours child care is provided by the age of the child. Clearly, children under the age of six spend more time with care givers than do school-age children. To illustrate, nearly 30 percent of all children under the age of six spend 30 or more hours a week with a care provider as compared with six (6) percent of their school-age counterparts. By contrast 74 percent of school-age children in a child care arrangement spend less than ten hours with a care provider as compared with 43 percent of the children under six years of age.

Table 2-9:
Number of Total Hours Each Week Child Care is Provided

Weekly Hours	Age of Child					
	Under 2	2 – 3	4 – 5	6 –7	8 – 9	10 – 12
1 – 5	31% (18)	29% (22)	22% (17)	65% (34)	66% (37)	50% (38)
6 – 10	29% (17)	14% (10)	13% (10)	13% (7)	11% (6)	22% (17)
11 – 19	17% (10)	6% (5)	17% (13)	10% (5)	14% (8)	9% (7)
20 – 29	13% (8)	18% (13)	17% (13)	4% (2)	2% (1)	— (0)
30 – 39	17% (10)	11% (8)	6% (5)	— (0)	— (0)	1% (1)
Greater than 40	10% (6)	19% (14)	22% (17)	8% (4)	2% (1)	7% (5)
Missing Data	2% (1)	1% (1)	3% (2)	— (0)	5% (4)	11% (6)

Nearly 80 percent of households utilizing some form of child care arrangement keep the child at home or within five miles of home (see Table 10). Younger children are frequently kept in the home or within a short distance from the home in comparison with their school-age counterparts. While children six to twelve years of age are frequently cared for at or near their homes, considerably higher proportions are with providers six or more miles from home.

School-age children, those six to twelve years of age, who are placed in child care arrangements typically receive care after school. Forty-one

Table 2-10:
Number of Miles from Child's Home that Care is Given

Miles from Home	Age of Child					
	Under 2	2 – 3	4 – 5	6 –7	8 – 9	10 – 12
Home Care	43% (25)	32% (23)	32% (25)	31% (16)	27% (15)	34% (26)
0-5	40% (23)	48% (35)	57% (44)	50% (26)	57% (32)	46% (35)
6-10	9% (5)	8% (6)	4% (3)	17% (9)	11% (6)	16% (12)
11-19	2% (1)	8% (6)	4% (3)	2% (1)	5% (3)	3% (2)
Greater than 20	7% (4)	4% (3)	3% (2)	— (0)	— (0)	1% (1)

percent of these children arrive at the child care site via a school bus, while 47 percent are picked-up at school, and 12 percent walk to the site. The average distance from school to the child care location is two miles, with 90 percent of all locations being under ten miles from the child's school.

Child Care Needs by Income Level and Single-Parent Status.

The mean household income level for West Virginia is $20,795, according to the U.S. Census Bureau (1990), a figure comparable to that found in the 1992 WVSIS. Among its neighboring states, West Virginia has the lowest median family income level at $25,225, the highest percentage of children living below the poverty level at 25.9 percent, and the highest percentage of families living below poverty level at 16 percent. Kentucky is a close second, with the other states having much different characteristics.

Table 11 reveals that 51 percent of the state's households with children under six and requiring some form of child care earn less than $30,000 per year. With annual costs of professional child care averaging between $3,000 and $6,000 for each child, households earning less than $30,000 a year would have to spend ten to twenty percent of their gross income to afford such care. Utilizing the inferences drawn at the beginning of this report, 61,970 households in the state with children below the age of six would need to rely on child care. This translates into 31,605 households earning less than $30,000 and requiring child care provisions. Likewise, 44 percent of households with children aged six to twelve earn less than $30,000 per year, translating into 54,534 households in West Virginia.

Table 2-11:
Child Care Needs by Income Levels and Single Parent Status

Household Income	Statewide Child Care Needs for Persons Under 6	Statewide Child Care Needs for Persons 6–12	Single Parent HH with Child Care Needs for Persons Under 6	Single Parent HH with Child Care Needs for Persons 6–12
Under $10,000	9% (15)	7% (11)	30% (7)	22% (7)
$10,000 – $19,999	21% (35)	16% (24)	30% (7)	28% (9)
$20,000 – $29,999	21% (34)	21% (30)	25% (6)	16% (5)
$30,000 – $39,999	15% (24)	20% (29)	— (0)	16% (5)
$40,000 – $49,999	12% (20)	14% (20)	4% (1)	13% (4)
$50,000 – $59,999	5% (8)	8% (11)	— (0)	3% (1)
$60,000 or More	13% (22)	12% (17)	— (0)	3% (1)
Don't Know	1% (2)	— (0)	4% (1)	— (0)
Refused	3% (4)	2% (3)	8% (2)	— (0)

Also noteworthy in Table 11 is the proportion of single-parent households that require child care provisions. Many studies have noted that single-parent households are disadvantaged in two ways; very low income levels and scheduling problems. Findings from the WVSIS reveal that 27 percent of all households in the sample (506) have children under 13 years of age. Eighteen percent of these households are headed by a single parent. Moreover, 79 percent of all single-parent households in West Virginia are headed by a female. Using earlier figures derived in this report would suggest that approximately 18 percent, or 33,129 of the 184,051 households containing children would be headed by a single parent. Table 11 shows that 62 percent of the single-parent households in the sample rely on some child care provisions. In addition, 75 percent of households with children under six and 66 percent with children between six and twelve respectively earn less than $30,000 in gross annual income.

Single-parent households are likely to require child care for greater numbers of hours each week than two-parent households (see Table 12). Seventy (70) percent of all single-parent households require child care provisions between 11 and 50 hours per week in comparison to 54 percent of two-parent households. Children six to twelve receive less formal care, with 83 percent of two-parent households and 62 percent of single-parent households reporting that their children receive less than ten hours of care each week. But even here, over twice the proportion of single-parent households, in comparison to two-parent households, require child care provisions that surpass 11 hours a week.

Table 2-12:
**Number of Hours Per Week Children Receive Care
by Single Parent Status**

Weekly Hours	Two-Parent household with children under 6	One-Parent household with children under 6	Two-Parent household with children 6 – 12	One-Parent household with children 6 – 12
Under 10	46%	30%	83%	62%
11 – 50	54%	70%	17%	38%
20 – 50	42%	56%	6%	21%
Number of Cases	142	24	113	32

Discussion of Findings and Conclusions

Nine key factors emerge from the preceding analysis. First, child care is widely used and needed throughout the state. Frequently, such care is needed because both parents are employed; sixty (60) percent of households in West Virginia with children under the age of six regularly rely on some form of child care provision while the same is true for 42 percent of households with children between the ages of six and twelve. Second, nearly 60 percent of this care is currently provided by relatives of the child. Third, as expected, pre-school children require the greatest amount of care; spending an average of 20 hours per week in the care of others. Fourth, much of the care provided to children is strategically located within five miles of the child's home and ten miles of one parent's workplace. Fifth, a majority of the care given to children occurs in a home other than the child's own. Fifty-seven (57) percent of children under the age of two were found to receive care outside of their homes versus 62 percent of school-age children. Sixth, one-quarter of all households (15,493) with children were found to rely on three or more care providers, thereby creating a very unstable social environment for the children. Seventh, thirteen (13) percent of all households (23,927) with pre-teenage children reported one parent left a job due to difficulties associated with child care. Eighth, very little information or financial assistance is provided by employers in the state of West Virginia. Ninth, single-parent households are more likely to require child care for longer intervals of time but are the group least likely to be able to afford it.

Key concerns emerge from the analysis of West Virginia's child care patterns and their impact on economic programs: access, quality care provisions, affordability, and flexibility of work and child care arrangements. These issues and trends are quite similar to those found in other surveys across the United States. These four concerns (access, quality care, affordability, and flexibility), rather than being independent of one another, are closely interconnected to economic progress. Access is critical, especially for parents who must participate in the labor force. Without access, individuals are severely impeded in terms of their economic options and opportunities. The provision of quality child care is closely tied to access. Parents want more than a temporary holding tank in which their kids can be placed for extended intervals of time. They want places that are safe, stable, and stimulating. Such care requires that centers be regulated and accredited by governmental agencies, that they hire staff who are educated, experienced, and paid comparatively competitive wages to ensure their retention, and that they are able to actively engage children through low staff/child ratios. Affordability suggests that those in need of child care are not restricted from using these services because of cost. The data showed that households in West Virginia with the greatest need for quality child care provisions are the least able to afford it (e.g., household earnings of less than $30,000 annually). Finally, scheduling flexibility requires that centers and employers operate in sync with one another, maximizing flexibility so that people can utilize the care when they are expected to work.

In West Virginia, while nearly 60 percent of care is routinely provided by relatives of the child, over 40 percent is not. Care for children who cannot rely on relatives is typically left to friends of the family (19%), in-house providers (6.8%), or child care centers (11%). While friends probably provide care that is quite good, it is unlikely that most of these situations involve a single friend. More common would be the expectation that children are transported from one friend to another according to availability, producing an environment that is less likely to offer the type of long-term stability necessary for childrens' physical and intellectual development (Volling and Belsky 1995; Belsky 1991). Given that professional care facilities and in-house providers are generally expensive by comparison to alternative providers, such care is the least likely to be utilized, leaving the vast majority of child care providers unregulated (Schwenk 1993).

This last area is one in which governments and employers can make a tremendous difference. Child care is typically needed due to parents' employment obligations. Yet, as noted in these findings, employers in West Virginia are unlikely to accommodate their employees with information or financial assistance. This finding, which parallels the trend throughout the United States (Schwenk 1993), may be even more critical in West Virginia because of the comparatively depressed economic conditions within the state. Governments can and should establish policies that require accreditation and regulation in order to ensure the quality of child care. Businesses, in cooperation with governments, can help to subsidize the cost of such care or provide locations where care can take place. This does not require that each business, regardless of size, assume the onerous responsibility of child care. Businesses can network, either directly or through their local chamber of commerce organizations, to provide appropriate care facilities (Schwenk 1993). Such trends, while recent, are beginning to become more pronounced.

Public Policy Recommendations

The findings and conclusions underscore several key issues can be stated as policy recommendations. The following statements are derived directly from the preceding discussion, which offer five challenges to public policy planners:

(1) Governments at all levels can and should be routinely involved in the licensure and regulation of all child care providers.

(2) Governmental representatives need to work closely with communities and local businesses to ensure that quality care is available for working parents, particularly for single-parent households.

(3) Businesses should be encouraged to offer creative job flexibility plans for their employees. Employees will need to be involved in these discussions to ensure the best possible fit.

(4) Businesses need to formulate, with governmental representatives, creative strategies that provide paid maternity leave with job protection. Such policies enhance employee satisfaction and morale.

(5) Local Chamber of Commerce organizations, in partnership with their respective communities, should be encouraged to sponsor cooperative child care facilities that pool resources across many small businesses locally.

References

Amott, Teresa L. and Julie A. Matthaei. 1991. *Race, Gender, and Work: A Multicultural Economic History of Women in the United States.* Boston, MA: South End Press.

Belsky, Jay. 1991. "Parental and Nonparental Child Care and Children's Socioeconomic Development." in Alan Booth (ed.), *Contemporary Families: Looking Forward, Looking Backward.* Minneapolis: National Council on Family Relations. Pp. 122–40.

Ferree, Myra Marx. 1995. Beyond Separate Spheres: Feminism and Family Research. in Gary L. Bowen and Joe F. Pittman (eds.), *The Work and Family Interface: Toward A Contextual Effects Perspective.* Minneapolis: National Council on Family Relations. Pp. 122–37.

Gormley, William T., Jr. 1995. *Everybody's Children: Child Care as a Public Problem.* Washington, D.C: The Brookings Institution.

Hochschild, Arlie R. 1983. *The Second Shift: Working Parents and the Revolution at Home.* New York: Viking.

Keith, Bruce. 1993. *1992 WVSIS Methodology Report: Sample Design, Questionnaire, and Technical Forms.* Morgantown, WV: West Virginia University Survey Research Center.

Presser, Harriet B. 1989. "Can We Make Time for Children? The Economy, Work Schedules, and Child Care." *Demography.* 26(4):523–43.

Schwenk, Nancy E. 1993. Child-Care Trends. *Family Economics Review.* 6(2): 8–16.

Skold, Karen. 1988. "The Interests of Feminists and Children in Child Care." in Sanford M. Dornbusch and Myra H. Strober (eds.), *Feminism, Children, and the New Families.* New York: Guilford. Pp.113–36.

Volling, Brenda L. and Jay Belsky. "Parent, Infant, and Contextual Characteristics Related to Maternal Employment Decisions in the First Years of Infancy." in Gary L. Bowen and Joe F. Pittman (eds.), *The Work and Family Interface: Toward A Contextual Effects Perspective.* Minneapolis: National Council on Family Relations. Pp. 281–92.945,545 (8.7%)

Chapter 3

Physical Activity Among West Virginians: Bridging Barriers to Promote Health[1]

Jessica Gamponia Wright

Abstract

Although physical activity in West Virginia has been increasing, the state's prevalence rates for physical inactivity and obesity remain among the highest in the nation. Consistent with empirical research documenting the relationship between the lack of physical activity and cardiovascular disease, stroke and other various chronic diseases, West Virginians have a higher rate of heart disease mortality than the national average. In a state that known for it's rugged beauty and varied recreational outdoor activities, why are West Virginians still not physically active? This chapter outlines several potential barriers to physical activity and exercise among West Virginians. These include, time constraints, health problems, work responsibilities, poor motivation and childcare issues. Policy recommendations to assist in bridging these barriers should focus on the development of a long-term plan to build and direct policy initiatives, further trails development, support for community recreation/wellness centers, and further support for health care provider counseling in support of physical activity.

Introduction

The first Surgeon General's Report to address physical activity and health, released in July 1996, stated that Americans can substantially improve their health and quality of life by incorporating moderate amounts of physical activity into their daily lives. Additional benefits can be obtained by further increasing activity levels. Inactivity causes several chronic diseases, which becomes a powerful predictor of early mortality.

Physical activity, defined as "any bodily movement produced by skeletal muscles that results in energy expenditure" has been associated with a decreased incidence of coronary heart disease, stroke, colon cancer, diabetes, osteoporosis, and depression (Pate 1995). Various studies have also

---

1　*I gratefully acknowledge assistance with the data analysis by Robert Galbreath and Bill Reger.*

shown that, in addition to the positive health outcomes derived from regular physical activity other significant social and economic benefits result, including improved employee performance, reduced absenteeism, and increased productivity (U. S. Department of Health & Human Services 1996).

Physical activity and fitness have been placed as a top priority by the U. S. Department of Health and Human Services, acknowledged as such in, *Healthy People 2000: National Health Promotion and Disease Prevention Objectives*. Regular physical activity that is performed on most days of the week reduces the risk of developing or dying from some of the leading causes of illness and death in the United States. According to *Physical Activity and Health: A Report of the Surgeon General* (1996), regular physical activity improves health in at least seven important ways. These include, a reduction in the risk of (1) premature death, (2) death from heart disease, (3) diabetes, (4) high blood pressure, (5) colon cancer, (6) depression and anxiety, and (7) obesity.

According to the West Virginia Department of Health and Human Resources (1995), during the years 1984 through 1991, nearly nine (9) percent of West Virginian adults reported "no physical activity". Those most likely to report no leisure-time physical activity were women with less than a high school degree, widowed women, African-American women, retired persons, homemakers, unemployed individuals, and women with incomes of less than $10,000. In addition, a markedly higher prevalence of obese persons (40.8%) reported no physical activity than in comparison to individuals who are average-weight (30.0%) or underweight (34.7%).

Physical activity trends among West Virginia's youth are not much better. Although young people are more active than adults, many youth do not engage in recommended levels of physical activity. In addition, among adolescents, physical activity declines precipitously with age. Futhermore, the percentage of young people who are overweight has more than doubled in the past 30 years (U. S. Centers for Disease Control & Prevention 1997). Comprehensive school health programs have the potential to slow this age-related decline in physical activity and help students establish lifelong, healthy physical activity patterns.

Why are such trends more evident today than in the past? Modern technology has wiped physical activity out of our typical workday because of the increased use of computers, elevators, TV remote controls, electric garage door openers, riding lawnmowers, etc. These sedentary devices are all now standard features of our lifestyle. Could it be that our current lifestyle does not make it easy to find time for physical activity, or is it more a matter of self-motivation? What barriers actually exist when it comes to living a physically active lifestyle?

Review of Relevant Literature

Yankelovich Partners, Inc. (1995), surveyed 1,599 urban residents, stratified by income, in order to compare attitudes and concerns of lower-income Americans with the rest of the general public. In so doing, they identified several barriers that make it more difficult for poorer men and women to be physically active. The study found that, regardless of income, child care responsibilities are an obstacle to getting more physical activity. Second, neighborhood safety and lack of access to parks, sidewalks and recreational areas are major deterrents for lower-income Americans trying to be more physically active. Third, low-income Americans are less active than their higher-income counterparts.

The U. S. Centers for Disease Control and Prevention (1995) conducted a focus group study as part of the development of a national campaign to encourage healthier eating and to increase physical activity. Lack of time and internal motivation were found to be the primary barriers to maintaining a healthy diet and regular physical activity. Benefits from physical activity included having more energy to do the things one wants and needs to do in life, losing/controlling weight, averting chronic diseases, feeling good, and looking good. Motivational reasons offered included the desire to set a good example for children, wanting to live a long life for grandchildren, and having someone else in one's life implemented changes.

What are possible reasons West Virginians are not physically active. A primary culprit may be the lack of time, particularly for leisure time or physical activity. Any time spent beyond work is usually spent taking classes, working on or around the house, or with children. Stress in everyday life may in itself be another reason for the lack of physically activity. Certainly, the lack of sidewalks and streetlights, where applicable, present potential safety concerns and impede physical activity that may be undertaken after work. In addition, costs associate with mountain bikes, rafts, and the mode for which one would need to transport this type of equipment may impede regular activities in these areas. These are some of the potential reasons for the lower physical activity among West Virginians. This chapter will examine the extent to which West Virginians report these, and other, reasons for choosing not to engage in regular physical exercise.

Data and Analysis

Data were drawn from 1995 Social Indicators Survey (Keith 1996). Survey questions are listed in Appendix C, item numbers 55-71. Discussions of the survey and sample design are detailed in Appendix A.

Survey questions on exercise were developed by the West Virginia Bureau for Public Health and were reviewed by members of the West Virginia Coalition for Physical Activity. These questions were included for the first time in the 1996 WVSIS. Questions included in this survey were unique when compared to many similar survey instruments in that they focused primarily on the characteristics and beliefs of individuals who indicated that they did not exercise or participate in physical activity at least 20 minutes/day, three times/week.

Variables

The data in this study were analyzed with respondents grouped with respect to race, sex, age, education, household income, marital status, employment status, and body mass index. Although a total of 922 adults participated in the survey, only the 360 respondents who indicated that they were non-regular exercising individuals were asked questions about why they did not exercise. This sample of 360 was relatively small; therefore, some grouping of response categories was necessary. The two variables that require some special grouping were Marital Status and Employment Status.

Within Marital Status there were initially six divisions in which the respondents were placed. Two of the divisions, "Separated" and "Married, Apart" contained few non-regular exercising respondents, with seven and three respondents, respectively (unweighted data). Because it was assumed that most of these individuals were living an independent life, without the ongoing companionship of a "significant other," the responses from these two groups were combined with those who were "Never Married."

Within the Employment Status variable there were initially 10 divisions in which respondents were placed. Categories of "With a job, but not currently working" and "Working" were combined and given the title, "Employed." Those in the divisions "Laid off," "Looking for work," "Unable to work due to a disability," "Unable to work due to work for other reasons," and "Not working, not looking for work" were combined and classified as "Unemployed." The "Keeping house," "Going to school," and "Retired" categories maintained their original classifications.

With the present report those who had BMIs (body mass index) that were equal to or greater than identifiable limits were categorized as "Obese" and all others represented as "Non-Obese".

The results of many of the questions within the study were based upon a relatively small sample of 360. Some of the questions that the individuals answered had as many as 20 possible responses. With such questions, and relatively few respondents, it cannot be assumed that each category represents a valid sample of the population per the possible responses. Therefore, it is important to caution the reader to some of the results provided in this report.

Findings

Respondents were asked if they take part in any physical activities or exercises such as walking, dancing, gardening or stair climbing [and if so] do they regularly participate in activities for at least 20 minutes, 3 or more times per week (Appendix C, questions 55 & 56)? Sixty-one percent of those surveyed indicated they were physically active for at least 20 minutes, three or more times per week. Thirty-nine percent reported being inactive or irregularly active.

The results of this question indicated a greater percentage of regular exercisers than had been reported by similar surveys. Several factors may have contributed to the apparent inflation of the number of those reporting regular physical activity. The WVSIS did not discriminate between leisure and non-leisure time physical activity. Although the respondents were asked whether they participated in physical activity at least 20 minutes (duration), three times per week (frequency), activities such as gardening and work related exercise were accepted for the surveys. The Behavioral Risk Factor Survey has historically restricted exercise to leisure time physical activity. The purpose for making these comments is not to discount the present or other surveys but to indicate a reason for the differences in the results. However, those reporting no regular physical activity in this survey likely represented the segment of the population most at risk.

When respondents were asked, "was there ever a time in their adult life when they considered themselves a regular exerciser" (Appendix C, question 57), a little over half of the non-regular exercisers (51%) reported having regularly exercised in the past.

Participants were then asked what caused them to stop exercising on a regular basis (question 59). Respondents reported health problems, time constraints, work responsibilities, family responsibilities, and poor motivation as the five most common reasons for stopping exercise or not being active on a regular basis. These facators accounted for 68% of the impediments identified.

Participants were asked what were the main reasons they do not currently exercise (question 60). The five top reasons given were time constraints (25.7%), health problems (16.5%), work responsibilities (11.9%), poor motivation (10%) and child care issues (4.6%). Although work responsibilities, "child care issues, and family responsibilities are forms of time constraints, the latter category reflected responses in which more than one responsibility was felt to be the cause of not participating in regular exercise. If all of the time-limited respondents were placed in the "time constraints" category, they would represent 44% of the sample.

An unexpected response pattern was observed for education and income variables. One would expect less education and low income to show similar responses. However, 32% of the lower income (<$30,000) and 20% of higher income respondents (>$30,000) cited time constraints as the most significant impediment to regular exercise, compared to 14% of the respondents with less than 12 years of education. Similarly, 8% of the lower income group and 24% of the higher income group cited health problems as a deterrent, compared to 40% of those with less than 12 years education. The results are shown in Table 1.

Respondents were also asked what would personally motivate them to be physically active on a regular basis (question 61). The number one reason given was to feel healthier (23%) and the second most popular reason was lose weight (16%). Eighteen percent responded that they didn't know what would motivate them to exercise. This might indicate that many non-regular exercising individuals are simply not interested in physical activity (see Table 2).

Eighty-six percent of the non-regular exercising individuals surveyed were confident that if they decided to exercise regularly, they would continue to do so. This result appears to be high in light of the research that has been done on other unhealthy behaviors, such as smoking cessation and overeating. However, exercise is different from many other health-related behaviors in that it is a positive habit that should be a part of one's life rather than a negative, addictive habit, such as smoking or compulsive overeating, which needs to be eliminated from one's life. Public health educators would do well to build on this confidence and provide community members more opportunities to plan and implement exercise programs.

Few respondents (7%) reported they would not receive support from people of most importance to them if they began an exercise program (question 62).

When asked what particular activities they would like to become involved with that they are not currently doing (question 64) the following top five responses were given: walking (18.6%), don't know (15.9%), cycling (7%), jogging (6.2%), and swimming (5.7%).

Because there are so many activities with which persons can become involved, the results to this question appear to be spread out over many

Table 3-1:
Percentage of Respondents Who Report Barriers to Regular
Physical Activity by Selected Demographic Categories

Category	Time Constraints	Health Problems	Work Responsibilities	Poor Motivation	Child Care Issues
Total	25.7	16.5	11.9	10.0	4.6
Sex					
Male	29.9	16.9	17.3	7.9	1.3
Female	22.4	16.2	7.3	11.7	7.1
Age					
18-24	37.6	6.1	15.1	14.2	7.9
25-34	32.0	3.3	16.1	8.2	13.0
35-44	32.8	4.2	18.6	15.6	3.4
45-54	28.2	16.3	9.0	10.0	2.0
55-64	15.6	33.0	6.4	3.2	0.0
65+	1.8	48.3	0.9	4.8	0.0
Education					
< 12 Years	14.4	39.9	7.6	3.1	3.6
12 Years	29.1	11.3	12.3	9.6	4.1
13-15 Years	29.4	10.7	13.0	14.5	6.7
16+ Years	27.6	5.1	15.5	14.9	4.8
HH Income					
< $30,000	32.1	7.6	15.6	13.5	4.6
> $30,000	20.4	23.7	9.2	6.3	6.8
Marital Status					
Married	27.8	13.4	13.1	10.0	5.1
Divorced	32.5	14.1	12.6	9.7	5.6
Widowed	3.5	44.5	0.0	5.7	0.0
Alone	26.8	47.3	14.2	13.1	3.5
Employment					
Employed	36.1	3.3	17.6	10.9	5.0
Unemployed	6.1	43.3	9.2	9.6	3.8
Homemaker	20.7	21.0	1.4	10.9	13.4
Student	44.3	24.9	0.0	5.2	12.8
Retired	3.6	37.2	4.2	7.2	0.0
Body Mass Index					
Not Obese	26.4	16.5	12.4	9.0	5.0
Obese	27.7	15.6	11.9	10.6	3.8

Number of cases is 360 non-regular exercisers

Table 3-2:
Percentage of Respondents Who Report Motivators to Regular Physical Exercise by Selected Demographic Categories

Category	To Feel Healthier	To Lose Weight	Extra Time	Not Sure
Total	22.9	16.3	5.5	17.6
Sex				
Male	25.3	11.8	5.1	18.0
Female	21.0	20.0	5.9	17.4
Age				
18-24	15.3	11.0	5.0	27.5
25-34	25.2	18.4	6.9	20.6
35-44	30.4	19.1	8.5	13.0
45-54	22.8	18.3	5.9	12.2
55-64	26.0	11.9	0.0	22.6
65+	13.0	14.4	3.6	17.7
Education				
< 12 Years	12.0	12.8	3.8	24.8
12 Years	21.5	14.8	6.5	23.3
13-15 Years	29.6	19.7	5.1	5.3
16+ Years	32.6	21.2	6.2	9.0
HH Income				
< $30,000	29.8	19.3	12.4	12.8
> $30,000	18.6	13.4	11.3	18.9
Marital Status				
Married	25.2	19.1	6.9	16.0
Divorced	27.6	15.3	2.5	17.6
Widowed	8.9	11.0	1.7	22.0
Alone	17.7	8.9	4.6	21.9
Employment				
Employed	24.4	20.3	6.2	17.4
Unemployed	19.5	6.0	1.5	15.7
Homemaker	23.7	16.4	5.1	23.5
Student	20.3	9.0	22.4	0.0
Retired	16.8	13.0	4.0	17.8
Body Mass Index				
Not Obese	21.7	14.4	4.3	19.2
Obese	26.2	21.3	6.0	13.4

Number of cases is 360 non-regular exercisers

different activities. The most important observation is that most of the individuals indicated an interest in some type of activity. However, within some activities, the most frequently answered response was don't know, a possible indication that that the respondent has no interest in participating in any form of exercise (see Table 3).

Approximately four out of five respondents (81%) indicated an interest in engaging in physical activities that they could do with their families (question 66). Family participation was indicated to be important across all categories. In addition, family activities may well be more motivating, since time constrains of family responsibilities and child care issues would be somewhat mitigated.

Fifty-four percent (54%) of the respondents answered that they would use exercise facilities if they were available near where they worked or lived (Question 67). Females (60%) were more likely than males (47%) to answer that they would use exercise facilities if proximate to work or home.

Approximately two-thirds (68%) of all respondents indicated that no health care provider had recommended that they participate regularly in physical activity (question 68). An additional nine questions (questions 63a through 63h) focused on the beliefs of the health advantages of regular physical activity. Very few respondents (an average of 6.6%) disagreed with any of the statements regarding the relationship between health and physical activity.

Discussion of Findings and Conclusions

The results of this survey provide some useful feedback for policy purposes. While time constraints are noted as an important impediment to physical activity, it is clear from these results that many people want to regularly engage in such activity. To encourage physical activity, communities must enhance access. For example, among those who want to become more involved in walking, jogging, roller blading/skating, horseback riding, and cycling (37.2%) these activities can be accommodated by trails.

Another way to motivate those persons who would like to walk and jog, etc., would be the incorporation of sidewalks within rural neighborhoods. Inclusion of streetlights along these sidewalks would provide added security not only to pedestrians but to drivers as well.

An additional issue regarding access concerns proximity to facilities. Fifty-four (54) percent of the respondents indicated that they would use an exercise facility or participate in exercise classes if it were available near where they lived or worked. Creating a funding mechanism for the cre-

Table 3-3:
Percentage of Respondents who Report Desired Physical Activities as Those They Would Like to Begin by Selected Demographic Categories

Category	Walking	Cycling	Jogging	Swimming	Not Sure
Total	18.6	7.0	6.2	5.7	15.9
Sex					
Male	13.4	5.9	8.8	2.8	13.7
Female	23.2	7.9	3.9	8.3	17.7
Age					
18-24	6.9	5.7	16.1	2.5	7.7
25-34	11.9	9.2	9.3	8.0	11.4
35-44	23.9	6.7	4.4	5.3	11.3
45-54	22.9	9.3	3.0	7.0	14.3
55-64	25.4	8.4	5.3	4.7	19.2
65+	19.1	2.5	1.5	5.2	32.8
Education					
< 12 Years	17.3	6.4	2.2	2.7	31.8
12 Years	19.4	6.6	7.2	5.1	13.2
13-15 Years	20.4	7.8	5.9	7.5	8.8
16+ Years	15.9	7.8	9.6	9.1	9.7
HH Income					
< $30,000	15.9	7.1	8.1	5.4	8.1
> $30,000	19.1	5.6	4.6	6.2	23.9
Marital Status					
Married	21.1	7.3	4.9	6.1	11.2
Divorced	20.6	14.1	6.9	8.5	13.3
Widowed	18.0	0.0	0.0	6.0	47.9
Alone	9.8	6.3	13.7	2.6	17.0
Employment					
Employed	18.4	8.1	8.1	5.2	7.8
Unemployed	13.5	8.0	1.1	5.8	25.5
Homemaker	32.4	5.1	3.4	6.8	9.0
Student	0.0	3.9	19.6	6.2	7.9
Retired	16.9	4.4	4.5	6.4	33.8
Body Mass Index					
Not Obese	16.5	7.0	8.5	4.1	17.9
Obese	20.8	6.2	3.3	7.9	14.0

Number of cases is 360 non-regular exercisers

ation of community wellness centers may be one of the most significant steps towards reducing physical inactivity in West Virginia.

It would also be wise to take advantage of the counseling opportunity that physicians have to encourage their patients to exercise. Health care providers are often provided the unique opportunity of seeing their patients at times when they might be more receptive to the suggestion of participating in exercise. An exercise consultation reimbursement system might also fuel a desire for providers to carry this out. Based upon these findings and results, the following policy recommendations are postulated to enhance physical activity.

Public Policy Recommendations

(1) Local communities should be encouraged to further trail development.

This involves zoning to include walking/biking/blading/stroller areas in or along shopping areas, residential subdivisions, worksites, etc. Subsidizing sidewalks and streetlights on rural roads would also promote pedestrianism. Designing all public buildings with easy, accessible, well-lit and user-friendly stairways is also a form of creating "trails" in a most "urban" sense. In addition to further "urban trail" development, incorporation of policies to allow walking/activity breaks as part of the business day would allow use of these trails.

(2) Local communities should be encouraged and supported, to the extent possible, in the development of recreation/wellness centers.

This would also be another way to facilitate physical activity, particularly in rural communities where none of these centers currently exist. These centers should be available at little or no cost to community members in order to allow for access for those who cannot afford health club memberships. In order to create new social norms for physical activity, subsidization of opportunities such as dance lessons, gymnastics, etc., need to be developed similar to the format for which Little League has been subsidized throughout the years. One idea to support funds for statewide health promotion initiatives such as these, would be raising taxes on tobacco products. Zoning to protect open land use for recreation is also another area critical to creating community-friendly avenues for physical activity.

(3) Communities and medical educators should be challenged to promote the active role of the health care provider in physical activity counseling.

The establishment of a reimbursement process for physical activity counseling for all health care providers (nurse practitioners, dietitians, physicians, physician assistants, etc.) could directly affect their clientele. In addition, issuing insurance incentives for individuals and families who maintain regular physical activity can be done. Physical conditioning training of all health professionals would also help in providing a basic background for counseling and much needed role modeling of an active lifestyle.

Conclusion

West Virginia, like many other states, has a long way to go in creating effective environments in support of physical activity for the general population. This effort will require collaboration among many non-traditional partners, considerable prior planning, and much support from policy makers. An overarching, long-term plan through which to build and direct state and national policy initiatives would greatly assist in developing an infrastructure for promotion of physical activity in West Virginians' everyday lives. Grass-root efforts at the local community will need to "make a case" in support of sidewalks and lighting for rural roads, local community recreation centers, access to specialized instruction such as dance & gymnastics opportunities. Employers will need to support the development of role model policies for physical activity opportunities within the workday and workplace. Daily physical education, physical activity and comprehensive school health education in grades K-12 must be supported in all schools and communities to increase the efforts already in place by the West Virginia Department of Education and the West Virginia Bureau for Public Health. There needs to be a collective push in momentum for efforts at every level (federal, state, local, in schools, work-sites, and communities). Leveraging funding for all of the above strategies has become a priority for which there are no easy solutions. In order for these recommendations to succeed, policy makers will need to both understand and buy into their role in the creation and support of local infrastructures.

References

Centers for Disease Control and Prevention. 1997. *Guidelines for school and community programs to promote lifelong physical activity among young people.* MMWR 46(No. RR-6).

_____. 1995. "Health Communication Evaluation Services Project Task 08: Formative Research for a Nutrition & Physical Activity Health Communication Campaign." *Healthy Eating and Physical Activity: Focus Group Research with Contemplators and Preparers.* National Center for Chronic Disease Prevention and Health Promotion, Centers for Disease Control and Prevention. Atlanta, GA. (July).

R.R. Pate, M. Pratt, S.N. Blair, W.L. Haskell, C.A. Macera, C. Bouchard, D. Buchner, W. Ettinger, G.W. Heath, A.C. King, A. Kriska, A.S. Leon, B.H. Marcus, J. Morris, R.S. Paffenbarger, K. Patrick, M.L. Pollack, J.M. Rippe, J. Sallis, and J.H. Wilmore. 1995. "Physical Activity and Public Health: A Recommendation From the Centers for Disease Control and Prevention and the American College of Sports Medicine." *Journal of the American Medical Association.* 273:402–407.

U. S. Department of Health and Human Services. 1994. "Even Some Exercise Offers Health Benefits." In: *Prevention Report.* (Oct/Nov):1–3.

U. S. Department of Health and Human Services. 1996. *Physical Activity and Health: A Report of the Surgeon General.* Atlanta GA: Centers for Disease Control and Prevention, National Center for Chronic Disease Prevention and Health Promotion.

U. S. Department of Health and Human Services, Public Health Service. *Healthy People 2000: National Health Promotion and Disease Prevention Objectives.* DHHS Publication No. (PHS) 91–50213.

West Virginia Department of Health and Human Resources, Bureau for Public Health, Office of Epidemiology and Health Promotion. 1997. *West Virginia Healthy People 2000 Midcourse Review 1995.*

West Virginia Department of Health and Human Resources, Bureau for Public Health, Office of Epidemiology & Health Promotion. 1995. *The Status of Leisure-Time Physical Activity in West Virginia.*

West Virginia Department of Health and Human Resources, Bureau for Public Health, Office of Epidemiology & Health Promotion. *1995 West Virginia Behavioral Risk Factor Survey.*

Yankelovich Partners, Inc. 1995. Shape Up America! C. Everett Koop Foundation, Healthy Weight for Life. *Barrier Survey, Identifying the Obstacles to Activity and Healthy Eating.*

Chapter 4

Access To Health Care in West Virginia

Renate E. Pore and Daniel M. Christy

Abstract

Tracking the status of health insurance to understand the characteristics of the population without coverage is important in order to evaluate and design policies and programs that enhance access to health care. A number of national and statewide studies track health insurance status and other indicators of health care access and health status. These studies indicate that both insured and uninsured West Virginians have difficulty receiving health care when they need it but that the uninsured are at greater risk of not being able to access health care. The high cost of health services is cited as the major barrier to care for both insured and uninsured West Virginians. In order to effectively address problems of health insurance coverage and health care access, West Virginia should consider adoption of five planning initiatives: (1) creating a health care financing system that supports affordable access to preventive and primary care, (2) establishing effective consumer protections for managed care, (3) promoting the development of community-based services and use of non-physician health care workers, (4) developing and supporting a variety of strategies to expand health insurance coverage, (5) focusing on incremental health system change, and (6) continuing to conduct surveys which track access at the local and sub-population level.

Introduction

Universally, health insurance coverage is an important indicator of access to health care services. Because of the high cost of health care, lack of insurance often presents a serious barrier to care nationally. Uninsured persons visit the doctor less often, use more emergency room care, and are more likely to be hospitalized for chronic conditions that could be better controlled with reliable access to physician services, all of which may increase the risk of mortality (Franks et al. 1993). In West Virginia, these problems are compounded by the low supply of primary care practitioners, their geographic distribution, and cultural barriers that keep people from seeking care.

This chapter analyzes the issue of universal health insurance coverage and access to health care among West Virginians. Data are examined from four studies recently commissioned by various state agencies in West Virginia, including the West Virginia Social Indicators Survey (Keith 1994; Foster and Wadsworth 1997), Harris and Associates (1992), Keith, Beaumont, and Derk (1993), and the Behavioral Risk Factor Surveillance System Survey. The results of this analysis lead to the postulation of six public policy recommendations, which, if implemented, will enhance West Virginians' access and coverage to health care.

Overview of Literature Related to National Trends

Nationally, more than 40 million Americans including 10 million children have no health insurance coverage. The Kaiser Family Foundation (1996) finds that 19 percent of American adults report being uninsured sometime in the previous year, 18 percent report problems getting medical care, and 16 percent report problems paying medical bills. The lack of coverage and good access to basic health care for many children in their developmental years is of special concern on a national level.

Uninsured children frequently miss annual visits to doctors. Almost 37 percent of long-term uninsured children do not visit a doctor. Even children age five and younger, who should receive annual doctor visits to monitor their growth and development, go without such care at three times the rate of insured children. When long-term uninsured children see a doctor, they are twice as likely as insured children to receive care in emergency rooms. Uninsured children are also less likely to be in excellent health than insured children; in effect, they are more likely to be in fair or poor health.

The United States currently has a mixed system of private and government-sponsored health insurance. Medicare, a federally sponsored health insurance program, covers all Americans over age 65. Medicaid, a federal-state partnership covers disabled and poor Americans. Most Americans, however, receive coverage through their employer. Nearly two-thirds of the population under 65 years old (approximately 150 million people nationally), receive health insurance through an employer-sponsored plan. While employers continue to express a commitment to providing health insurance benefits, employer financial support for employee health insurance, and especially for families, has declined over the past several years, causing an overall decline in private health insurance coverage. Between 1987 and 1995, the percentage of Americans under 65 years old with private health insurance coverage decreased from 75.9 percent to 70.7 percent. Employment-based insurance declined from 69.2 percent to 63.8 percent during the same period. Likewise, employer-based coverage for children declined from 73 percent to 66 percent (U. S. Government Academy Office 1997).

These trends are due, in part, to the hidden cost of unreimbursed care employers must pay through higher premiums and charges. For example, in West Virginia, the cost of unreimbursed hospital care in 1995 was $210,243,354 or 6.12 percent of all hospital costs (Health Care Cost Review Authority 1996). If we assume that the cost for most unreimbursed care is shifted primarily to the approximately 900,000 privately insured individuals and their employers through higher premiums, then the privately insured West Virginia population in 1995 paid $233 per person on health care to cover the cost of unreimbursed care.

Without thoughtful policy and concerted action to support the availability, affordability, and expansion of health insurance coverage, we can expect increasingly more people to be uninsured for long periods of time during their lives. The larger number of uninsured people has serious consequences for the viability and quality of the health care system as well as public health. The advent of managed care and efforts by government and private employers to control health care costs will only magnify the crisis. Consequently, tracking and understanding trends in insurance coverage at the national, state, and local level is important in the development of government and private sector initiatives to protect the health of the public, to promote efficiency in the delivery system, and to assess the impact of federal and state policy. Long-term trends in the decline of employer-based health insurance, recently enacted welfare reform legislation, and the emergence of managed care all have profound implications for the health care system generally and for the health and well being of West Virginians in particular.

Data and Analysis

Most of the health insurance trends reviewed thus far represent national samples, many of which may not be entirely relevant to West Virginia. How well do West Virginians fare with regard to access and coverage of their health care needs? To address this concern, several studies were recently commissioned by various state agencies in West Virginia. The findings of these studies serve as the focal point of this chapter.

Louis Harris and Associates, Health Care Experiences in West Virginia (1992)

The Harris survey was used as a one-time telephone survey of 1,250 West Virginia adults age 18 and older. The survey employed a stratified and unclustered systematic random selection sample method, using random-digit-dialing procedures. The sample is highly representative; unlisted telephone numbers have the same probability of inclusion as listed numbers. Respondents were geographically dispersed, rather than clustered; and households with multiple phone listings had the same probability of being selected in the sample as those with a single listing. During tabulation, the data were weighted to reflect Bureau of the Census parameters for age, race, sex, education level, and insurance status, and to adjust for the number of adult residents in the household, and number of telephone lines in the household. The study asked questions from the following 11 categories: (1) Political Salience of Health Care Reform, (2) Health Status, (3) Salience of Different Health Care Issues, (4) Access, (5) Insurance Coverage, (6) Demographics, (7) Employer Experiences and Behavior, (8) Managed Care, (9) Cost Experiences, (10) Worries, (11) Reform Option.

A Survey of Health Insurance Coverage Among West Virginia Businesses

This survey was sponsored by the West Virginia Health Care Planning Commission and was completed under contract with the West Virginia University Survey Research Center (WVUSRC) by Bruce Keith, Lee Beaumont, and Susan Derk (1993). The study employed a disproportionate stratified random sample designed to examine how businesses in West Virginia manage health care benefits for their employees. Businesses were stratified according to the number of employees maintained by the firm. Three strata were constructed: firms with 3–9 employees, firms employing between 10 and 49 persons, and businesses that had 50 or more employees. Justification for this procedure was based on access to health care coverage. Firms with fewer than ten employees are frequently not eligible for coverage in most group insurance plans while those employing more than 50 persons are more likely to offer health insurance plans to their employees.

Data for the survey were obtained from the March, 1992 quarterly report on statewide West Virginia employee compensation records. In order to have a margin of error of plus or minus five percent at the 95 percent confidence level, 400 completed interviews were needed from small and medium size firms respectively, and 300 completed interviews were needed from large firms. The smaller sample of large-size firms relative to the other strata is the result of a population correction factor that takes into account the small number of large firms in the total population. In order to obtain appropriate sample sizes, the sample size was increased to account for refusals, incorrect telephone numbers, and dissolved businesses. Since more problems were expected to occur among smaller businesses, it was estimated that a sample of 880 small firms would be needed to reach the target of 400 completed interviews. Samples of medium and large firms were estimated at 589 and 378 respectively to reach the projected targets. The initial sample contained the names, addresses, and telephone numbers of 1,847 firms. The Bureau of Economic Research provided the WVUSRC with three samples, stratified by size of firm, containing the names, addresses, and telephone numbers of firms within each of the three strata. All firms were mailed initial contact letters indicating that they would be called about the availability of employee health insurance coverage.

Behavioral Risk Factor Surveillance System (BRFSS)

The Behavioral Risk Factor Surveillance System survey has been conducted annually by telephone since 1984 and represents a collaborative effort between the West Virginia Bureau for Public Health (WVBPH) and the Centers for Disease Control (CDC). The core questions were developed and field-tested by CDC. Phone calls and interviews are conducted by the WVBPH during a seven-to-12-day period each month. The sample was selected by random digit dialing (RDD) rather than through telephone directories since the latter do not include unlisted or new numbers. Sampling procedures incorporated a multistage cluster design based on the Waksberg Sampling Method for RDD.

Respondents were asked if they have any kind of health care coverage including health insurance, prepaid plans such as HMOs, or government plans such as Medicare. Individuals responding in the negative were asked how long it has been since they had health care coverage. Respondents were also asked if there was a time during the past 12 months when they needed to see a doctor, but could not because of the cost. The analyis in this survey was based on these three questions in combination with other questions on income, health risk behavior and self-reported health status.

West Virginia Social Indicators Survey (WVSIS)

The West Virginia Social Indicators Survey methodology and analysis techniques have been detailed in Appendix A. Like the Louis Harris survey, this sample is drawn from a population consisting of non-institutionalized persons residing in the state of West Virginia and living in households with telephones during the survey period. The 1996 survey asked the same question about coverage as the Behavioral Risk Factor Surveillance System survey: "Do you have any kind of health insurance coverage, including private health insurance, prepaid plans such as HMOs or government plans such as Medicare or Medicaid?" A follow-up question asked respondents if there was a time in the past twelve months when they were without health insurance coverage. When children were present in the household, respondents were asked if any of those in the household had coverage through Medicaid? Two follow-up questions included in the survey were, if there was a time in the past twelve months when such child was without health insurance and how many of the children were without coverage in the past twelve months.

Summary of Findings of West Virginia Studies

This section describes the findings regarding insurance coverage and health care access derived from the four West Virginia studies cited in the previous section. Since each of the studies reflect slightly different methodologies and time intervals, their results have been presented separately. Presentation of the findings is further grouped into two subsections: (1) West Virginians' access to heath care and (2) health insurance coverage among West Virginia businesses.

West Virginians' access to heath care

The Harris and Associates survey (1992) found that 30 percent of West Virginians reported putting off or postponing care they felt they needed in the twelve months prior to the survey because they could not afford it. Twelve percent of all West Virginia adults living in households with children said they postponed seeking care for a child in the past twelve months because they could not afford it. Ten percent of those needing care in the previous year reported that they had been refused health care because they did not have insurance and could not pay.

Fourteen percent of West Virginia adults reported being without health insurance at the time the Harris (1992) survey was conducted while an additional 10 percent said they had an episode of going uninsured in the past two years. These findings suggest that one in four West Virginian adults is at risk of being uninsured for some period of time. If the dependents of these adults are presumably also uninsured, then this finding suggests that upwards of 25 percent of West Virginians (approximately 500,000) is at risk of being uninsured for some length of time. Among these persons, 20 percent said they had never had health insurance coverage. Almost half of all West Virginians without health insurance coverage indicated that their lack of coverage was because they lost their job, were between jobs, or were unemployed. Forty-six (46) percent had been uninsured for less than 12 months, while 54 percent had been uninsured for more than 12 months.

In West Virginia, as in the nation, private (non-government) health insurance is predominantly employment-based. Of those West Virginians who hold private insurance, 73 percent reported receiving coverage through their own work or union or through someone else's work or union. Another 27 percent were covered by insurance they or their families have purchased directly.

While health care coverage is generally related to employment status, not all employed workers have health insurance. In West Virginia, 50 percent of all uninsured people, are employed, 32 percent are employed full-time.

Out-of-pocket costs are of concern to West Virginians. The uninsured and those with a lapse in coverage bear greater out-of-pocket costs than the insured population. Privately, the insured have greater out-of-pocket expenses than do individuals covered by Medicare or Medicaid. Eleven percent of West Virginians surveyed reported out-of-pocket costs of $2000 or more in the year preceding the survey. High out-of-pocket expenses were generated by the factor of chronic and acute illness (34 percent) and by accidents (15 percent). Among individuals with high out-of-pocket costs, 78 percent said these costs represented a serious financial problem for them.

One-half of those who said that out-of-pocket costs were a serious problem indicated they had to change their lives significantly as a result of the expenses. Some said they had to cut down food and clothing (42 percent), or entertainment and recreation (30 percent), while others had to cut down on everything (21 percent). These data show that insured West Virginians are not necessarily protected from high health care costs. The results of the Harris survey further showed that most West Virginians do not feel secure about their ability to pay for medical care and to retain their health insurance coverage. About two-thirds of the respondents worried that "health insurance will become so expensive you won't be able to afford it." More than half worried that they would not get the necessary health care because of cost, while more than one-third worried that their current health insurance coverage would be cut.

West Virginia Behavioral Risk Factor Study Results (BRFSS)

In 1991, the BRFSS for the first time included questions on health insurance coverage, access and cost. In that year, one in five non-elderly, adult West Virginians (age 18–64) reported no health insurance coverage and 14.3 percent reported that they had difficulty seeing a doctor because of cost. The number of uninsured West Virginians has remained approximately the same between 1991 and 1995, as shown in Table 1. However, the number finding it difficult to see a doctor because of costs increased from 14.3 percent in 1991 to 17.1 percent in 1995. These data may reflect increases in health care costs in general and increased cost sharing for families or individuals covered by private health insurance.

Table 4–1:
Percentage of West Virginian Adults
Without Health Insurance Coverage or Who Have Difficulty
Seeing a Doctor Because of Cost by Year.

Year	No Health Insurance Coverage – Adults 18-64	Difficulty Seeing Doctor Because of Cost – Adults 18–64
1991	20.1	14.3
1992	23.0	17.9
1993	19.4	17.3
1994	19.5	16.4
1995	19.9	17.1

Source: West Virginia Behavioral Risk Factor Surveillance Survey (BRFSS)

The West Virginia Behavioral Risk Factor study is especially valuable for policy formulation because with multi-year data aggregation it permits county-level analysis of health insurance coverage and access to care. While the sample size at the county level is small, five years of merged data at the county level ensures a reliable predictor of information on coverage and access to health care. The county level data show enormous variation of coverage and access in West Virginia ranging all the way from a low of 9.3 uninsured in Ohio county to a high of 36.2 percent uninsured in McDowell County. In a number of the state's most rural areas, the number of unin-sured is at or above 30 percent including the counties of Doddridge, Fayette, Jackson, Lewis, Logan, Mingo, Ritchie, and Wirt.

Difficulty of seeing a doctor because of cost was reported by a low of 6.2 percent in Ohio county to a high of 27 percent in Mingo county. The merged data for 1991–95 is presented for each county in Appendix A. Among the uninsured, 53.2 percent reported not being able to see a doctor compared to 11 percent of individuals with coverage.

The BRFSS study also permitted comparing insurance status with in-come and self-reported health status and health risk factors. About 36 percent of West Virginians without health insurance reported household incomes below $10,000; approximately 34 percent had incomes in the $10,000 to $24,999 range, while 8 percent had income above $25,000. Income was unknown for 20 percent of the survey sample.

In correlating insurance status with self-reported health status, the survey found that more uninsured West Virginians (21.1 percent) as compared to insured (17.2 percent) West Virginians reported their health status as fair/poor. With the exception of smoking, West Virginians without health insurance generally do not report worse health risk factors. However, uninsured West Virginians are 50 percent more likely to smoke than individuals with coverage.

The West Virginia Social Indicators Survey Results (WVSIS)

This survey obtained responses from 961 West Virginia adults on health care coverage and access during 1994 (see Appendix E, questions 108–114). Eighteen percent of those surveyed, reported that they had no insurance coverage. Of those without coverage, 30.5 percent reported that they or a household member needed medical care but did not receive it. The 1995 and 1996 surveys contained no questions on health care access and its relation to cost.

Health care questions, including items on coverage for children, were included in the 1997 survey (See Appendix B, questions 28–32). In that study, 16.4 percent of West Virginians or 295,000 reported being without insurance. When those with coverage were asked if they had been uninsured sometime in the past twelve months, 7.1 percent said yes. This supports the Harris survey data suggesting that almost one in four West Virginians are uninsured or at risk of being uninsured at any time.

The 1996 survey indicated that 14.3 percent or about 63,300 West Virginia children lacked health insurance coverage. This finding supports comparable data reported by the Southern Institute on Children and Families (1996) on uninsured children in the South. That survey estimated that 59,800 West Virginia children were uninsured.

All of the 1,041 businesses surveyed in this study were asked if they currently offered health insurance coverage to their employees. Of the 1,041 businesses surveyed, 68 percent indicated that they offered some type of health insurance to their employees, while 32 percent indicated that they offered no health insurance benefits. Most businesses that provide insurance only offer it to full-time employees. Only 17 percent of the businesses indicated that they offered coverage to part-time employees.

More than half (53 percent) of West Virginia businesses who offered insurance coverage paid the entire monthly premium for the employee while the remainder reported the presence of a cost-sharing arrangement. Overall, the average monthly premium in 1993 was $175 for employee coverage. Of that amount, the average employee paid $34 monthly, or 19 percent of the total average cost.

Large firms in West Virginia, in comparison to small firms, were found to more frequently offer health care coverage. Overall, 98 percent of large firms offered employee coverage, while only 78 percent of medium-sized firms and only 45 percent of small firms offered employee coverage.

Most West Virginia businesses offering health insurance coverage to their employees also make coverage available to dependents (92 percent). More than two-thirds of these businesses require the employee to pay all or a substantial part of the cost of dependent coverage. In 31 percent of the firms surveyed, the employer paid the full cost of dependent coverage. In 25 percent of firms surveyed, the employee paid the full cost; in 44 percent of firms, the cost was shared between the employer and the employee.

Ninety-five (95) percent of all employers surveyed expressed concern about the ability of their firms to continue to provide health insurance coverage because health insurance premiums were too expensive for the organization. Sixty-nine (69) percent expressed concern that the premium was too expensive for the employee. Eighty-two (82) percent of the firms not providing coverage at the time of the survey had never provided their employees with health insurance coverage. The remaining 18 percent not providing coverage indicated that they had done so previously. Almost all non-providers indicated they had stopped coverage because premiums were too expensive. A full 89 percent of the firms not offering health insurance coverage stated that the cost of premiums was too high for the company and/or for the employee. A comparable percentage of employers, who did not offer coverage, believed that employees preferred higher wages to insurance coverage.

Discussion of Findings and Conclusions

This chapter initially reviewed health care access data for West Virginia in 1994 and observed that access to health care was a problem for many West Virginians. We noted that, while surveys tend to provide slightly different results depending upon their methodology and the manner in which questions are framed, all of the surveys report that, for many West Virginians, the cost of health care is a barrier to seeking and obtaining necessary health care services (Harris and Associates 1992). The survey data made available since the Harris survey suggests that not much has changed since 1992 and that, health insurance coverage and access to health care remains a serious problem for many West Virginians. Several common themes are evident from the results of these four studies.

Health Insurance Coverage

Health insurance coverage provides families with the security of knowing that in a medical crisis, they won't have to mortgage the family home to pay for the cost of health care. While some West Virginian families have the additional security of knowing that a substantial part of outpatient care — doctor visits and pharmacy costs — will be paid by their insurance plan, many West Virginians do not enjoy such security. Some are without coverage for only a few months, others for a year or more, and others have never had health insurance coverage.

In developing policy and programs to expand coverage, it is important to understand the differences in these segments of the population. Individuals and families who lose coverage for a few months between jobs present a different problem from the population which has never had insurance.

The United States is virtually the only developed country that has not been able to provide its citizens with the security of universal health insurance coverage. This anomaly is not so much because of a lack of money, for the U.S. spends considerably more on health care than any other nation in the world, but more because of a lack of consensus about the role of the government versus private sector in assuring and providing coverage.

In 1966, Congress and President Lyndon Johnson hoped to usher in universal coverage for Americans by passing Medicare and Medicaid. Medicare provided for health insurance for all people over age 65 and Medicaid was designed to provide for poor people. In the robust economy of the 1960s, it was believed that employer-sponsored health insurance would provide coverage for all other Americans. Thirty years later, universal coverage remains an elusive goal. Structural changes in the nation's economy have led to a decline in employer sponsored coverage rather than in the expansions expected during the 1960s. Clearly, this problem will not solve itself. Without renewed effort by the private and public sectors to find new solutions, we can anticipate a growing number of uninsured children and adults and increasing anxiety about the ability to access health care when needed.

Most of the uninsured, both nationally and in West Virginia, are people who work or who are the dependents of labor market participants. They have no coverage because their employer does not provide it or the cost-sharing arrangement makes health insurance prohibitive. A solution for these workers lies in a partnership between government and business to make health insurance affordable for both the employer and the employee. Similarly, for the long-term uninsured, both adults and children, government-sponsored solutions will have to be generated.

Access to Health Care.

The West Virginia surveys show, in terms of access, that being covered by health insurance is better than not being covered. Coverage, however, does not necessarily bring with it peace of mind nor access to a doctor when it is needed. High deductibles, co-payments, and outpatient care that are often not covered create barriers to care for many insured West Virginians.

Most West Virginians are covered through indemnity plans which traditionally have not been designed to encourage preventive and primary care. Since a doctor's office visit can cost $100 or more, many West Virginians find such out-of-pocket costs prohibitive. In the last decade, many employers have sought to control high health care costs by shifting more of the burden to employees through higher deductibles and co-payments. This change has only made health care access more difficult for many West Virginians.

The trend towards managed health care may help those West Virginians who report that they have difficulty seeing a doctor because of cost in the following two ways. First, enrollees in managed care plans do not pay deductibles and co-payments are generally minimal. Managed care plans save money by controlling the high-tech, high-cost end of health care services. Thus managed care subscribers gain by more affordable access to preventive and primary care but give up some choice and access to higher cost specialty and hospital services. Second, a study by the Lewin Group estimated that, in 1966, managed care saved an average of $304 to $406 per family for households headed by a person under age 65. Managed care has helped keep insurance more affordable and has helped many employers and families maintain their insurance coverage (Sheils and Haught, 1997). The authors' estimated that without managed care and lower costs, the numbers of uninsured families and individuals in the United States would have increased by an additional 3.1 to 5 million people.

There is a dilemma associated with long-term reliance on managed care toward which we are evolving nationally. Individuals and families that remain uninsured in a managed care system will have an increasingly difficult time finding care that is free or available at reduced cost. Doctors and hospitals have always provided unreimbursed care through a practice referred to as "cost-shifting." In the fee-for-service system, health care providers covered the cost of care to uninsured and underinsured people by charging higher prices and shifting the cost of unreimbursed care to those with the ability to pay. Under managed care arrangements, the ability for these agencies to shift costs is greatly reduced. Consequently, health care providers will no longer be able to pass on the cost of caring for the uninsured. Hospitals will be especially affected by this change. Addressing the concerns of their constituents, the American Hospital Association is now making the expansion of health insurance coverage to all Americans a priority.

The Unique Problems of West Virginia.

West Virginia health care experiences are unique among states for a number of reasons: (1) West Virginia is one of the most rural states in the nation, (2) the state's per capita and average household incomes and the health status of its population are among the lowest in the nation, (3) relative to its income, the state's health care costs are high, and (4) as a percent of the state's gross product, West Virginia has the highest health costs in the nation. To illustrate, in 1992, 15.7 percent of the state's gross product was spent on health care — the highest percent of any state in that year (Morgan, et al., 1997).

A combination of low wages, chronic disease, high rates of the uninsured in rural counties, and high health care costs, all combine to create a special problem of access to health care for West Virginia's rural citizens. Consequently, it is no surprise that almost one-third of West Virginians reported in the 1992 Harris poll and one in five adults below age 65 reported in the BRFSS (U. S. Centers for Disease Control, 1991) that they have difficulty seeing a doctor because of cost.

One issue, which deserves further study and analysis, is the availability of free and reduced health care services and access to care. Both the federal and state governments have invested large sums to develop West Virginia's rural health infrastructure. In many of the state's rural counties, government supported primary care services are available to anyone regardless of ability to pay. It would be valuable to know if access to care is reported as better, the same, or worse, in those counties where subsidized services are widely available. If free services are available and the public perceives that cost is a barrier to care, what are the factors which support that perception? Are people not aware of these services? Are they reluctant to ask for subsidized care? Do they feel that subsidized services do not meet their specific medical needs? The following public policy recommendations are offered:

Public Policy Recommendations

(1) Develop a health care financing system that supports access to preventive and primary care.

The surveys and studies of health insurance coverage within the state indicate that even people with health insurance coverage have difficulty paying for the high cost of health care. Traditional health insurance systems were designed to pay for major acute illnesses or accidents. They were not designed to support preventive care and chronic disease management. High deductibles and high co-payments for primary care and outpatient care are counterproductive and keep people from seeking appropriate medical care that can keep them healthy, independent and productive.

From this perspective, the trend towards managed health care, nationally and within the state, is a positive development. Managed care plans typically have no deductibles and low or no co-payments for doctor office visits. An explicit goal of effective managed care plans is to provide services which will keep members of the plan healthy and to treat plan members in lower cost settings. As West Virginians enroll in managed care, their ability to access preventive and primary care should improve. It should be noted, however, that those West Virginians who remain in traditional indemnity plans will increase their out-of-pocket costs. West Virginians who have no insurance coverage will have increasing difficulty finding health care that is free or available at reduced cost. Financing systems that pay for outpatient care for both the insured and uninsured may help to improve the health status of West Virginians over time by encouraging people to seek necessary care.

(2) Establish effective consumer protection systems for managed care.

Managed care holds great promise to control costs and to promote access to preventive and primary care. Managed care, however, also has financial incentives to deny specialty and hospital care. To insure that managed care in West Virginia develops in the best interests of the citizens of the state, strong consumer protection processes must be put in place. Such processes can help assure that individuals get the care they need.

A related challenge for managed care is the measurement of quality and consumer satisfaction. In a fragmented fee-for-service system, there are not many opportunities to measure quality and monitor consumer satisfaction. By taking responsibility for managing the care of individuals, managed care organizations also take responsibility for assuring quality of care and consumer satisfaction. Meaningful measurements in the health industry are still a work in progress. However, West Virginia should begin to develop its expertise and competence in the area of health care quality monitoring and measurement.

(3) Promote the development of community-based services and use of non-physician health care workers.

Most of the basic medical care that West Virginians need can be provided in community settings by mid-level providers or physician extenders such as nurse practitioners and physician assistants. Even registered nurses can provide much basic care. In regular consultation and under the supervision of a physician, these health care professionals can meet most of the medical needs of West Virginia's rural communities. For outreach, health education and preventive care, lay health workers may also be a sound source for West Virginia's communities.

(4) Develop and support a variety of strategies to expand health insurance coverage.

As the cost of health care increases, employer-based health insurance coverage especially among small employers will continue to erode unless policies are designed to support the current system. While health insurance premium increases have slowed during the past three years, many health care analysts are predicting an increase in premiums within the next few years. If inflationary pressure increases health insurance premiums, we are likely to see a continued decline in employer-based health insurance coverage and an increase in the number of the uninsured (Employee Benefits Research Institute, 1997).

To address the needs of small employers, some states have created health insurance purchasing cooperatives to pool the purchasing power of employers and to help them negotiate better rates. West Virginia's efforts to promote coverage among small employers have failed in the past. For example, during the 1980s, a Robert Wood Johnson project to create a small employer pool through the Public Employees' Insurance Agency (PEIA) failed when the agency encountered major financial problems. In 1991, so-called "No-Frills" or "Bare Bones" legislation [Senate Bill 535] was passed directing the Insurance Commissioner to create a basic health policy for individual and group accident and sickness insurance. The new policy covered hospital care but not preventive or primary care. Rates to providers were substantially below the prevailing rates in the state. This effort failed when physicians refused to participate. It is important to understand the failures of these attempts to expand coverage, but they should not discourage state policy makers from trying other strategies.

Many states have also provided public funding to subsidize insurance coverage for children and the working poor. With welfare reform and efforts to place welfare recipients into jobs, the issue of insurance coverage for low wageworkers becomes even more critical.

(5) Focus on incremental health system change.

Given the failure of the 1993 national comprehensive efforts to provide for major health care reform and given the power and importance of the health care industry in the United States, it is not likely that major efforts at reform can succeed in the near future. Implementation of incremental changes may gradually support the goals of controlling costs, improving access, and assuring quality.

Incremental reforms have met with some success at both the state and federal levels. At the federal level, the 1996 passage of the Kennedy-Kassebaum Legislation provided for portability of health insurance coverage and a greater uniformity of health insurance policy across the states. In 1997, the Budget Reconciliation Act provided $24 billion in federal funding over five years to support state programs to expand health insurance coverage to children. Many states have moved forward on their own to expand health insurance coverage and to regulate managed care organizations.

(6) Routinely administer surveys to provide county and population specific data.

While West Virginia is a small state, it is still a very diverse state. In terms of health status and health care access, the problems of McDowell County in the southern coal fields are very different from the problems of Monongalia County. In terms of health insurance coverage, the five-year merged data of the BRFSS, paints a varied picture. In McDowell County over 36 percent of adults below age 65 lack insurance coverage; in Ohio County, in contrast, less than 10 percent lack coverage.

To develop positive policies and programs to address the state's health care needs, these differences need to be understood. National surveys will not provide the detail that West Virginia policymakers need to address state and local problems. West Virginia state government pours millions of dollars into trying to improve access to health care. A wise allocation of resources requires accurate county-level data and evidence that these efforts have their intended effect. In particular, the BRFSS and WVSIS studies provide state legislators and policy planners with essential information on how to manage the heath care problems. In this regard, resources should be made available annually to conduct the health access portion of the surveys and to expand the scope of the questions to allow for analysis of health care access by county, age, gender, income, employment status, and health status.

Both for better and for worse, health care at the end of the 20th century is a powerful industry which impacts the life of every American in many profound ways. Sorting out the economic interests of the industry from the public interest for affordable quality medical care will continue to be a challenge. To meet this challenge, the state will need valid data and thorough analyses to stimulate public discussion and to influence public policy.

References

Agency for Health Care Policy and Research, 1996. The Medical Expenditure Panel Survey; *Questions about the Medical Expenditure Panel Survey,* Pub. No96-Ro72.

Bureau of the Census, *Current Population Survey.* Conducted annually in March.

Employee Benefit Research Institute, 1997. "Trends in Health Insurance Coverage," *Issue Brief,* Number 185 (May).

Foster, Christa and Michael Wadsworth. 1997. *1996 WVSIS Methodology Report: Sample Design, Questionnaire, and Technical Forms.* Morgantown, WV: West Virginia University Survey Research Center.

Franks, P., C.M. Clancy, and M.R. Gold. 1993. "Health Insurance and Mortality," *Journal of the American Medical Association,* vol. 270, pp. 737–741.

Government Accounting Office (GAO). 1997. *Employment-Based Health Insurance, Costs Increase and Family Coverage Decreases.* HEHS–97–35. (February 24)

Harris, Louis and Associates, 1992. *West Virginia Health Care Experiences,* New York, New York. Unpublished report, p. 7.

Health Care Cost Review Authority, West Virginia Department of Health and Human Resources, 1995. *"Overview of West Virginia Hospitals FY 1995,"* p. 33. Unpublished report.

Kaiser Family Foundation. 1996. *"Getting Behind the Numbers on Access to Care",* October 22.

Keith, Bruce. 1993. *1992 WVSIS Methodology Report: Sample Design, Questionnaire, and Technical Forms.* Morgantown, WV: West Virginia University Survey Research Center.

Keith, Bruce, Lee Beaumont, and Susan Derek. 1993. *A Survey of Health Insurance Coverage among West Virginia Businesses.* Morgantown, WV: West Virginia University Survey Research Center.

Morgan, O'Leary, Kathleen Morgan, and Scott Morgan, editors, 1997. *Health Care State Rankings.* Lawrence, KA: Morgan Quitno, p. 260.

Sheils, John F., Randall A. Haught, 1997. "Managed Care Savings for Employers and Households: Impact on the Uninsured." *Follow-Up Report, The American Association of Health Plans,* p.1.

The Southern Institute on Children and Families, 1996. *Uninsured Children in the South* Columbia, SC.

U. S. Centers for Disease Control. 1991. *Behavioral Risk Factor Surveillance Survey.*

"Washington Health Briefs," *Health Legislation and Regulation.* 1996. Volume 22, Number 39, Faulkner & Gray, p. 3.

Chapter 5

Household and Local Labor Market Determinants of Economic Well-Being in the State of West Virginia: A Multi-Level Analysis

Josh Masnick Kim and F. Carson Mencken

Abstract

The determinants of household economic well-being are analyzed in this study using both household data from the West Virginia Social Indicator Survey (WVSIS) and county level variables measuring the quality of the local labor market and the degree of employment growth. Economic well-being is measured subjectively through self reports whether or not the household's basic needs were met by income, and objectively by a measure of income per person in the household. Using logistic and OLS regression techniques, we found that local labor market variables are only significant in increasing economic well-being in households that are endowed with above average levels of education and which are headed by a married parent. West Virginians who do not have any education beyond high-school and who live in a single-parent household do not receive any significant benefits in their levels of economic well-being through residence in counties with a growing and high quality local labor market. These findings suggest that policies aimed at attracting and recruiting industries may not be effective in raising the standards of living for households already operating under multiple disadvantages of low education and single parenthood. Levels of economic inequality in the state are bound to increase unless balanced economic policies that stress both labor market development and the provision of services to low-income households (such as health insurance coverage and child care) are pursued.

Introduction

The emergence of a global service economy has concentrated economic activity in the major urban areas of key economic powers (Sassen 1994; Goe 1994; Dicken 1992; Mencken and Singelmann forthcoming). This transition has caused alarm among leaders concerned about the socioeconomic well-being of rural people and places. The global transition has taken its toll on rural states, such as West Virginia. Over the last 15 years, the economy in West Virginia has shifted from traditional manufacturing (primary metals and chemicals) and extractive industries (coal in particular) to a service-based economy. From 1977–1987, the state lost almost 70,000 jobs in coal mining and manufacturing (primarily in metals and chemicals). The average salary had been $20,000 per annum in manufacturing and $36,400 in coal mining (Maggard, 1994). During this same period, almost 32,000 new service jobs were created, with an average salary of only $15,000 per annum.

Consumer services (entertainment, social, health, personal, education, public administration, repair, retail) dominated growth in West Virginia's service sector, but new jobs in these industries provided low wages. For example, the dominant service industry in the state is now health services, but 62% of the new health services jobs are in the low waged non-profit health services sector (W. V. Center for Economic Research 1991a). The over 9,000 new jobs created in retail averaged wages of only $13,000 per annum. Growth in producer services was also low-waged. Of the 4,784 new jobs created during this period in finance, insurance, and real estate, wages averaged $14,500 per annum (W. V. Center for Economic Research 1991b).

The transformation to an industry characterized primarily by service has had important negative effects on the socioeconomic well-being of West Virginia's citizens. Population declined by 8% between 1980 and 1990 (U.S. Bureau of Census, 1990), causing West Virginia to lose a congressional representative. Concurrently, median household earnings fell by almost 15% during the 1980s. (Maggard 1994; Center for Economic Research 1991b). While it is true that West Virginia ranks at the bottom of states in median household income (50th at $23,564 in 1994) and employment to population ratio (50th at 50.1% in 1994), and towards the top in percent of individuals in poverty (5th at 18.6% in 1994) these figures mask wide variation in economic well-being across the state. Some areas in West Virginia are doing relatively well. Median family income in Jefferson county ($34,887) is more than twice that of Webster county ($15,489) while in Clay, McDowell, and Webster counties, close to one-third of families live on less than $10,000 a year. This compares to Berkeley, Brooke, Hancock, Jefferson, Morgan, and Putnum counties in which less than one-tenth of the families share this low income (WVU Bureau of Business Research 1996). Therefore, West Virginia is better understood as an economically stratified state rather than exclusively as a poor state.

Each state in the nation has programs and policies to help alleviate the problems that such economic transformations create for its citizens. Currently, public policies designed to increase the standard of living for West

Virginian's at the bottom end of the economic ladder can be divided into two categories. The first category is policies that attempt to increase the equality of economic ends. These policies include cash payments to households (TANF, formerly AFDC) as well as payments in services such as Medicaid, Food Stamps and housing assistance, child care and job training. Yet, political support and funding for programs designed to directly impact economic well-being has substantially decreased in recent years. The federal Personal Responsibility and Work Opportunity Reconciliation Act of 1996 ended federal entitlement of income support for the poor. West Virginia will now have very wide latitude in deciding how moneys previously earmarked for income support for children living in low-income, mother-only families (the bulk of Aid to Families with Dependent Children recipients) can be spent. Funds previously earmarked to the state as cash payments can now be used for programs such as job training (Welfare-to-Work) or child-care. Major restrictions include a five-year lifetime limit and mandatory work requirements for receiving benefits, although residents of counties with very high unemployment will be temporary exempted.

A second set of current public policies is designed to increase economic opportunities. These policies include both programs to stimulate local economic development (demand side) and policies to increase levels of human capital (supply side). The philosophy behind local economic development is that the needs of citizens are best met through an expansion of employment opportunities in local areas. The stress in this policy is on creating jobs, preferably jobs that pay good wages and provide benefits. Local economic development is undertaken at the state, county, and city level. According to Bartik (1993), strategies include direct subsidies for firms to locate in a particular area, such as the building of plant specific infrastructures such as roads or sewer lines, the transfer of public land or the use of eminent domain, and/or tax abatement. Indirect subsidies include non-firm specific funding of infrastructure, such as highways and road networks.

Policies that attract industry through direct (tax abatements, road building) or indirect (infrastructure spending) aim to increase the demand for labor in the local labor market and thereby create jobs and raise wages. Critics of these demand-side policies argue that investments in the overall level of human capital, as well as targeted job training and education for low-income workers, is more efficacious in raising living standards of low-income families (see Lichter et al. 1993; Bartik 1993). Demand side policies aim at increasing the supply of high productivity workers so that wages will increase and firms will be attracted to the local labor market. Upgrading the skills of low-wage workers has proved difficult for a number of reasons. Studies of worker training programs have shown only marginal benefits for the costs incurred. Increased resources in West Virginia, especially for statewide education, is hampered by a funding structure that relies on local property taxes. Making education available to older workers has been difficult given the high opportunity costs of subsidies incurred by not working, as well as the lack of affordable child care and transportation for potential recipients.

Policy initiatives, which were essentially aimed at direct support for individuals and households (e.g. Food Stamps, AFDC), have lost political support in recent years. The perception is that such policies create more problems (i.e. dependency on the welfare state) than they solve. Given this political reality, policies in the future will need to focus more on the demand and supply factors mentioned above. That is, more emphasis (if not resources) will need to be placed on policies that are designed to improve the opportunity structure of local places and empower individuals with skills to take advantage of new opportunities. Moreover, in an era of scarce resources, it is important to evaluate which of the policy directions (supply vs. demand) are most likely to succeed in providing increased economic opportunity-particularly for those households at the lowest income levels.

We found no recent studies on West Virginia households which attempted to test supply and demand factors simultaneously. This analysis is, therefore, designed to fill that void. In the present inquiry, we examined household well-being in West Virginia using a multilevel model that includes household measures, such as education level of household, age structure of household (which would be considered supply side factors) and place level measures (such as county unemployment rate, recent county employment change, local industry structure) to predict household well-being. The benefit of this type of analysis is that it allows us to estimate simultaneously the effects of place (demand) and household (supply) characteristics. Most importantly, these data will tell us the relative strengths of each set of variables; which, in turn, should allow us to make informed contributions to policy debates on demand and supply issues.

Economic Perspectives on Labor Force Participation: A Literature Review

Supply and demand policy perspectives are grounded in theoretical models of attainment at place, household and individual levels. Supply side policy focuses on characteristics of the labor force, individuals in the labor force, and household constraints on labor force participation (see Lichter et al. 1993). Supply side perspectives are grounded in theories of human capital, where the well-being of individuals and the households in which they are embedded are directly linked to the bundle of skills and education individuals bring to the labor market. Supply side policies which aim at improving well-being through increased human capital seek to increase the value of individuals in the labor market, through skill enhancement. However, there are problems with measuring well-being at the individual level. Households are the primary unit of social organization in all societies, and we believe that well-being should be assessed at the household level. In addition to skills of the particular individuals living in a household, there are characteristics of households that will affect household well-being. The presence of children may mean that one family member (typically women) must forego labor market participation in order to provide child care. This is particularly true when affordable child-care is not available. The family structure of the household may also affect well-being. Single parent households, especially single mother households, do not fare as well economically as two-parent families, the net of human capital variables (see Biblarz et al. 1997 for a recent review). The lack of affordable child-care compounds the problems of a single parent household. Household size is also a confounding factor. Larger households require greater resources for sustenance than smaller households. The age structure of the household may also be another confounding factor. Older or retired households may report lower levels of income, but require less income to meet household needs.

Demand-side policy perspectives are grounded in the idea that the attainment and well-being of individuals and households are not independent of the well-being of places in which they are embedded. The fortunes of individuals and their households are dependent upon the labor market opportunities available to them. Places that are doing well economically offer opportunities to local citizens that other less fortunate locales cannot (Lyson et al. 1993; Snipp and Bloomquist 1989). The economic plight of households are ultimately linked to conditions in the local labor market. This is particularly true for households in rural states (Lichter and McLaughlin 1995; Kassab et al 1995).

There are a variety of studies, from different theoretical perspectives, which show that household well-being (poverty, income, unemployment) is largely affected by local economic conditions, particularly the industry structure of local communities. For example, human ecologists show that the ecological structure of local communities affects their ability to attract and retain jobs. The human ecology perspective views industry structure as a measure of the sustenance base of a local ecosystem. It is a dimension of how local populations interact with their environment for sustenance or survival (Frisbie and Poston 1978; 1976; Nord and Luloff 1993; Murdock et al. 1993). One of the assumptions of human ecology theory is that sustenance activity directly affects the carrying capacity of the local ecosystem (Poston 1984). Ecosystems with differentiated or complex sustenance functions have greater potential for growth than ecosystems with simple or singular sustenance activities (Hawley 1986). Moreover, ecosystems with singular sustenance activities are at greater risk of "system shock" should organizational or technological changes cause a contraction in the particular niche from which the system draws sustenance (Kasarda and Irwin 1991). Proponents of the industrial restructuring hypothesis in rural sociology make similar arguments (Lichter and McLaughlin 1995; Lyson et al. 1993; Brown and Hirschl 1995; Kassab et al. 1995; Mencken 1997). These scholars maintain that shifts in the industrial structure over the last 20 years have caused changes, drastic at times, in household well-being in rural America.

Urban sociologists now generally maintain that local opportunity structure is not necessarily a function of community structure, but is directly linked to political power and political alliances. Specifically, urban sociologists are interested in how political economic systems work, how groups acquire and monopolize power, who gains and who loses. The perspective is based on several assumptions (Smith 1995: 440–1; Gottdiener and Feagin 1988: 172–74), one of which is that the ability to attract new jobs results from a pro-business climate that is forged through an alliance of state and local government and local business elites. In rural areas, places with cheap labor, anti-union sentiments, and low business costs make attractive sites to locate businesses (see also Dicken 1992; Glasmeier and Howland 1995).

In addition to the political economy of business location decisions, some urban sociologists maintain that the state plays a very important role in affecting the flow of capital (state disparity hypothesis— see Smith 1995: 440–1; Gottdiener and Feagin 1988: 172–74; Gottdiener 1994). The federal government has the power to make substantial economic investments and divestment in communities. According to Mollenkopf (1983), since WWII, one-third of all manufacturing jobs created in the high-tech electronics and computer industries (primarily in the suburbs of large cities) have been the direct result of federal defense spending. Mencken (1996) shows that federal spending was more important in determining earnings growth in the poor counties of Central Appalachia than in other Appalachian counties. Falk and Lyson (1993) contend that the socio-economic spatial disparities in the 1980s were created partly by the transfer of dollars from successful nonmetro development programs to defense contracts (see also Castells 1988; Markusen 1994). During the 1980s, over 8 billion dollars were cut from nonmetro development programs, such as FMHA business loans,

Economic Development Administration, Community Development Block grants, and over 6 billion in General Revenue Sharing (see Falk and Lyson 1993: 268). In short, new urban sociologists maintain that government spending, particularly federal spending, is an important determinant of the types and quality of jobs available in local economies.

If industrial structure is an important determinant of place well-being, as the above review suggests, then industrial recruitment strategies are important players in this equation. Since the full transformation from an agrarian to an industrial society in the U.S. (defined as 50% of the labor force employed in manufacturing), many states have embarked on economic development strategies that attempt to attract industries to their respective state. Isserman (1994) points out that the most frequently adapted model, particularly among rural states (Mississippi, South Carolina, Alabama), is one of "smokestack chasing," where states attempt to recruit manufacturing plants away from other states.

While states have been criticized for this strategy (see Falk and Lyson 1993; 1988; Bartik 1993; Isserman 1994), rural states are often at a disadvantage in the industrial recruitment game. Rural places have few competitive advantages, but one of them is cheap labor (Summers 1982; Bloomquist et al. 1993; Mencken and Singelmann Forthcoming). Therefore, in the industrial recruiting process, rural states and communities are apt to attract industries in the mature stage of the product cycle (i.e. declining or sunset industries), or those industries which are seeking short-term profits through reduced labor costs (Markusen 1985). Typically, these are thought of as manufacturing enterprises, but recent research shows that this model can be extended to services, as well (see Maggard 1994; Glasmeier and Howland 1995). Therefore, the types of industries that are recruited to places will also affect place and household well-being.

In this chapter we examine the effects of place (demand) and household (supply) characteristics through a multi level analysis of household level economic outcomes with household and county level explanatory variables. Variables from the West Virginia Social Indicator Surveys (WVSIS years 1994 through 1996) are merged with county level data gathered from a number of sources. A multi-level research design allows for direct comparisons of the relative importance of household and place level variables in determining economic well-being. The WVSIS is well set up to explore how the economic context in which West Virginians live effects their own economic outcomes. The goal of this research is not to examine the effects of particular policies or programs, but rather to provide information on *what types of economic development strategies* are likely to have the greatest impact on the household level (demand or supply). The inclusion of explanatory and control variables at the county level allows for the effect of economic context to be considered in explanations of economic need. These place level variables are often missing from individual/household analysis of income and poverty. It is at the place level (political boundary) however where most of the economic policy action operates. Failing to include contextual level variables severely limits policy implications that can be drawn from individual and household level research.

Data and Analysis

The task of combining both household and contextual levels of analysis is complicated by the structure of the WVSIS. While the WVSIS is representative of West Virginia's population for ages 18 to 65 (Keith 1996), the WVSIS was not designed to be representative by county. See Appendix A for a discussion of the survey and sample methodology employed by the WVSIS. In order to overcome this difficulty we merged three years of WVSIS data into one data file (1994, 1995, 1996). This increased the number of cases available for analysis to 4,115 and allowed a greater distribution of cases across counties. The geographic population distribution in the newly merged data set was then compared with the actual population distribution by county taken from the U. S. Census (1990). A t-test for paired samples showed that the geographic distribution was for the merged data set and the actual geographic distribution was not significantly different (t value – .77; two-tail sig= .444).[1]

Dependent Variables

Economic well-being is assessed both subjectively and objectively in this analysis. The subjective measure of economic well-being was taken from a question on the WVSIS survey that asked *"Has the income your household earned during the past year allowed you to meet your basic needs?"*[2] This variable was coded as a dichotomous categorical (dummy) variable (BASICY). Fifteen (15) percent of respondents answered that their basic needs were not met by income. This figure corresponds closely to the pov-

---

1 *The tradeoff for increasing the sample size so that county level variables could be included in the analysis was the loss of a range of variables due to changes in the survey over the years covered. From year to year, the survey questions that provide detailed information on a range of household level economic strategies and outcomes have changed, leaving a core set of questions to be analyzed. For instance, questions about means tested transfer payment and informal economic activity are not consistent across the years that were pooled in order to construct the data set.*

2 *See, for example, Appendix C, question 15, Appendix D, question 16, and Appendix E, question 21.*

Table 5–1:
Descriptive Statistics of Survey Data

Variable	Variable Description	Mean	Std Dev	Min.	Max.	Valid N
Dependent Variables						
BASICY	Dummy variable for basic needs met by income	0.15	0.36	0	1	4092
HHNEED	Household income / household size	12,648	10,236	313	85,000	3801
Independent Variables *Household Level*						
YRSED	Respondent years of education completed	12.8	2.95	0	30	4106
SINGLEP	Dummy variable, unmarried with one or more children = 1	0.12	0.32	0	1	4115
AGER	Respondent's age	45.1	16.71	21	70	4115
GENDER	Dummy variable, female = 1	0.52	0.50	0	1	4115
MARITAL	Dummy variable, married = 1	0.60	0.49	0	1	4103
NOADULT	Number of adults in household	2.04	0.80	1	9	4115
NOCHILD	Number of children aged 12 and under living in household	0.50	0.86	0	7	4115
NOTEENS	Number of teenagers living in household	0.25	0.55	0	4	4115
HHSIZE	Number of persons living in household	2.79	1.38	1	11	4115
HHINCR	Household income	29,977	20,075	2,500	85,000	3801
County Level						
SUNSET	Continuous variable for shift industries	0.18	0.09	–0.07	0.41	4112
SUNRISER	Dummy variable, share industries = 1	0.42	0.49	0	1	4112
HSPLUS	Percentage of persons in county with more than high school education	0.29	0.08	0.14	0.45	4112
UNEMRATE	Unemployment rate, 1990	8.52	2.62	5	18.1	4112
POPDEN	Population per square mile, 1990	149.91	107.19	9.6	479.1	4112
SUSDIV	Diversity of industry structure	–3.04	22.76	–174.2	6.16	4112
METRO	Dummy variable, MSA = 1	0.41	0.49	0	1	4112
ADJ	Dummy variable, adjacent to MSA = 1	0.20	0.40	0	1	4112
FEDCAP	Per capita federal spending in county for 1989	3,125	665	1,683	7,229	4112
FEDEMP89	Percentage of labor force employed by federal govt.	0.02	0.02	0.01	0.09	4112
HOUSE90	Percentage of houses built before 1939	0.24	0.08	0.10	0.46	4112
INTSTAT	Dummy variable, presence of interstate highway = 1	0.60	0.49	0	1	4112
MANUF$	Manufacturing compensation / total salary	35.29	38.78	6.22	240.2	4112

• Data are weighted by the household weight variable.

erty rate in the state. The largest category of basic need reported as not met by income for the respondents was general bills (13.5%), followed by medical/health expenses (13.4%), utilities (12.6%), housing/rent (10.1%), and food (9.6%). The second dependent variable specified in this research was a measure of the income available to each member of the household (HHNEED). This was constructed by dividing household income by household size. Household income in the WVSIS is measured as a categorical (14 categories) rather than a continuous variable. Therefore it was necessary to recode this variable at the midpoints (see, e.g., Appendix E, questions CINC1 through CINC3). A respondent who reported a household income between $30,000 and $40,000 was assigned a value of $35,000. The household income variable was topcoded at $85,000, as the highest category possible was $80,000 or more (see Table 1 for descriptive statistics).[3]

Independent Variables

The predictor variables included in this analysis were categorized by key household and county variables and control household and county variables. The key household independent variables were a measure of human capital and a key measure of household structure. At the county level, the key variables were the measures of industry earnings growth and the measure of local labor market quality. The county level variables were intended to operationalize demand policies (industry structure) and some supply policies (labor market quality) that are pursued to encourage increased economic well-being for low-income households.[4] These variables model the intended effect of these polices, but not the policies themselves. In other words, counties with a high level of growth in fast growing industries should theoretically enjoy lower levels of economic need.

The main predictor variables were measures of human capital and household structure. The education of the respondent served as a proxy for the human capital level of the household (Appendix E, question 1F). The education variable (YRSED) was measured as a continuous variable with a mean of 12.8 (standard deviation 2.95). Household structure was measured using three variables. The most important variable of interest was a measure for unmarried parents (SINGLEP); this was a dummy vari-

---

3 *The BASICY and HHNEED variables are complementary measures of economic well–being. The two variables are highly correlated with each other and the use of two measures of economic well–being increases the validity and reliability of the analysis.*

4 *The education measure is also used as a measure for the demand for skilled labor, given that better educated workers are likely to migrate to prosperous labor markets.*

able coded 1 in cases where the respondent reported children in household age 18 or under and was not currently married. Eleven and six-tenths (11.6) percent of households and 16.2 percent of the families in the survey were coded as single parent households.[5]

Two measures of local industrial quality were computed for each county with a shift-share analysis. Shift-share analysis decomposed earnings into two categories: share of nationally growing industries and shift of nationally declining industries (see Loveridge 1995). The share of nationally growing industries was computed by comparing earnings growth from all industries in a county over a period of time to the national growth rate for all industries for that period of time. We subtracted the national growth rate from the county growth rate for the 1989-92 business cycle. The shift of nationally declining industries was computed as the sum of earnings growth from all industries in a county less the national growth rate for the sum of all those industries. A positive share value represented a county industry mix where earnings were growing faster than the national growth rate, and these are referred to as *sunrise industries* (SUNRISE). A positive shift value represented a county industry mix where earnings were growing faster than the national growth rates only for those particular industries. This typically happens in nationally declining industries (i.e. those in the mature stage of the product cycle). We refer to these as *sunset industries* (SUNSET).

The key county level variables analyzed were measures of change in industry structure (SUNRISE) and (SUNSET) and a measure of labor force quality based on the educational level of the county (HSPLUS). Forty-two (42) percent of all counties in the West Virginia (23 counties) were classified as SUNRISE counties (see Table 1). While this may appear to be good news for the counties classified as SUNRISE, it should be kept in mind that the mean increase above the national average was only .01 (1 percent) and the maximum is only .03. For the state as a whole, the mean SUNRISE score is -.01. In other words, the majority of West Virginia counties that have experienced employment growth in fast growing industries nationwide have done so only marginally. No county in West Virginia stands out as a center of rapid industrial growth. The mean score for SUNSET was .18 with a standard deviation of 0.09 and a range from -0.07 (Hancock county) to 0.41 (Wayne county). In comparison, the SUNRISE variable was very narrowly distributed with a mean of -0.01, a standard deviation of 0.03 and range from -0.07 (Hancock county) to 0.03 (Monongalia county). Overall,

---

5 *These percentages are very close to the state averages. In 1990,15.5% of all families in the state with children under age 18 were headed by women.*

counties in WV experienced more earnings growth from nationally declining industries during the late 1980s and early 1990s. The data for shift-share
analysis was derived from the Regional Economic Information Systems, of
the Bureau of Economic Analysis.

The second key county level variable was a measure of labor force
quality operationalized as a percentage of the population 25 and older with
greater than a high school education in 1990. In practice, this means that
anyone in the county with 1+ years of technical, vocational or college training and a high school degree was counted in this category. Statewide, the
mean percentage of adults with greater then a high-school education is 29
percent (see Table 1). Monongalia county has the most educated workforce
in the state where 45 percent of the over 25 population has some sort of
education beyond high school. Lincoln county is the least educated with
only 14 percent of the age 25+ attaining greater than a high school education.

The variable HSPLUS was intended to operationalize local labor market quality (supply side policies). Theoretically, counties with a higher
quality labor market should be able to attract high productivity/high-pay-
ing industries. In the regression models, this variable has typically been
left as a continuous variable.

Control Variables

Control variables at the household level were standard controls for
estimates of income and economic well-being (Atkinson et al. 1992). The
age of the respondent proxied for the age of the adults in the household
(Appendix E, question 1D). Controlling for age was necessary as age was
correlated with both income and family formation behavior. Other measures of household structure included as controls were the number of
children, teenagers and adults in the household. Economic well-being
should not be evaluated apart from economic need. Children and teenagers consume more than they produce in the household, where more adults
in the household should be associated with higher levels of economic well-
being. Respondents' sex was also included in the analysis to control for the
possibility that men and women may answer questions regarding household need differently (Appendix E, question 1C).

Control variables at the county level were drawn from both human
ecology and the new urban sociological theory. Human ecology variables
included population density in 1990, metropolitan status (binary 1=yes),
adjacency to metropolitan area (1= yes), and an interstate in the county
(1=yes). The underlying economic infrastructure of the county of residence
was measured by the percent of 1990 housing stock built prior to 1939.
This measure served as a proxy for infrastructure as it is highly correlated

with the age and condition of physical assets such as roads, water, and sewer systems (Kasarda and Irwin 1991). Counties with high levels of infrastructure (e.g. low percentage of homes built before 1939) are thought to be at a competitive advantage in recruiting capital intensive industries—industries that tend to pay higher wages. The diversity of the industry structure (sustenance diversity) has been identified as an important component of ecological models (Murdock et al. 1993). Areas with greater industrial diversity are generally cushioned against economic downturns and other dislocations (such as increases in energy prices). Greater industry diversity is associated with higher levels of productivity as labor is more specialized (Frisbie and Poston 1976). These measures were taken from the Census of Population and Housing for 1990.

Controlling for the underlying business climate is important to evaluating the impact of local economic development initiatives. Unlike human capital or infrastructure levels, business climate cannot be measured directly and must be done through proxy measures. The new urban sociology suggests that measures such as labor force quality, existing infrastructure, and public (e.g. federal) investments, constitute a large part of the business climate equation. Labor force quality was one of the main variables of interest (see above) and was operationalized as percentage of population age 25 and over with some education beyond high school. Average earnings per manufacturing employee (MANUF$) is a measure of labor market wage rates, and relative importance of manufacturing in the county. Places with higher manufacturing wages are said to be poorer locations for new business because labor costs are too high (Kasarda and Irwin 1991). Public investment was measured by capita federal spending less transfer payments (FEDCAP) and the percent of the labor force that is employed by the federal government (FEDEMP). These measures were taken from the County Statistics File 4. Descriptive statistics of all measures are presented in Table 1.

Both household level and contextual level variables were examined in order to determine their relative effect on the socioeconomic well-being of households in West Virginia. A set of means tests differences were performed on all predictor variables (both key and control) using the dependent variables as the grouping variables. For this set of tests, the continuous HHNEED variable was recoded as a dichotomous variable at the sample mean. We estimated a logistic regression model for the dependent variable BASICY, which asked if the household's basic needs were met by income. The determinants of income available per household member (HHNEED) were modeled using a standard OLS model. Both the logistic and OLS models for the dependent variables were measured using the same household and county level key and control variables.

Findings

Difference of Means Tests

Table 2 shows the difference in means tests for all independent variables by the dependent variables BASICY and HHNEED. Respondents who reported that their basic needs were not met by income differed significantly from those whose basic needs were not met on almost every household level variable and a few county level variables. On average, respondents who reported that their income did not meet their families basic needs were younger, less likely to be married, less educated, had more children, and more teenagers in the household, as compared with households whose basic needs were met (see Table 2 below). Not surprisingly, respondents whose basic needs were not met had significantly lower household incomes ($15,211 vs. $32,573), had less income per capita in the household ($6,122 vs. $13,766), and were more likely to be classified as a single parent household (23% vs. 9%).

Differences at the county level for households in which basic needs were not met as compared to households in which basic needs were met are statistically significant for five of the thirteen county level variables. Households that reported that their basic needs were not met by their income, on average, live in counties that also have lower levels of the adult population who have more than a high school degree. These households were less likely to live in a metropolitan county, and on average lived in counties that were less densely populated per square mile than households whose basic needs were met. The average county unemployment rate was also slightly higher for households in which basic needs were not met than for those households in which income did meet basic needs.

The mean score for the HHNEED variable (per capita household income) was $12,648 with a standard deviation of $10,236 (refer to Table 1). Dividing the HHNEED variable at its mean allowed for the difference of means tests to run on lower and higher income-to-needs households (see Table 2). Households in the lower half of the income-to-needs category were on average less educated (respondent 12.1 vs. 14.1) and more likely to include a single parent (16% vs. 4%) than households on the top half of the income-to-needs distribution. Households with less income per person were both younger (respondent 43.8 vs. 46.2), larger (3.1 vs. 2.3) than better off households.

Using the sample mean of the HHNEED as the grouping variable revealed larger differences in the county level measures than those observed by using BASICY as the grouping variable. The industry growth measure (SUNRISE) was significantly different across household types. Forty per-

Table 5–2:
Means–Test Differences for Selected Variables

Variable Description	Basic Needs		Household Needs	
	Met	Not Met	Less Than Sample Mean	Greater Than Sample Mean
Household Level				
Household income/ household size	13,766	6,122*	6,825	22,751*
Respondent's years of education	12.9	11.8*	12.1	14.1*
Dummy variable, unmarried with one or more children = 1	0.09	0.23*	0.16	0.04*
Respondent's age	45.6	42*	43.8	46.2*
Dummy variable, female = 1	0.05	0.61*	0.55	0.44*
Dummy variable, married = 1	0.06	0.44*	0.59	0.63*
Number of adults in household	2.0	2.0	2.1	1.9*
Number of children under 13 years of age in household	0.48	0.61*	0.67	0.25*
Number of teenagers in household	0.23	0.32*	0.32	0.13*
Number of persons living in household	2.7	2.9*	3.1	2.3*
Household income	32,573	15,211*	20,160	47,010*
County Level				
Shift industries	0.184	0.186	0.18	0.18
Dummy variable, shared industries = 1	0.42	0.4	0.4	0.44*
Percentage of residents with more that 12 years of education	0.30	0.28*	0.28	0.30*
Unemployment rate, 1990	8.4	8.8*	8.8	8.0*
Population per square mile, 1990	151.4	140.6*	141.8	163.9*
Diversity of industry structure	−2.7	−4.5	−4.1	−1.1*
Dummy variable, MSA = 1	0.43	0.34*	0.37	0.48*
Dummy variable, adjacent to MSA = 1	0.2	0.21	0.22	0.17*
Per capita federal spending, 1989	3,128	3,100	3,118	3,143*
Percentage of labor force employed by federal government	0.021	0.021	0.021	0.023*
Percentage of houses built before 1939	0.23	0.23	0.23	0.23
Dummy variable, interstate highway in county = 1	0.6	0.57	0.58	0.63*
Manufacturing compensation / total salary	35.6	33.2	33.5	37.3*

* Mean difference is statistically significant at $p < .05$

cent (40) of the counties were classified as SUNRISE counties for respondents whose income per household member fell below the sample mean compared with 44 percent of counties for households with incomes-to-need ratios above the sample means. As with the basic needs variable, households whose income-to-needs was below the sample mean were less likely to live in a metropolitan county (48% vs. 37%) and more likely to live in counties with a higher unemployment rate (8.8 vs. 8.0). These households were also less likely to live in a county that had an interstate running through it (63% vs. 58%), but more likely to live in a county adjacent to another county that does have an interstate (22% vs. 17%).

Logistic Regression Results

In order to determine the relative effect of the study's household and county level variables on economic well-being, we estimated both logistic and OLS models. Table 3 below shows the R value and the odds ratios (Exp B) for the logistic model with the dichotomous dependent variable BASICY. [6]

When the full set of household and county level predictor and control variables were entered into the logistic model to predict whether or not income met household needs, only 6 out of the 20 variables reached statistical significance. The variable with the highest R value was the respondent's years of education (YRSED). For each additional year of education, the likelihood that a respondent's household would not be able to meet its basic needs with current income decreased an average of 17.6 percent (ExpB = 0.85). The overwhelming effect of education on economic well-being was consistent with our expectations and with an enormous body of human capital literature.

Households that contain an unmarried parent carried an elevated risk of not meeting their needs with income. Controlling for no other variables, the being a single parent raised the odds of having income below needs by 70 percent (ExpB = 1.7). Within the full model (all other household and county variables held constant) this increased relative risk dropprd to 1.48. With an R value of .10 the SINGLEP variable was the second most impor-

---

6 *The R value is analogous to a standardized coefficient in an OLS model in that it shows the relative effect of the independent variable on the dependent variable for measures with different metrics. The value of the R statistic can range from –1 to +1. The higher the R value the more effect the variable has on increasing the likelihood that a respondent will report that the households basic needs are not met. The odds ratio can be interpreted as measuring the relative risk implied in moving from one value or category of a given independent variable on the dependent variable. For instance, controlling for all other variables in the equation households that are headed by a single parent are 1.48 times as likely (or 48 percent) to report that their basic needs are not met by income than all other households.*

Table 5–3:
Logistic Regression of Basic Need Variable
on Household and County–level Variables
(Basic Needs Not Met coded as 1) Variable Description

Variable Description	R	Exp (B)
Household Level		
Respondent's years of education	0.15	0.85***
Dummy variable, unmarried with one or more children = 1	0.10	1.48***
Household Level Controls		
Respondent's age	0.07	0.98***
Dummy variable, female = 1	0.06	1.18***
Number of children under 13 years of age in household	0.00	1.04
Number of teenagers in household	0.00	1.11
Number of adults in household	0.00	0.92
County Level		
Shift industries	0.00	1.29
Dummy variable, share industries = 1	0.00	0.94
Percentage of residents with more than 12 years of education	0.02	0.10
County Level Controls		
Unemployment rate, 1990	0.00	1.02
Population per square mile, 1990	−0.04	1.00
Diversity of industry structure	0.00	1.00
Dummy variable, MSA = 1	0.07	0.70***
Dummy variable, adjacent to MSA = 1	0.03	0.85***
Per capita federal spending, 1989	0.00	1.00
Percentage of labor force employed by federal government	−0.01	0.00
Percentage of houses built before 1939	0.02	0.24
Dummy variable, interstate highway in county = 1	0.00	0.98
Manufacturing compensation / total salary	0.00	1.00

*** $p < .001$, * $p < .05$

tant predictor after education. Households with children and an unmarried adult face an economic disadvantage that is only slightly attenuated by education, age of respondent, and household size. Re-running the logistic model on households that had one or more children less than the age of 13 increased the magnitude and relative effect of the single parent variable to R= 0.19 and the ExpB to 1.76. Controlling for education and every other household and county measure — families with children and a non-married parent were at increased relative risk of 76 percent of not having their basic needs met as compared with families that contain married parents. For households that contained children, the non-marital parent variable was the most important predictor of whether or not basic needs were met by income.

None of the county level key variables achieved statistical significance in determining a households ability to afford basic needs. In bivariate regression models, the only key county level variable that achieved statistical significance was the measure of labor market quality HSPLUS. This suggests that households do benefit from living in a county in which the population is more educated-but only if those households have some resources to take advantage of the higher quality labor market. If the full model was run for households that did not contain a single parent (SINGLEP=0), the county labor market quality variable gained marginal significance (HSPLUS p< .0876). When the same model was run for households that did not contain an single parent and whose respondents had 12 or more years of education, (YRSED) than the labor market quality variable becomes highly significant (HSPLUS p < .0093).

The failure of the comparative industry growth measures, SUNSET and SUNRISE, to achieve statistical significance suggests that either 1) industry composition does not determine household economic well-being, or 2) that no county has experienced yet enough growth to show up as significant at the household level. The lack of counties that have experienced rapid growth in high productivity industries within the state made it difficult to test the hypothesis that this sort of growth increases chances for households to avoid economic distress. It may very well be true that recruiting high productivity industries is beneficial for the households in the county in which these industries are located. It would be beneficial from a policy point of view to reanalyze this data at a point in which counties in the state have been successful in industrial recruitment.

Among the county level controls, only the metropolitan and adjacency measures gained statistical significance. No matter what a household's educational level or household structure, they decreased their risk of having incomes below need if they live in or adjacent to a metropolitan county.

The other way to look at this finding is that West Virginian's who do not have access to metropolitan labor markets have a significantly increased relative risk of having inadequate incomes. Given the fact that 26 out of the 55 counties in the state are not metropolitan or adjacent to a metropolitan county, this is a significant finding.

OLS Regression Results

Table 4 shows the unstandardized and standardized regression coefficients for the full model in which the level of income per household member (HHNEED) was estimated. This model explains 33 percent of the variance for the HHNEED variable. As with the logistic analysis, the most important determinant of household income per capita was years of education of the respondent (YRSED). Each year of additional education increased the amount of dollars available to each household member by $1,340. Education explains 15 percent of the variance HHNEED. Households headed by a single parent have on average $2,766 less income per household member then any other household type, when all other variables are held constant. This figure is considerably below a loss of income of $6,536 per household member when the regression model is run with no other variables (bivariate regression results not shown). As expected the number of children, teenagers, and adults in the household were strong predictors of household need. This was not surprising given the fact that the dependent variable was constructed using the household size in its denominator.

The most striking difference between the logistic and OLS models was that the industry structure variables, SUNSET and SUNRISE, achieved significance in the OLS models where in the logistic model they did not. Households that resided in counties that experience earnings growth above the national average in either sunrise or sunset industry types reported losses in income per household. There may be two explanations for these effects. First, the negative effects of SUNSET earnings change were not wholly unanticipated. This measure generally reflects the influx of mature, labor intensive jobs, where employers were looking for short-term gains through reduced labor costs. Therefore, while there may be more jobs in the area, they are not necessarily jobs that are going to improve household well-being. In fact, there is an established literature in sociology which suggests that this type of employment is generally cyclical, short-term and low paying (Hirschl et al. 1989).

The negative effects of SUNRISE industries may reflect mining dependence. During the 1989–92 period, mining made a brief rebound, due to increases in crude oil prices as a result of the Gulf War. With a short-run

increased demand for domestic coal, earnings grew at a much faster rate in
these sectors. However, our analysis models household income-to-size in
the years following the Gulf War (1993–95), where the price and demand
for coal returned to pre-war levels. Since coal counties have had high unemployment rates since the early 1980s (Maggard 1994), it is reasonable to
expect households in these counties to have lower income to size ratios.
Therefore, it is possible that the SUNRISE measure was capturing the effects of being a coal county in a brief period when there was increased
demand for coal production.

Table 5–4:
Regression of Household Need on Household and
County–level Variables

Variable Description	Unstandardized B	Standardized Beta
Household Level		
Respondent's years of education	1,340	.383***
Dummy variable, unmarried with one or more children = 1	–2,766	–.086***
Household Level Controls		
Respondent's age	7	.012
Dummy variable, female = 1	–2,190	–.170***
Number of children under 13 years of age in household	–3,200	–.272***
Number of teenagers in household	–2,135	–.117***
Number of adults in household	–2,859	–.223***
County Level		
Shift industries	–3,768	–.033*
Dummy variable, share industries = 1	– 739	–.036*
Percentage of residents with more than 12 years of education	–4,165	–.032
County Level Controls		
Unemployment rate, 1990	– 247	–.064***
Population per square mile, 1990	– 3	–.032
Diversity of industry structure	– 10	.022
Dummy variable, MSA = 1	–2,074	.100
Dummy variable, adjacent to MSA = 1	– 733	.029
Per capita federal spending, 1989	0	–.013
Percentage of labor force employed by federal government	–1,678	–.003
Percentage of houses built before 1939	–1,025	–.008
Dummy variable, interstate highway in county = 1	351	.017
Manufacturing compensation / total salary	– 3	.010
CONSTANT	9,111***	

*** p < .001, * p < .05

Discussion of Findings and Conclusions

A sizable proportion, about 15 percent, of households in West Virginia cannot meet their basic needs for general bills, medical/health expenses, utilities, housing/rent, and food. Among certain types of households the probability that income will fall below basic needs is very high. Almost one-third (30.2 percent) of single parent households was found to have income below their basic needs. Close to one-in-five households (18.1 percent) in which the WVSIS respondent had less than or equal to 12 years of education reported that their basic needs were not met. The majority of households in the WVSIS (57.5%) fall into this education category.

Households that face multiple disadvantages such as having 12 or less years of education and an unmarried parent are at the highest risk to have low-incomes which do not meet their basic needs. The average income per person for these households is under $5,000 annually, as compared with an average annual income per household member of over $11,000 for households that have both a married couple and which the respondent had more than 12 years of education. Households that were headed by an unmarried parent who did not have a high school diploma (one fifth of all single parent households) reported an average income per household member of just over $4,500 per year.

Beyond living in a metropolitan or adjacent county, the type of county in which single parent and less educated households resided made very little difference in determining their economic well-being. These households were no more likely to have their basic needs met or to have significantly more income per household member even when they lived in counties that had experienced employment growth rates in high productivity industries that were above the national average. Only households that already have some advantages such as higher levels of education and headship by a married adult did labor market quality variables make a significant difference in household level economic well being.

We found that policies designed to improve the opportunity structure at the county level, through either industry recruitment or upgrades in the skills of the local labor market, were largely ineffective in making any material difference in the lives of households in the lower quintile of income distribution. We based this conclusion on two findings. First, education level and single parent status had negative effects on earnings, net of place effects; and they were more likely to report that their basic needs were not met, net of place effects. The implications are that single parent and low educated households in counties that are doing well will not benefit from general increases in the quality of the labor market. In further analyses not reported here, we restricted the analyses to heads of households with a high school diploma and those non-single parent households. This analysis showed that place effects were more important, especially the quality of the local labor force (education level of local labor force). This finding implies that policies aimed at increasing the opportunity structure at the place level are effective for households that have higher levels of education and are not single parent households. Households that are operating under the multiple disadvantages of low education levels and single-parenthood are not likely to see the benefits of a well-developed labor market. Policy makers should be clear about what their economic development policies can realistically accomplish. This research empirically demonstrates that specific segments of the population do not see any economic improvement in their well-being (both perceived and actual) in counties that have both the most educated and highly trained labor markets and the strongest degrees of job growth.

Policy makers are now faced with a fundamental choice between policies that promote economic growth and policies that promote economic equality. Targeting resources at recruiting and retaining new industries in the state may pay off in terms of employment and economic growth. However, these policies, while effective in creating jobs, will also command state and local funds; hence lowering the amount of resources available to direct subsidies aimed at the household level. In short, policy makers may succeed in improving overall levels of economic growth only to find that those households with low levels of education or other difficulties, such as headship by single-parent, are unaffected by this economic growth. A rising tide of economic growth will not lift all boats in the state. A West Virginia economy with lower unemployment and higher average wages could also mean higher levels of income inequality across households.

The other difficulty that policy makers will face in decreasing the numbers of families whose income is too low to meet basic needs is that demographic trends are moving in a direction that all but guarantees the proportion of economically distressed families will increase. The main trend is the growth in the number of families that contain an unmarried parent due to both increases in the divorce rate and increases in the rate of non-marital childbearing. Starting in the early 1970s, West Virginia has seen a "divorce revolution" with the divorce rate increasing from 3.2 per 1,000 in 1970 to 5.4 per 1,000 in 1993. During these same years the marriage rate declined from 9.1 per 1,000 to 6.4. Changes in marital patterns have largely driven the increase in births to unmarried women. In 1975 just under one-in-ten births were to unmarried women. Today that figure is close to one-in-three. Where as most efforts to reduce non-marital pregnancy in the state have been aimed at teenagers, this group constitutes a minority of all non-marital births (36% in 1993 — a figure that has stayed relatively constant since 1965). Due to growth in the divorce rate, declines in the marriage rate, and the attendant increase in non-marital fertility, today close to 1 in 5 children in the state lives in a single-parent family. This proportion is up from less than 1 in 10 two decades ago.

Even if the trend towards non-marital fertility does stabilize, the trend will be difficult to reverse. One of the most effective strategies in reducing the level of economic need among West Virginian families would be to reduce the proportion of one-parent families. The ability, however, of policy makers to legislate family formation decisions is severely limited. Programs to increase the availability of birth control, sex education and abortion are extremely controversial. Education about the dangers of single-parenthood is expensive and not very effective in isolation from other programs that aim to increase the options of young women. Mandating tougher marriage counseling and divorce laws is popular but is not likely to make much of a substantive difference as cohabitation and separation rates increase to fill the gap.

The results of this analysis of the determinants of household need are somewhat distressing. The current focus on policies designed to increase worker opportunities in local labor markets may be effective in the aggregate, but the benefits of these programs will accrue primarily to those with skills and the resources to take advantage of increased opportunities. Entry into the local labor market of people formerly on public assistance will increase the labor supply, but will also drive down the wages of all low-skilled workers. There is very little chance that jobs reflective of low-skill and high-pay, such as mining or manufacturing, will be brought into the state at anywhere near the levels necessary to make a significant impact in the proportion of households with low-income. The majority of anticipated new manufacturing jobs, such as the Toyota engine plant opening in Putnam county, requires workers with higher levels of education and skills in order to operate the machinery. Demographic trends such as decreases in the marriage rate and increases in divorce and non-marital childbearing have increased the percentage of households headed by a single parent. These households are among the most vulnerable to having incomes below their basic needs. Based upon these findings, the following recommendations are essential to improving the conditions of household incomes in the new labor market:

Public Policy Recommendations

(1) Policy makers should be clear on what local economic development projects *can and cannot* accomplish.

All too often the recruitment of a new manufacturer to the state is seen as a panacea to address the needs of low-income families. Industrial recruitment may be a good thing in its own right in that new industries raise average wages and increase employment. However, the households that benefit most from these policies are those that are not at the bottom quintile of income to needs.

(2) Policies aimed at recruiting and retaining industries must be balanced with policies aimed directly at helping low-income households meet their basic needs for medical care, housing, and child-care. In par - ticular, legislators should resist the urge to attract new businesses at the costs of eroding the tax base to a degree that direct services such as child-care and continuing education cannot be offered.

Industry recruitment programs that diminish state revenues through direct subsidies (such as infrastructure building) or indirect subsidies (such as tax abatements) will primarily benefit West Virginian's who are already relatively well off. Conversely, mother-only and less educated households are extremely vulnerable to even small cutbacks in state sponsored social services. The potential economic impact of state sponsored economic development programs (whether they be industry recruitment or infrastructure investment) must be assessed for all citizens in the effected area. This research has demonstrated that economic development strategies do not impact all groups equally, and that households with less education and/or fewer wage earners must be directly considered in assessing the efficacy of state funded investment opportunities. Families with greater initial resources will continue to prosper in a competitive economic climate with or without state interference in the market. On the other hand, families with fewer resources stand to lose the most if direct social services are cutback in order to fund industry recruitment. Achieving growth with equity must be a primary objective of social and economic policy within the state of West Virginia as we enter the 21st Century.

References

Atkinson, A.B., F. Bourguignon and C. Morrisson. 1992. *Empirical Studies of Earnings Mobility.* Chur, Switzerland: Harwood Academic Publishers.

Bartik, Timothy J. 1993. "Who Benefits from Local Job Growth: Migrants or the Original Residents?" *Regional Studies* September: 297–311.

Biblarz, Timothy J, Adrian E. Raftery and Alexander Bucur. 1997. "Family Structure and Social Mobility." *Social Forces* 75:1319–1342.

Bloomquist, Leonard, Christina Gringeri, Donald Tomaskovic-Devey; and Cynthia Truelove. 1993. "Work Structures and Rural Poverty." Pp 68–105 in *Persistent Poverty In Rural America* Edited by the Rural Sociological Society Task Force on Persistent Rural Poverty. Boulder, CO: Westview Press.

Brown, David and Thomas A. Hirschl. 1995. "Household Poverty in Rural and Metropolitan Core Areas of the United States." *Rural Sociology* 60: 44–66.

Center for Economic Research. 1991a. "West Virginia Service Industries." Morgantown: West Virginia University.

Center for Economic Research. 1991b. "Bearfacts: West Virginia 1979–89" and Bulletin 7. Morgantown: West Virginia University.

Dicken. Peter. 1992. *Global Shift* 2nd ed. New York: Guilford Press.

Falk, William and Thomas Lyson. 1988 *High Tech, Low Tech, No Tech.* Albany: SUNY Press.

_____. 1993 "Restructuring Local Labor Markets" Pp. 257–278 in J. Singelmann and F.A. Deseran (eds.) *Inequalities in Labor Market Areas.* Boulder: Westview Press.

Frisbie, W. Parker and Dudley L. Poston, 1978. "Sustenance Differentiation and Population Redistribution." *Social Forces* 57:42–56.

_____. 1976. "The Structure of Sustenance Organization and Population Change in Nonmetropolitan America." *Rural Sociology* 41: 354–370.

Glasmeier, Amy and Marie Howland. 1995. *From Combines to Computers* Albany: SUNY Press.

Goe, Richard 1994 "The Producer Services Sector and Development within the Deindustrializing Urban Community." *Social Forces* 72:971–1009.

Gottdiener, Mark and Joe Feagin 1988. "The Paradigm Shift in Urban Sociology." *Urban Affairs Quarterly* 24: 163–87.

Hawley, Amos. 1986. *Human Ecology: A Theoretical Essay.* Chicago: Univ. Press.

Isserman, Andrew, 1994. "State Economic Development Policy and Practice in the United States: A Survey Article." *International Regional Science Review.* 16:49-100.

Hirschl, Thomas A., Gene F. Summers, and Leonard E. Bloomquist. 1989 "Right-to-work legislation and local labor market growth." Pp 223–240 in W.W. Falk and Th.A. Lyson (eds.), *Research in Rural Sociology and Development.* JAI Press.

Kasarda, John D. and Michael D. Irwin. 1991 "National Business Cycles and Community Competition for Jobs." *Social Forces* 69:733–61.

Kassab, Kathy, A.E. Luloff, Fred Schmidt. 1995. "The Changing Impact of Industry, Household Structure, and Residence on Household Well-being." *Rural Sociology* 60:67–90.

Keith, Bruce, 1996. *1995 WVSIS Methodology Report: Sample Design, Questionnaire, and Technical Forms.* Survey Research Center, West Virginia University, Morgantown, WV.

Lichter, Daniel T. and Diane K. McLaughlin. 1995. "Changing Economic Opportunities, Family Structure, and Poverty in Rural Areas." *Rural Sociology* 60:688–706.

______, Lionel J. Beaulieu, Jill Findeis and Ruy A. Teixeira. "Human Capital, Labor Supply, and Poverty in Rural America." Pp. 39–67 in *Persistent Poverty In Rural America* Edited by the Rural Sociological Society Task Force on Persistent Rural Poverty. Boulder, CO: Westview Press.

Maggard, Sally W. 1994. "From Farm to Coal Camp to Back Office and McDonald's: Living in the Midst of Appalachia's Latest Transformation." *Journal of Appalachian Studies Association* 6:14–38.

Markusen, Ann R. 1985. *Profit Cycles, Oligopoly and Regional Development.* Cambridge, MA: MIT Press.

Mencken, F. Carson 1997. ""Regional Differences in Socioeconomic Well-being in Appalachia" *Sociological Focus* 30: 79–97.

______. 1996 "Income and Employment Change in Appalachia during the 1983–88 Business Cycle Recovery: Locating Differential Effects in North, Central and South Appalachia." *Journal of Appalachian Studies* 2(1): 77–86.

______ and Joachim Singelmann. Forthcoming. "Socioeconomic Performance in Metropolitan and Nonmetropolitan Areas during the 1980s." *Sociological Quarterly.*

Mollenkopf, John H. 1983 *The Contested City.* Princeton University Press.

Murdock, Steve H., Md. Nazrul Hoque, and Kenneth Backman. 1993. "Determinants of 1980–1990 Net Migration in Texas Counties." *Rural Sociology* 58:190–209.

Nord, Mark and Al Luloff. 1993. "Socioeconomic Heterogeneity of Mining-Dependent Counties." *Rural Sociology* 58:492–500.

Sassen, Saskia. 1994. *Cities in a World Economy* Newbury Park, CA: Pine Forge.

Smith, David A. 1995. "The New Urban Sociology Meets the Old: Rereading Some Classical Human Ecology." *Urban Affairs Review.* 30:432-457.

Snipp, C. Matthew, and Leonard E. Bloomquist. 1989 "Sociology and labor market structure." Pp. 1–28 in W.W. Falk and Th.A. Lyson (eds.), *Research in Rural Sociology and Development.* JAI Press.

Summers, Gene F.1982 "Industrialization." Pp. 164–174 in D. Dillman and D.J. Hobbs (eds.), *Rural Society in the U.S.* Boulder: Westview Press.

U.S. Bureau of Census. 1990. *Characteristics of the Population.* Washington, DC: Government Printing Office.

WVU Bureau of Business Research, 1996. *West Virginia Statistical Abstract 1995–96.* West Virginia University, Morgantown, WV.

Chapter 6

Informal Economic Activity In West Virginia: A Descriptive And Multivariate Analysis[1]

F. Carson Mencken and Sally Ward Maggard

Abstract

This study investigates the extent to which households in West Virginia participate in informal economic activities. The recent transformation to a service based economy has negatively affected the state, long dependent upon primary and secondary economic sectors. Informal economic activity offers one strategy for adapting to economic restructuring. Using data collected from a random sample of West Virginia households in 1996, this study found that approximately 22% of West Virginia's households engage in informal economic activities (such as house repair, yard work, crafts, child care, raising farm animals) for income or exchange. However, we also found that very few West Virginia households depend on these activities for substantial proportions of total household income. Among those that participate for income/exchange, only 8% reported that 20% or more of their total household income comes from informal economic activities. Our analysis shows that economic status of the household is an important determinant of which households participate in informal economic activity. However, the data also shows that it is not the poorest households that participate in this activity, but the near poor.

Introduction

Rural and urban economies have gone through important transformations during the last three decades. This transformation has been difficult for rural areas, particularly over the last 15 years, where poverty rates have increased dramatically (U.S. Department of Agriculture, 1993; Lichter and

---

1 *A previous version was presented at the annual meeting of the Rural Sociological Society in Des Moines, Iowa. Institutional support for this project was provided by a grant from the Eberly College of Arts and Sciences, West Virginia University. We wish to thank Ralph Brown, Charles Tolbert, II, William Falk and Ann Tickamyer for comments on earlier drafts.*

McLaughlin, 1995). As part of an overall adaptation strategy to new forms of production, rural families are expected to turn to non-standard forms of production for sustenance (Jensen et al, 1995; Campbell et al., 1993; Duncan, 1992).

This study explores the extent to which households in West Virginia engage in, and rely upon, informal non-standard forms of production. West Virginia is an interesting and unique case study because it is a rural state without a major metropolitan area, with a history of non-standard or home production that traces back to the earliest coal camps (Pudup, 1990; Lewis, 1989). Economic restructuring has taken its toll on West Virginia's economy, where unemployment rates continue to rank among the highest in the nation. West Virginia also has one of the lowest female labor force participation rates in the nation, and one of the highest public assistance rates (Rogers et al. Forthcoming), two factors which others have directly related to participation in the informal economy (Oberhauser 1995a; 1995b; Campbell et al. 1993).

Informal or non-standard forms of production in West Virginia have been the subject of past investigations, but past attempts have relied upon qualitative case studies and historical research. As informative as these studies are, they lack generalizability, and therefore may not paint an accurate picture of informal economic activity (eg. who does it, why, and how much of it is going on). The present analysis builds on past nonparametric and qualitative attempts to understand this activity by using the West Virginia Social Indicator Survey, a 1995 survey of over 500 households in West Virginia.

West Virginia's Recent Industrial Transformation

The "better" jobs in a service economy are located in urban areas (U.S. Department of Agriculture, 1993; Singelmann et al., 1993; Glasmeier and Howland, 1994). Business or producer services (banking, communications, utilities, insurance, transportation, wholesale) are an important component of urban economies because they provide integrative functions for local multinational corporations, local government agencies and local manufacturing establishments, which help locales achieve a greater position of dominance in a hierarchy of urban systems (Goe 1994; Irwin and Kasarda 1991). Moreover, producer services are hypothesized to lead to economic development in urban areas because they employ a large proportion of highly skilled workers, and producer services allow multi-national corporations with headquarters in urban areas to better control the geographical distribution of capital and achieve favorable positions in nonlocal trade exchanges (Goe, 1994; Irwin and Kasarda, 1991).

Rural areas, in contrast, are at a disadvantage to attract high quality service jobs. Dillman and Beck (1986) argue that nonmetro communities lack the telecommunications hardware to support the high-tech communications technology necessary to establish and maintain links with other geographical areas. Also, tasks involved in service production are less easy to standardize and routinize (Singelmann and Mencken, 1992), and this is particularly true for producer service production. Therefore, producer service transactions may be based on face-to-face interactions, thus requiring certain functions to be spatially located near markets (i.e. near clients in metro areas— see Irwin and Kasarda, 1991). Fuguitt et al. (1989) maintain that workers in many rural communities lack the human capital to occupy producer service jobs.

Proponents of the service spatial division of labor model, however, argue that certain producer service tasks can be standardized and routinized (i.e. data entry), and "back-officed" to nonmetropolitan areas to take advantage of low-skilled labor (Glasmeier and Howland, 1994). Recent evidence from Appalachia suggests that producer services involve back-office routinized tasks (see Maggard, 1994; Couto, 1994; Dickstein 1992). The problem for Appalachian communities, however, is that these back-officed services do not represent the high-quality producer service jobs that are capable of generating economic growth. Typically they are low- wage, low/no benefit jobs, which are often temporary in nature (Maggard, 1994). Evidence from the southeastern U.S. also support that this phenomenon this is happening. In her study of householders in rural labor markets in five southeast states (Kentucky, North Carolina, Tennessee, Virginia, West Virginia), Tickamyer (1992) found the highest poverty figures among householders working in producer service employment.

Evidence specifically from West Virginia supports this urban bias in industrial transformation trends. Over the last 15 years, the economy in West Virginia has shifted from traditional manufacturing (primary metals and chemicals) and extractive industries (coal in particular) to a service-based economy. From 1977-1987, the state lost almost 70,000 jobs in coal mining and manufacturing (primarily in metals and chemicals). The average salary had been $20,000 per annum in manufacturing and $36,400 in coal mining (Maggard, 1994). During this same period, almost 32,000 new service jobs were created, with an average salary of $15,000 per annum.

Consumer services (entertainment, social, health, personal, education, public administration, repair, retail) dominated growth in West Virginia's service sector, but new jobs created in these new industries provided low wages. For example, the dominant service industry in the state is now health services, but 62% of the new health services jobs are in the low waged non-profit health services sector, typically earning less than $13,000 per annum

(WVU Center for Economic Research, 1991a). The over 9,000 new jobs created in retail between 1979 and 1989 averaged only $13,000 per annum. Growth in producer services has also been low waged. The 4,784 new jobs created during this period in finance, insurance, and real estate have averaged $14,500 per annum (WVU Center for Economic Research, 1991b).

The industrial transformation has had important negative effects on socioeconomic well-being in West Virginia. Population declined by 8% between 1980 and 1990 (U.S. Bureau of Census, 1990), causing West Virginia to lose a congressional representative. Median household earnings fell by almost 15% during the 1980s, while the number of families in poverty grew to 16% between 1979 and 1989. Currently, about 25% of the state's population lives in poverty (WVU Center for Economic Research 1991b).

Given that quality service jobs are primarily based out of large, metropolitan areas (Glasmeier and Howland 1994), West Virginia, which lacks a well-defined metro core, has not been able to attract high quality service sector jobs (Maggard, 1994).[2] Therefore, households in West Virginia that are now relying upon service work for sustenance find it increasingly difficult to stretch those wages to cover expenses (Oberhauser, 1993; Maggard, 1994). With more and more households dependent upon low-wage service employment for subsistence, households must adapt survival strategies. Theoretically, one strategy may be to engage in informal economic activities to supplement income, or to substitute informal activities for formal activities (Jensen et al., 1995; Oberhauser, 1995; Duncan, 1992; Portes, Castells and Benton, 1989; Portes and Sassen-Koob, 1987; Mingione 1991).

Informal Economic Activity in West Virginia

Much of the past research on informal economic activity (especially in West Virginia) has been conducted with qualitative data. Researchers have relied upon in-depth interviews with small snowball samples (Oberhauser, 1993; 1995a; 1995b; Duncan, 1992) or analysis of historical documents (Pudup, 1990; Lewis 1989) for sources of information. Oberhauser's recent research on informal economic activity among 50 female homeworkers in West Virginia shows that households rely upon a variety of agricultural (crops/livestock) and household production activities (domestic services, crafts, sewing, etc) to generate income.

Oberhauser (1995a; 1995b) links informal economic activity to a lack of formal job opportunities. In particular, she argues that women are the main players in the informal economy in West Virginia, primarily because

---

2 *Charleston is the largest city, with a population of 55,000.*

of a lack of formal job opportunities. Other research documents a gendered-based effect on economic opportunity from the particular mix of industrial history and culture which dominated Appalachia's mining regions (Maggard 1994). If men and women face different kinds of economic vulnerabilities and opportunities during restructuring, they may respond differently to the emerging regional economy. Research on economic activity by males in informal economic activity, as well as females, is needed to test for significant differences by gender and determine who in the household is likely to participate.

Context of Informal Economic Activity

One pertinent question identified by Jensen et al. (1995) in their analysis of informal economic activity among Central Pennsylvania households is which households actually participate in informal activities. The image portrayed by some is that non-formal activities are performed by the very poor to stretch pensions and/or public assistance (Duncan, 1992; Campbell et al., 1995). However, Jensen et al. (1995:92) point out that many nonformal economic activities can be quite capital intensive, requiring land, tools and skills. Moreover, since poor people tend to lack these forms of capital, they may be less likely to engage in informal economic activity. They report only a slight variation in participation across income categories and note that while lower income households are somewhat more likely to participate, the data suggest a curvilinear relationship, with informal activity dropping off with the lowest income group (Jensen et al 1995:98).

Another issue concerns the needs of households. Some may engage in informal economic activity because their needs are not met by current income (from job, entitlements, public assistance, etc.). Many of these activities are labor/time intensive (high opportunity costs). If people feel that their needs are met, they may be less likely to engage in such activities, despite their overall financial situation (Jensen et al., 1995). Oberhauser (1995a) argues that effective social networks are essential resources for informal activities to be beneficial. Finding a market for home produced goods/services can be difficult, and locating clients or customers often involves social dynamics that match people to jobs in the formal economy (i.e. social contacts). Therefore, the image of informal participants portrayed in Duncan's (1992) analysis of Central Appalachia (very poor, unconnected community members) may not be consistent with who is actually participating.

Theoretically, informal economic activities are part of an overall adaptation strategy that financially stressed families and households use to supplement income in a transformed economy, where the economic opportunities of the past (manufacturing, steel, and coal) are no longer available. We can now turn to an analysis of West Virginia households, to examine to what extent households in one of the nation's most rural and poor states engage in such activities.

Data and Analysis

Data for this analysis were derived from the West Virginia Social Indicator Survey (see Appendix C, questions 29–39). A discussion of the survey and sample design is detailed in Appendix A. The sample was weighted to adjust the distribution of households for age, sex, and regional biases. Weights were calculated based on 1990 Census data for West Virginia (see Keith 1996).

Jensen et al. (1995) have pointed out a number of validity and reliability issues in defining and measuring informal economic activity. People who do not claim informal economic activity as earned income might be suspicious and reluctant to provide such information. Others may engage in these activities for a hobby (growing crops, for example) and sell the extras (Wood and Tickamyer 1995). The authors of the present inquiry were primarily interested in those "extra" activities or odd jobs in which individuals engage to earn extra money to help them "get by."[3]

As one aspect of a larger project on economic restructuring, researchers in several states affiliated with U.S.D.A. Regional Project S-259 are studying informal economic activity. Our measures of informal activity and preamble are modifications of questions and language developed by those researchers (see Wood and Tickamyer, 1995; Tolbert et al., 1996). The changes made to the survey instrument made in a better fit with the particular informal activities pertinent to West Virginia.[4] The preamble for the West Virginia survey reads:

> I am going to read a list of extra work some people do to help
> them get by. You might be doing one or more of these things

---

3 *Systematic research on informal economic activity is developing and researchers are currently working to address pressing conceptual and measurement issues (Jensen et al., 1995; Wood and Tickamyer 1996; Wright 1995). This study is a first attempt to measure the extent, range, and economic importance of such activity in West Virginia households. We focus on activities which reduce household expenditures through labor exchanges and which increase household income from labor which is not legally regulated or documented.*

4 *For example, we included rattlesnakes in the questions concerning hunting and trapping, because there is a market for rattlesnakes in West Virginia and Ohio.*

> to save yourself money, earn extra money, or in exchange or
> trade for something else. In the past 12 months, have you or
> any member of your household done any of the following
> things to save money, earn extra money, or in exchange for
> something else? Please do not include doing something as
> part of your main occupation, purely for recreation, as a hobby,
> or as part of regular household chores.

The respondents were read a list of eight (8) activities and were in-structed to indicate if they engaged in these activities to (a) save money, (b) earn money, and/or (c) for exchange. The eight (8) activities were: (1) handi-work/household repair; (2) yardwork/landscaping; (3) hunting/fishing; (4) raise farm animals; (5) raise nonfarm animals; (6) crafts, sewing, knit-ting; (7) personal services (housework, child care, etc.); (8) bookkeeping/typing (see Appendix for actual questions). The respondents were also asked a question concerning how much income from these informal activities contributed to total household income.

Informal economic activity was measured with a dummy variable (1=yes for income/exchange). We defined those that engaged in any of these activities for income generation, or for exchange of labor or services to reduce household expenditures as engaging in informal economic ac-tivities. Respondents who reported that they engaged in informal economic activity "to save money" were removed from further analysis. It is realized that individuals may engage in any of these activities to avoid paying some-one else to do them (such as yardwork), but this does not necessarily qualify as informal economic activity (see Wood and Tickamyer, 1995).

Findings

Table 1 presents a descriptive analysis of the results. Almost 22% of the West Virginia households sampled reported engaging in some form of informal activity for exchange or income. The percentage was far less than the 56.3% of households sampled by Jensen et al. (1995), or the 49% from the Fall 1994 survey from a study of Kentucky households (Wood and Tickamyer 1995). However, the percentage is consistent with a 1995 survey of Kentucky households reported by Wood and Tickamyer (1995).[5] Among the activities that West Virginia households reported engaging in for money

---

5 *See Wood and Tickamyer (1996) for a discussion of the use of open–ended versus closed–ended questions in measuring survey data on informal economic activity. They concluded that specific questions regarding formal and informal labor force participation generated the most useful data on informal work.*

or exchange, handiwork/home repair (9.7%) and personal services (8.3%) were the most popular. These categories were followed by crafts/sewing (6.4%) and landscaping/yardwork (5.4%) activities. When only households that participated for income or exchange are examined, the percentages of households participating in the activities change as follows: household repair (48.3%), personal services (38.6%), crafts (30.5%) and landscaping/wood or coal gathering (26.7%).

Table 6–1:
Percentage of Informal Economic Activities Among All West Virginia Households (N=521) and Participating Households (N=112)

Variable Description	All Households	Participating Households
Household repair for money/exchange	9.7	48.3
Collect wood, coal, or do landscaping or yardwork for money/exchange	5.4	26.7
Hunt or fish for money/exchange	1.2	4.8
Raise farm animals for money/exchange	2.3	11.5
Grow non–farm animals for money/exchange	1.3	6.5
Make crafts, sewing, or other handiwork for money/exchange	6.4	30.5
Perform personal services such as child care, nursing, or housework for money/exchange	8.3	18.2
Perform bookkeeping or other services for money/exchange	3.4	16.5
Percentage of total households performing some type of informal economic activity for money/exchange	21.4	

Table 2 presents a brief analysis of which households are participating in informal economic activities for income/ exchange. The analysis shows that 5.8% come from low income households (less than $10,000 per year), 34.3% from low/medium income households ($10,000 to $20,000), 34.3% from medium income households ($20,000 to $40,000), and 26.4% from high income households ($40,000 +). Almost 12% of those households participating for income/exchange report being on public assistance. More than

Table 6–2:
Percentage of Households that Engage in Informal Economic Activity for Money/Exchange by Selected Demographic Characteristics

Variable Description	Percentage of Households
Annual income less than $10,000	5.8
Annual income between $10,000 – $20,000	34.3
Annual income between $20,000 – $40,000	34.3
Annual income greater than $40,000	26.4
On public assistance	11.7
Does not meet basic household needs	15.6
Presence of children in home	51.9
Primary income earner employed full–time	79.4
Primary income earner retired	10.7
Primary income earner not employed full–time	10.7
Household located in open–country, not town	53.9

15 percent (15.6) of households participating in the activities reported that the basic needs of the household in the previous year were not met by income.

Almost 80% of the households that participated in these activities report that their primary income earner worked full-time the week prior to the interview, while 10.7% reported that their primary income earner was not working, and 10.7% reported that their primary income earner was retired.

Table 3 examines differences in participation by household characteristics. The analysis shows that 19.5% of high income households participate for income/exchange, 28.9% of medium income households, 48.6% of low/medium households, and only 8.2% of low income households participate for income/exchange. Related to this, 20% of households receiving public assistance participate for income/exchange. Twenty-five percent of households in which the primary income earner worked full-time the previous week participated for income/exchange, compared to 12% of retired households, and 15.2% of households in which the primary income earner did not work full-time the previous week. These descriptive data do not suggest that the lowest income households in West Virginia participate in the informal economy at a substantially higher rate than other households. In fact, it is low/middle income households (between $10,000 and $20,000)

Table 6–3:

Percentage of Households that Engage in Informal Economic Activity for Money/Exchange by Selected Demographic Characteristics

Variable Description	Percentage of Households
Annual income less than $10,000	8.2
Annual income between $10,000 – $20,000	48.6
Annual income between $20,000 – $40,000	28.9
Annual income greater than $40,000	19.6
On public assistance	20.0
Does not meet basic household needs	24.2
Presence of children in home	26.1
Primary income earner employed full–time	25.0
Primary income earner retired	12.2
Primary income earner not employed full–time	15.2
Household located in open–country, not town	24.4

that are most likely to participate in informal activity.

The data presented in Table 4 below also show that West Virginia households do not engage in informal economic activity for a substantial portion of total household income. Twenty six (26) percent of the households that report engaging in these activities for income/exchange report that infor-

Table 6–4:

Percentage of Household Income Derived from Informal Economic Activity Among Participating Households in West Virginia (N=112)

Percentage of Household Income	Percentage of Households
Less than 10 percent	71.4
10 – 20 percent	17.8
20 – 30 percent	4.5
30 – 40 percent	1.0
40 – 50 percent	1.0
Greater than 50 percent	2.6
No response	1.6

mal economic activities constitute greater than 10% of total household income, and 8% claim that these activities contribute to more than 20% of total household income. Only three (3) households reported that greater than 50% of total household income comes from these activities. These findings would suggest that households in West Virginia do not substitute informal activities for formal activities, but that about 20% of all households use informal activities to supplement other sources of income. During restructuring, members of households appear to be packaging together a variety of economic resources to support households.

Bivariate and Multivariate Results

The literature reviewed suggested that participation in the informal economy is dependent upon certain context (size of place, household income, household size, etc.). This study investigated to what extent participation among West Virginia households were dependent upon the context identified in other studies (namely Jensen et al., 1995). Table 5 presents correlation and logistic regression results from this comparison. The correlation analysis showed that there are several household characteristics positively correlated with participation in informal economic activity for income/exchange (size of household, low/medium household income, primary income earner currently employed in West Virginia. Low income household status (< $10,000), age of respondent, retired households, and ratio of household income to household size were all negatively correlated with participation for income or exchange.[6]

Table 5 also presents logistic regression results. The analysis, somewhat exploratory, closely followed the model presented by Jensen et al. (1995). We used a number of household characteristics to predict which households engage in informal economic activity. The regression analysis supported the correlational analysis. It is not the lowest income households that are participating, but those that are close to the bottom (between $10,000 and $20,000 annual income). Low/medium income households were six (6) times more likely than low income households (less than $10,000) to participate for income/exchange. Medium income households ($20,000 to $40,000) were over three (3.3) times more likely than low income households to participate. The effects for high income households were significant

---

6 *Given that the dependent variable is a categorical dummy variable, we verified the correlations with cross-tab analysis. We report the correlations because they have more intuitive (i.e. linear) properties. The cross-tab analyses are available upon request.*

only at the p<.10 level, but showed that even higher income households (over $40,000) were more likely to participate than are low income households. In addition, none of the other indicators of financial hardship (public assistance, primary income earner not working, basic needs not met) have a significant effect. This pattern also suggests somewhat of a curvilinear trend.

We also controlled for the effects of household size, with the variable that measures the ratio of total household income to total household size. This variable had no effect on participation in informal economic activity, net of the effect of the other income measures. We also estimated a model (results not reported) with income measures removed, and income to size ratio variable included. This analysis showed that income to size had no

Table 6–5:
Results from the Correlation and Logistic Regression Analyses

Variable Description	Bi–variate Correlation with Informal Economic Activity	Logit	EXP(B)
Basic needs met in household, yes = 1	−.027	−.306	.736
Public assistance received, yes = 1	.019	.208	.812
Located in open–country, yes = 1	−.034	.045	1.046
Number of persons in household	.168*		
Annual income less than $10,000	−.144*		
Annual income between $10,000–20,000	148*	1.811*	6.116*
Annual income between $20,000–40,000	.012	1.201*	3.323*
Annual income greater than $40,000	−.034	1.170	3.220
Ratio of household income to household size	−.108*	−0.002	.998
Primary income earner employed full–time	.144*	0.363	1.437
Primary income earner not employed	−.068		
Primary income earner retired	−.112*	0.879	2.408
Respondent's years of education	.045	0.052	1.053
Respondent's age	−.248*	− 0.044*	.956
Constant		−1.202	
Model Chi–Square Statistic		56.33*	
Proportional Reduction In Error		11.5%	

For purposes of model identification, the dummy variables representing "annual income less than $10,000" and primary income earner not employed" served as the reference categories.

significant effect on participation in informal economic activity for income/ exchange at the p<.05 level, even when other household income measures were excluded from the analysis.

The other variable with a significant effect was age of respondent. For every year increase in age, the probability of engaging in informal economic activity for income/exchange decreased by 5.2%. This finding is somewhat at odds with the results presented by Jensen et al. (1995), which showed that age has a positive effect on participation up to a point, and a negative effect among the oldest respondents (curvilinear effect). We initially included a higher order polynomial (age squared) to detect for this curvilinear effect among West Virginia households, and found no significant effects.[7]

We also measured whether or not the primary income earner in the household was retired. This factor had no significant effect on the probability of engaging in the activities for income/exchange. This variable helped to capture some of the "age" of household issues raised by Jensen et al. (1995).

Discussion of Findings and Conclusions

This analysis of informal economic activity in West Virginia showed that about 20% of households engage in informal economic activities for income/exchange. However, very few households appeared to substitute informal economic activity for formal activity; that is, very few households depended on such activities for a substantial proportion of income (i.e. over 50%). What the data appeared to be telling us (at least initially) is that informal economic activities are used to supplement sources of income from the formal economy. This interpretation was consistent with the theme of this study, that informal economic activities are an adaptation strategy to a changing (and lower wage) formal economy.

However, these findings were somewhat contrary to the expectation that it is the most economically disadvantaged that are participating in the activities (Duncan, 1992; Campbell et al., 1993). Our results showed that the lowest income households (less than $10,000) are less likely to engage for income/exchange than households with higher incomes. However, as Jensen et al. (1995) point out, many informal economic activities are capital

---

7 *We took this term out because it was almost perfectly correlated with age of respondent (r=.92), and the effects for age of respondent disappeared when this term was in the model (we assume due to the collinearity). We conclude that this term has no significant effect on participation because adding the age–squared term to the model did not affect the overall fit of the model (no significant change in model chi–square).*

intensive. Land and/or equipment are needed to engage in many of the agricultural functions. Some of the household functions require human capital and equipment (bookkeeping, hairdressing, telephone). These are skills that many very poor households lack. In addition, successful participation requires an ability to tap into markets, which often requires being integrated into social networks (Oberhauser, 1995a; 1995b). Those at the bottom of the social hierarchy tend to be disconnected from the social network fabric (Lin et al., 1981). Perhaps the lack of skills/capital/networks that hurt many truly disadvantaged households in the formal economy (eg. Wilson, 1987) also have negative effects in the informal economy.

The findings from our study are somewhat different than those presented by Wood and Tickamyer (1995) and Jensen et al. (1995). To our surprise, the analysis showed significantly less activity among West Virginia households than was reported in Central Pennsylvania and Kentucky. We expected high levels of activity, given that West Virginia is still one of the most economically disadvantaged states in the nation. Sampling differences may explain the differences between West Virginia and Central Pennsylvania. The Jensen et al. (1995) study used a sample of over 500 disproportionately lower income households, with a snowball sample attached. It is interesting that they drew the same conclusions—it is not the most poor households who are engaging in these activities, but the near poor.

The Wood and Tickamyer (1995) study was a random sample of households in Kentucky. They found a much higher rate of informal economic activity for income/exchange (around 50%). But these differences could be due to differences in state levels of urbanization. They found that urbanization is an important variable (most households participating lived in a city of 50,000 or more). A lower percentage of West Virginia households are located in urban areas of 50,000+ compared to Kentucky. If urbanization is a key to informal economic activity (as the Wood and Tickamyer paper suggests), then the lack of urbanization in West Virginia, which has only one city of 50,000 people, may account for these differences.

The other factor that may account for differences between these two studies is the omission of questions concerning participation in yard sales or "flea markets" in the West Virginia survey. Yard sales are the most frequently cited informal economic activity in Kentucky. The omission of this question was an oversight (which we will include in subsequent surveys). But we are not sure that having included this question on the survey would have changed the results dramatically, especially in terms of how much such activities contribute to total household income. Research by Farnham et al (1996) suggest that yard sale activities may be an urban/suburban phenomenon. They found that only a small proportion of nonmetropolitan Wisconsin households engaged in these activities for income/exchange (less than 10%).

Tolbert et al. (1996) maintain that among rural households, a farm-nonfarm distinction must be made. They found that farm households are more likely to participate in informal economic activities than are nonfarm households in Louisiana. West Virginia is a rural state, but only a very small proportion of West Virginia households are farm households (less than 3%). As Maggard (1981) points out, industrialization replaced agriculture as a way of life in Central Appalachia. This is not, however, a phenomenon experienced by all states. Perhaps the low profile of agriculture in West Virginia explains the lower levels of participation. West Virginians may lack the "agrarian ideology" and farm culture cited by Tolbert et al. (1996), which will induce households to participate in informal economic activities during tough times. If this argument has merit, it would help explain lower levels of participation in a rural state. Unfortunately, very few households in the 1995 WVSIS were farm households, but it is an issue that we will pursue in future studies.

The possible reasons for the lower levels of participation in West Virginia, compared to other states, also indicate interesting research questions. Tolbert et al. (1996) found that the type of activity performed may vary by farm and nonfarm households in rural communities. While we believe that the farm/nonfarm distinction of inactivities may not apply in West Virginia—where farm households represent a low proportion of rural and total households—there may be other distinctions that are unique to the region that need to be investigated (i.e. coal vs noncoal; steel vs nonsteel). Perhaps current or former employment in one of these sectors (especially coal which tends to be cyclical) creates opportunities to participate in the informal economy—possibly doing activities not measured here. In addition, these activities may vary by time of year, and we believe that these samples should be conducted at various times (as opposed to late fall). This may also help establish the validity of measures used in the surveys.

To further understand the informal economy, this current study suggests investigation of the resources or forms of capital household members may possess or lack as they devise responses to the changed economy needs to occur. There is also a need to examine to what extent the now disassembling formal economy of the region provides participants with a repertoire of skills, resources, and occupational networks in the labor force.

We believe that in order to better develop a theoretical understanding of the nature and extent of informal economic activity in rural communities, more data need to be collected which will allow a more complete investigation of people's motivations for participation in the activities. It is assumed that people are participating to supplement or replace wages earned in the formal economy. But we currently have very limited data on people's motivations for participating. It could be that a substantial portion of informal economic activity that is attributed to household survival strategies in actuality is a by-product of hobbies, or other interests (despite the researchers' attempts to circumvent this problem). We may also systematically ignore important informal activities by excluding hobbies, which we asked respondents to do in this survey. Financial gains may be the by-product of individuals pursuing hobbies.

We were also surprised by the lower participation rates in West Virginia, given that our study found that the state has one of the lowest female labor-force participation rates. According to Oberhauser (1995a), this phenomenon should create more activity in West Virginia. One explanation may be that the women in the households sampled are the actual participants. We, therefore, need to further investigate who inside households engages in informal activities and how household composition and operation may affect participation and the pooling of generated resources. It may be that women in West Virginia lack access to both formal and informal opportunities, a finding which would be consistent with that reported in Duncan's (1992) study of Applachia.

Conclusion

This study was exploratory in nature. Little quantitative research has previously been published on informal economic activities in rural areas. Most studies have focused on informal economic activities in urban or ethnic enclave economies (Jensen, et.al. 1995). This study, and others like it, should encourage policy planners and researchers to consider the extent to which informal economic activities are or can be relied upon for income or exchange. It is our opinion that as workers are further supplanted from manufacturing and natural resource extraction employment, they will have to turn to informal economic activities to supplement low-wage service employment. More studies of this nature will be needed to accurately measure and analyze emerging household economic strategies. Such research, in turn, will contribute to more accurate measures of the economically active population since they incorporate nontraditional income generation and household provisioning strategies not reflected in market-based measures.

Given that this analysis was focused on the economic activity of informal production (i.e. production for income/exchange), we also maintain that the research has several important policy implications. For the first time, the extent of this type of informal economic activity in West Virginia has been documented with a representative sample. Our analysis showed that informal economic activity is not as pervasive as some might believe. Only a handful of households sampled relied on such activities for greater than 50% of total household income. Second, our research documented that it is not the poorest households in the state that participate in informal economic activities, but the near poor. We speculate that home production among the near-poor households is an attempt to supplement other forms of income. Other research has concluded that participation in informal economic activity is dependent upon access to markets. Given the prospects of reduced earnings from formal employment in a service based economy in the future, we might expect an increase in the number of households turning to informal types of production to supplement earnings. We offer the following policy recommendations as a way to assist state legislators in incorporating these activities as a part of a viable economic strategy.

Public Policy Recommendations

(1) The state should promote markets for home produced goods by establishing networks of producers and throughout West Virginia as well as between it and border states.

A model already exists for some forms of craft production in West Virginia (see Oberhauser 1995a). Policy makers may be able to help design such models for other goods. Should the state become involved in promoting home production, additional economic activity may be generated within its borders.

(2) The state could support future research in informal economic activity by allocating resources to undertake a longitudinal study.

How West Virginia's household participation covaries with changes in local economic conditions, and how the support needs of home producers change during these periods would be documented. We believe that it will be very important to monitor household survival strategies once recent welfare reform legislation takes effect. Home production may be one of the few options these households will have to deal with reduced or eliminated benefits.

(3) State policy makers may improve the quality of life of its citizens through active involvement and support of informal economic activities.

In a global service economy, home production will probably become a long-term reality that is here to stay, as more and more households use such activities to supplement inadequate wages from formal activities (Jensen et al. 1995).

References

Campbell, Rex R., John Spencer and Ravinda Amonker. 1993. "The Reported and Unreported Missouri Ozarks: Adaptive Strategies of the People Left Behind." Pp. 30–52 in T. Lyson and W. Falk (eds.), *Forgotten Places: Uneven Development in Rural America.* Lawrence, Kansas: University Press of Kansas.

Center for Economic Research. 1991a. *West Virginia Service Industries.* Morgantown: West Virginia University.

Center for Economic Research. 1991b. *Bearfacts: West Virginia 1979–89.* Bulletin 7. Morgantown: West Virginia University.

Couto, Richard A. 1994. *An American Challenge.* Dubuque, IA: Kendall/Hunt.

Dickstein, Carla. 1992. The West Virginia Public Affairs Reporter 9 (2):1–7.

Dillman, David and Donald Beck. 1986. "The Past is not the Future: Urban Quality of Life as We Approach the 21st Century." *Urban Resources* 3:43–47.

Duncan, Cynthia. 1992. "Persistent Poverty in Appalachia: Scarce Work and Rigid Stratification." Pp. 111–33 in C. Duncan (ed.) *Rural Poverty in America* NY: Auburn House.

Farnham, Jennifer, Leann Tigges, and Ann Ziebarth. 1996. "Informal Economic Activity among Nonmetropolitan Households." Paper presented at the annual meeting of the Rural Sociological Society, August, Des Moines, Iowa.

Fuguitt, Glen, David Brown and Calvin Beale. 1989. *Rural and Small Town America.* NY: Russell Sage.

Glasmeier, Amy and Marie Howland. 1994. "Service-led Rural Development: Definitions, Theories and Empirical Evidence." *International Regional Science Review.* 16:197–229.

Goe, Richard W. 1994. "The Producer Services Sector and Development within the Deindustrializing, Urban Community." *Social Forces* 72:971–1009.

Irwin, Michael and John D. Kasarda. 1991. "Air Passenger Linkages and Employment Growth in U.S. Metropolitan Areas." *American Sociological Review* 56:524–37.

Jensen, Leif, Gretchen T. Cornwell, and Jill L. Findeis. 1995 "Informal Work in Nonmetropolitan Pennsylvania." *Rural Sociology* 60:91–107.

Keith, Bruce, 1996. *1995 WVSIS Methodology Report: Sample Design,Questionnaire, and Technical Forms.* Survey Research Center, West Virginia University, Morgantown, WV.

Lavrakas, Paul. 1988. *Telephone Survey Methods: Sampling, Selection and Supervision.* Newbury Park, CA: Sage.

Lewis, Ronald. 1993. "Appalachian Restructuring in Historical Perspective: Coal, Culture and Social Change in West Virginia." Urban Studies 30:299–308.

Lewis, Ronald. 1989. "From Peasant to Proletarian: The Migration of SouthernBlacks to the Central Appalachian Coalfields." *Journal of Southern History* 60 (1):77–102.

Lichter, Daniel and Diane K. McLaughlin 1995. "Changing Economic Opportunities, Family Structure, and Poverty in Rural Areas." *Rural Sociology* 60:688–706.

Lin, Nan, Walter Ensel and John Vaughn. 1981. "Social Resources and Strength of Ties: Structural Factors in Occupational Status Attainment." *American Sociological Review* 46:393–405.

Maggard, Sally W. 1994. "From Farm to Coal Camp to Back Office and McDonald's: Living in the Midst of Appalachia's Latest Transformation." *Journal of Appalachian Studies* 6:14–38.

______. 1981. "From Farmers to Miners: The Decline of Agriculture in Eastern Kentucky." Pp. 25–66 in L. Busch (ed) *Science and Agricultural Development.* Totowa, NJ: Allanheld, Osum & Co.

Rogers, Cynthia. Kimberly D. Mencken and F. Carson Mencken. Forthcoming. "Female Labor Force Participation in Central Appalachia: A Descriptive Analysis." *Journal of Appalachian Studies*

Mingione, Enzo. *Fragmented Societies: A Sociology of Economic Life Beyond the Market Paradigm.* Cambridge, MA:Basil Blackwell.

Oberhauser, Ann M. 1995a. "Gender and Household Economic Strategies in Rural Appalachia." *Gender, Place and Culture* 2:51–70.

Oberhauser, Ann M. 1995b. "Towards and Gendered Regional Geography: Women and Work in Rural Appalachia" *Growth and Change* 26:217–244.

Oberhauser, Ann M. 1993. "Industrial Restructuring and Women's Homework in Appalachia: Lessons from West Virginia." *Southeastern Geographer* 33:23–43.

Portes, Alejandro, Manuel Castells, and Lauren A. Benton. 1989. *The Informal Economy: Studies in Advanced and Less Developed Countries.* Baltimore, MD: Johns Hopkins University Press.

Portes, Alejandro and Saskia Sasssen-Koob. 1987. "Making it Underground." *American Journal of Sociology* 93:30–61.

Pudup, Mary Beth. 1990. "Women's Work in the West Virginia Economy." *West Virginia History* 49:7–20.

Singelmann, Joachim and F. Carson Mencken. 1992. "Job Autonomy in Advanced Industrial Countries." *Social Science Quarterly* 73:829–843.

Singelmann, Joachim, Forrest A. Deseran, F. Carson Mencken, and Jiang H. Li. 1993. "What Drives Labor Market Growth?" Pp. 125–142 in J. Singelmann and F.A. Deseran (eds.), *Inequalities in Labor Market Areas.* Westview Press.

Tickamyer, Ann R. 1992. "The Working Poor in rural Labor markets: The Example of the Southeastern United States." Pp. 41–61 in C. Duncan (ed.) *Rural Poverty in America* NY: Auburn House.

Tolbert, Charles, Linda Tobin, Dana Haynie. 1996. "Informal Economic Activityin Louisiana Farm and Rural Households." Paper presented at the annual meeting of the Rural Sociological Society, August, Des Moines, Iowa.

U.S. Dept of Agriculture. 1993. *Rural Conditions and Trends* 4:3.

U.S. Bureau of Census. 1990. *Characteristics of the Population.* Washington,DC: Government Printing Office.

Wilson,William. 1987. *The Truly Disadvantaged.* Chicago: Univ. of Chicago Press.

Wood, Teresa A. and Ann R. Tickamyer. 1995. "Yard Sales Happen or: Identifying Participation in the Informal Economy: The Utility of Open-ended Versus Closed-Ended Questions." Paper presented at the annual meeting of the Rural Sociological Society, August, Washington, D.C.

Wright, Mareena McKinley. 1995. " 'I Never Did Any Fieldwork, but I Milked an Awful Lot of Cows!': Using Rural Women's Experience to Reconceptualize Models of Work." *Gender & Society* 9(2):216–235.

| Chapter 7 |

Shades of Green: Public Opinion and the Economics of Environmental Protection in West Virginia

Rory Fraser, Steve Hollenhorst, and Alan Collins

Abstract

Growing concern for the environment is often attributed to persons categorized as affluent, well-educated, urban, young, women, and in the case of rural areas, in-migrants to the region. This view holds that the environment acts as an "amenity," mostly of recreation or aesthetic value, for the middle and upper classes. In this study, we have analyzed this stereotypical view of environmentalism using public opinion data on environmental issues collected in the 1997 West Virginia Social Indicator Survey. As expected, women, democrats and independents showed high levels of environmental concern and activism. However, concern was highest among the state's traditionally marginalized groups: rural residents, households making less than \$30,000/year, people with lower levels of education, older people, non-professionals, and non-voters. While West Virginian's concern over 14 specific issues was uniformly higher than found in national surveys, it was highest for local health related environmental issues such as illegal dumping; pollution of lakes, rivers and streams, and; toxic and hazardous waste. The character of this environmental concern is attributed to historical resentment that the state's rural poor and working class hold towards the resource extractive industries. The findings also suggest a significant gap between the environmental concerns of most West Virginians on one side, and the direction of the legislature, state government, and state environmental organizations on the other.

Introduction

Numerous studies have documented the rise of environmental concerns in North America (Kunagy, Humphrey and Firebaugh 1994; Inglehart 1977, 1990; Milbrath 1989). Recent polls generally suggest that about a third of Americans consider themselves "active environmentalists" while another 50% are "concerned though not active." (Times Mirror 1992) Underlying Americans' environmental concerns is a strong emphasis on local problems and on protecting human health. This explains why issues such as water pollution, shortage of clean drinking water, air pollution, ozone damage, toxic waste dumps, and landfills are consistently identified as being the most serious problems.

Government actions to protect the environment work best when political leaders know their constituent's preferences for environmental quality. In this context, public opinion polls are a potentially valuable source of information on people's perceptions of environmental quality, their awareness of the severity and causes of environmental problems, and preferred solutions to these problems. While many polls have been conducted at the national level and in other states, little information has previously been collected about the environmental perceptions and opinions of West Virginians.

The purpose of this chapter is to examine West Virginians' environmental concerns by various demographic attributes, namely, income, age, education, gender, occupation, political party affiliation, level of political involvement, urban and rural dwellers, as well as differences in environmental perceptions of native West Virginians relative to those of recent in-migrants. This comparative perspective lends itself to a discussion of public policy in West Virginia through three distinct areas. These include, (1) the nature and extent of West Virginian's concern about environmental quality, relative to the nation as a whole, (2) the perceived causes of environmental problems, and the activities being blamed for those problems, and (3) West Virginian's willingness to bear the cost of environmental protection and their expectations of industry in these efforts.

Free Markets and Environmental Activism: A Literature Review

Historically, free markets have tended to work poorly in allocating resources for protecting and enhancing the environment. Indeed, all of the classic causes of market failure—negative externalities, public goods, and common property—are at the core of most environmental problems (Bloom 1995)[1].

---

1 *Bloom describes these three causes in detail.* **Externalities** *arise when one economic agent's consumption or production activities impose costs (i.e. water pollution) on another agent with no compensation.* **Public goods** *are goods like clean air whose consumption cannot be restricted and whose supply is undiminished by additional consumers. Since economic agents tend to "free ride" on the environmental protection activities of others, preferences for protecting these public goods tend to be understated in a free market economy.* **Common property** *is a resource whose consumption cannot be restricted, although its supply is diminished by additional consumers. Fisheries are an excellent example. Overuse of common property resources—the so called "tragedy of the commons"—occurs because individuals receive full benefits from their usage of common property but bear only a small share of the cost of any degradation they induce.*

In response, corrective government mechanisms such as tax incentives, legislation, regulations, and public resource management are often implemented to ensure that societal interests in environmental protection are addressed

Comparative public opinion research suggests that a new worldview is emerging in which citizens are placing increasing importance on "postmodern" ideas such as participatory democracy, protecting nature, quality of life issues, and attaining satisfying work (Olsen, Lodwick, Dunlop 1992). Specific to growing environmental concern, several interrelated theories have been advanced to explain this shift in interest. First, historical studies by Hays (1987) along with quantitative analyses by Buttel (1979), Honnold (1984), Mohai and Twight (1987) and Kanagy, Humphrey and Firebaugh (1994) have suggested that cohort replacement, or generational change, underlies the current surge in environmental concern. Growing up amidst the great spatial and environmental transformation brought on by the post World War II industrial expansion and suburban sprawl, Baby Boomers developed higher expectations with respect to personal health, fitness, and environmental quality (Hays 1987). Second, increased education and affluence have not only provided people with the time, energy, and civic skills to devote to environmental issues, but also to interact with the environment from a leisure/outdoor recreational perspective rather than a work/survival perspective (Hollenhorst and Salstrom 1994). Third, the continued population shift from rural to urban settings may also explain increased environmental concern. Repeated studies have found that urban/suburban respondents consistently express greater concern for most environmental problems, are more likely to support environmental reform, and are more likely to support land-use planning and control (Hays 1987, Christenson 1978, Lowe and Pinhey 1982, Rickson and Stabler 1985, Van Liere and Dunlap 1980). These theories underscore the presence of an emerging neo-conservative post-industrialism characterized by the declining influence of unions, cutbacks in government programs, growth of transnational corporations, deregulation, and declining influence of liberal parties (Kanagy, Humphrey and Firebaugh 1994; Buttel 1992).

Precipitated by animosity towards the "welfare state", high-wage labor, and increased international competition, trends toward neo-conservative post-industrialism have had a significant affect on the economic landscape of West Virginia. Indeed, economic development in West Virginia during the past decade has focused on corporations who invest heavily in automation (thus reducing dependence on unionized labor) and/or firms who relocate in order to take advantage of the state's low taxes, minimal environmental regulations, and inexpensive land. By contrast, a growing backlash to government policies and programs that favor corporate interests over environmental concerns of the citizens of West Virginia is apparent throughout the state. To illustrate, an increasing number of West Virginians have been joining environmental organizations; local environmental organizations are becoming more pronounced throughout the state, and development projects such as the Apple Grove Pulp Mill, the WTI Waste Incinerator, Corridor-H, landfill proposals in Barbour and Berkeley Counties, Morgantown Power Plant, and the logging of Kumbrabow State Forest and Blackwater Canyon are faced with strong opposition. Such activities reflect West Virginians' growing concern over the environment.

While this type of opposition to the development of natural areas has been examined at the national level (Hays 1987; Mitchell, Mertig, and Dunlap 1992), little is known about the dichotomies and roots of the movement at the state level. Nationally, environmental concern has been found to be greater among people with higher education and income, among women, among younger age groups (Times Mirror 1992, Inglehart 1990, Buttel 1979, Sahmdahl and Robertson 1989), urban dwellers (Lowe and Pinhey 1982, Van Liere and Dunlap 1980) and those who are more politically active (Hays 1987). In-migrants to rural areas—having higher affluence, education, and seeking certain lifestyle benefits (Bradshaw and Blakely 1981, Sofranko and Williams 1980)—are also attributed with having higher levels of environmental concern and activism (Fortmann and Kusel 1990). This chapter, in examining the history and social origins of the environmental movement in West Virginia, identifies potentially problematic gaps between the direction of recent state legislative policy initiatives and the environmental concerns reported by West Virginians.

Data and Analysis

As with the preceding chapters, data for this analysis have been derived from the 1997 West Virginia Social Indicators Survey (WVSIS), an omnibus study which annually assesses the quality of life of West Virginia's residents. Similar to a number of other state and national surveys, the WVSIS is designed to gather current information about the social and economic conditions of West Virginians and to monitor changes in the quality of their lives over time. Included in the survey is a set of "core" questions that are repeated annually, including basic demographic information on households and individuals within West Virginia as well as various quality of life indicators such as economic and political participation and residential mobility (Foster and Wadsworth 1997). The methodology of the survey is described in Appendix A.

In order to draw necessary comparisons with the U.S. population, questionnaire items measuring environmental concerns in the 1997 WVSIS (see, e.g., Appendix B, questions 48–59) were adapted from the Times Mirror Magazine's National Environmental Forum Survey, and various surveys developed by the Gallup and Lou Harris organizations. Environmental concern items included in the WVSIS covered a broad spectrum of national issues, as well as several issues specific to West Virginia.

The survey was designed to determine how concerned West Virginians are with the environment in general, as compared to other high profile public issues such as crime, education, roads, jobs, etc. Similarly, the respondents were asked whether they considered themselves "Active Environmentalists." Secondly, the survey explored respondents' perceptions of the relationship between economic development and environmental protection. Several questions were designed to explore their opinion regarding the degree of compatibility and relative importance of these two goals. Thirdly, the survey examined how serious respondents felt various environmental issues were, relative to each other. Fourteen issues were presented in the survey, namely, toxic waste pollution, global warming, coal mine subsidence, drinking water quality, air pollution, improper logging, illegal dumping, landfill space, acid mine drainage, ozone layer damage, extinction of endangered species, loss of open space and natural areas, and the loss of wetland areas. For each item, respondents were then asked whether state laws and regulations were too restrictive, not restrictive enough, or fine as written. Finally, because private property rights is a major consideration when developing environmental legislation and regulation, the survey asked whether property owners should be compensated when environmental laws and regulations restrict the use of their land. Property owners were divided into three categories: private individuals, small businesses, and large businesses and corporations.

Findings

Analysis of Environmental Concern

For all its logical consistency and status as conventional wisdom, the authors' prediction that West Virginians would express lower environmental concern than the general U.S. population was not borne out by the survey findings. On the contrary, the environment weighs heavily on the minds of West Virginians, with 63% indicating they were "very concerned" with environmental issues as shown in Table 1, and approximately 36% identifying themselves as environmentalists as shown in Table 2.

Table 7–1:

Percentage of West Virginians Who Reported That They are "Very Concerned" with Various State Issues, Including the Environment.

Issue	Overall
Drugs	83.9
Education	81.0
Jobs	78.5
Health Care	75.3
Crime	73.0
Economy	63.8
Taxes	63.7
Environment	63.0
Inflation	55.6
Roads	49.3

It should be noted that roads, long the principal focus for many politicians and bureaucrats, was rated least important among these state issues. Less than half of West Virginians surveyed indicated high concern with road issues. This might be indicative of a general disparity between politicians—who have the power to deliver on issues such as roads—and citizens, who generally have little choice in these matters. Alternatively, it might indicate a general satisfaction with the current extent of the highway system within the state.

Working Class Environmentalism

To identify the source of this higher than expected environmental concern, the demographic breakdowns were analyzed. As expected, a higher proportion of women indicated high environmental concern, as did Democrats and Independents (see Table 2). At this point, however, the findings deviated markedly from national surveys. While environmental concern was high among all groups (60.4% overall), it was highest among traditionally marginalized groups: rural residents, households making less than $30,000/year, people with lower levels of education, non-professionals, and politically inactive citizens. No difference in level of concern was found between native-born West Virginians and in-migrant residents, or between age cohorts.

Similarly, the findings were the opposite of national data with respect to West Virginians who identify themselves as environmentalists. Environ-

Table 7–2:

Percentage of West Virginians "Very Concerned" about The Environment, and the Percentage Who that Consider Themselves Environmentalists by Selected Demographic Characteristics.

Demographic Characteristic	% "Very Concerned" about the Environment	% Who Consider Themselves % Environmentalists
Household repair for money/exchange	9.7	48.3
Collect wood, coal, or do landscaping or yardwork for money/exchange	5.4	26.7
Overall	63.0	36.4
Gender		
Male	55.0 ***	37.0
Female	64.4	36.0
Education		
No High School Diploma	67.5 ***	48.7 ***
High School Graduate	63.1	35.8
Attended College	56.4	32.6
Age		
18–34	62.9	26.2 ***
35–54	58.9	37.3
55+	60.2	43.1
Residence		
Rural	61.6 **	40.8 ***
Urban	58.8	32.1
Income		
More than $30,000	56.1 ***	35.2 ***
Less than $30,000	65.6	38.6
Political Party		
Democrat	63.8 ***	40.1 ***
Republican	52.8	28.5
Independent or other	66.5	39.6
Politically Active		
Yes	64.0 ***	40.2 ***
No	70.8	29.4
Type of Job		
Professional/Technical	56.0 ***	30.9 ***
Service/Low Skill	61.6	42.9
Not in Workforce	65.3	37.2
Environmental Activist?		
Activist	75.9 ***	——
Not an Activist	51.8	

* Significant differences exist between groups at the .10 level
** Significant differences exist between groups at the .05 level
*** Significant differences exist between groups at the .01 level

mentalism—often stereotyped as the concern of affluent, well-educated, urbanites—takes on a surprisingly different form in West Virginia. In fact, those most likely to identify themselves as environmentalists were older, rural residents, non-professionals and those not in the workforce (i.e. homemakers, disabled, retired), and those making less than $30,000. Statistically, no difference was found by gender or between native born and in-migrant residents of the state.

It should be pointed out that while politically inactive residents held the highest level of environmental concern, they were also significantly less likely to consider themselves environmentalists. This is suggestive of a general feeling of futility or complacency regarding the capacity of state government and environmental organizations to deal with concerns central to their lives.

Conventional wisdom views the environment as an "amenity," mostly of recreation or scenic value to the middle class. Concern over such amenities supposedly arises once one has met other basic needs such as housing, child care, health, etc. The above findings offer scant support for this view, suggesting instead that environmental concern and activism is highest among those who might be regarded as least able to afford it.

Health-Related Environmental Issues

The survey examined how West Virginians viewed fourteen (14) specific environmental issues (see Table 3 below). Again, concern was uniformly higher among West Virginians than found in similar national surveys, in some cases by as much as 20 percentage points. The percentage of respondents indicating an issue was either "Extremely Serious" or "Very Serious" ranged from 49–84%. Highest concern existed for local and health related issues such as illegal dumping (84%), pollution of lakes, rivers, and streams (83.7%) toxic waste pollution (79.1%) drinking water quality (78.1%), landfill space (77.6%), air pollution (74.6%), acid mine drainage (72.6%), and ozone damage (67.4%). Issues of more moderate severity included state issues such as improper logging (61.6%), coal mine subsidence (60.6%) endangered species (57.1%) loss of open space and natural areas (56.9%), and loss of wetlands (52.5%). Only one issue, global warming (49.2%), was deemed of serious concern by less than half of West Virginians. In general, local and state issues were most important, and national/global issues were least important.

These results suggest that environmental concerns among West Virginians are primarily centered in the struggle for a healthier environment at home, in communities. Issues constituting the core of the modern environmental movement—protecting biodiversity, wild nature, wetlands, and

Table 7–3:

Percentage of West Virginians who Report "Extremely Serious" or "Very Serious," Concerns about Various Environmental Issues by Selected Demographic Characteristics [a]

Environmental Issue	All	U.S.	Income		Age			Political Party			Gender		Education		
			>$30K	<$30K	18–34	34–54	55+	Dem	Rep	Ind	Men	Women	<12	12	>12
Illegal dumping	84.0	—	85.9	82.3	88.7	86.3	77.9	85.3	81.3	86.3	81.6	85.6	81.8	86.6	82.9
Pollution of lakes, rivers, streams	83.7	77	84.0	84.3	91.0	86.9	74.3	86.4	77.5	87.3	85.3	82.5	80.5	85.1	84.3
Pollution from toxic waste sites	79.1	72	77.9	80.6	86.3	83.3	68.8	80.9	75.7	81.2	77.5	80.3	77.9	80.0	79.2
Drinking water quality	78.2	68	79.6	77.9	85.6	80.3	70.0	81.4	73.0	80.2	77.8	78.8	74.0	79.4	79.0
Landfill space	77.6	58	73.7	82.1	79.3	77.3	76.8	80.9	73.0	78.2	74.3	80.1	83.8	77.5	76.2
Air pollution	74.6	64	71.6	77.1	84.8	72.3	69.1	80.3	66.3	75.6	67.8	79.6	77.3	75.2	73.4
Acid mine drainage	72.6	—	73.7	72.6	75.8	74.5	67.9	72.6	69.7	77.2	56.8	58.6	70.1	73.2	73.4
Damage to the ozone layer	67.4	62	62.0	73.0	80.5	65.5	59.3	72.8	55.4	74.6	58.3	74.1	72.1	71.0	62.8
Improper logging	61.6	—	58.7	64.7	69.1	61.9	55.4	63.8	55.4	66.0	59.0	63.5	64.9	62.3	59.8
Coal mine subsidence	60.6	—	62.2	60.6	62.9	64.1	54.7	64.9	53.9	61.4	55.5	64.2	61.7	64.5	57.3
Endangered species extinction	57.1	45	56.6	59.8	73.8	60.6	42.2	60.3	50.2	64.5	56.8	58.6	54.6	58.3	58.7
Loss of open space and natural areas	56.9	46	57.3	57.7	66.4	58.9	47.1	61.6	49.1	58.4	54.0	58.9	53.9	57.2	58.4
Wetland loss	52.5	42	52.4	53.4	66.4	53.2	41.0	53.7	43.8	63.5	48.5	55.5	45.5	52.7	55.4
Global warming/ greenhouse effect	49.2	45	46.5	52.6	62.1	48.5	39.8	55.9	39.7	49.8	40.6	55.3	44.8	52.7	48.3

endangered species—were far less important than neighborhood issues such as clean air, water, and disposal of toxic waste.

An analysis of these issues by demographic characteristics revealed wide differences in the level of environmental concern. For instance, while concern over acid mine drainage cut across all political parties, on all other specific issues Democrats and Independents rated the concern of greater severity than did Republicans. On seven of the fourteen environmental issues, women indicated greater seriousness than men. In no cases were men's levels of concern significantly higher than those of women. Age was also an important indicator of the severity of an environmental issue, with younger people more likely to indicate an issues was serious in thirteen of fourteen cases. Only landfill space was considered of equal severity by all age groups. Lower income residents were also more likely to say an issue was serious, with significant difference occurring in five of the fourteen issues. No differences in severity ratings were found between urban and rural residence or between native born and in-migrant residents.

It's interesting to note that while there were no differences between age groups with respect to overall environmental concerns, younger people were more likely to say specific environmental problems were extremely serious. Older people were more likely to categorize themselves as active environmentalists. Explanation for this finding may be found in the work of Hays (1987) who suggests that environmental consciousness is most deeply ingrained in Americans born after 1965. With opportunity, income, and education necessary to appreciate concerns beyond immediate material needs, environmental thinking and activism have become the norm for the younger cohort. In turn, they are less likely than older generations to categorize their actions as those of an environmental activist. Conversely, older people who have made deliberate lifestyle changes (e.g., engage regularly in recycling) are more likely to categorize themselves as activists. The younger generation has been exposed through school and the media to a broad range of local and global environmental problems. Being conversant with specific environmental problems, they therefore are more likely to view specific issues as a serious threat. Also of note is that while women expressed higher concern overall as well as on specific issues, they were no more likely than men to categorize themselves as environmentally active.

Stronger Environmental Laws and Regulations

The survey explored whether West Virginians believe that current environmental laws and regulations are too restrictive, effective (or sufficient) as they are, or not restrictive enough (Table 4). The results of the data analysis indicated that current state environmental policies are substantially less rigorous than the preferences of its citizens. In five of the eight categories (air pollution, river protection, coal mining, timber harvesting, and water pollution), the largest proportion of West Virginians believe that the existing laws and regulations are not restrictive enough. In the other three categories (wild/natural area protection, endangered species protection, and wetland protection) the largest proportion of respondents indicated current laws were sufficient, while a sizable minority (approximately one-third of the sample) felt they weren't restrictive enough.

The percent who believe current laws and regulations are too restrictive was extremely small, ranging from 1.6% for water pollution to 7.1% for wetland protection. Compared to the U.S. population, West Virginians are more likely to be in the middle, believing that current laws were sufficient, with lower percentages indicating either that current laws were too strict or that they do not go far enough.

Similarly, a significant block—between 10 to 20 percent of the survey sample—indicated an ambivalence by not responding to the question. This is a much higher non-response rate than for other questions on the survey. It might be postulated that a general complacency or lack of faith in the effectiveness of the legislative process in dealing with environmental problems. The findings might also indicate solutions proposed by the environmental community do not focus on the local quality of life issues that are of concern to most citizens.

Major differences in this survey item were again evident by demographic group. While support for more restrictive environmental laws and policies existed in every demographic category, it was women, young people, Democrats and Independents, and low-income people who were most likely to call for tougher environmental protection. For instance, the percent of women who preferred to see stronger air and water pollution controls was 57.1% and 67.0%, respectively. Substantially lower numbers were found for men, at 41.9% for stronger air pollution control and 55.8% for stronger water pollution control respectively. In regards to wetlands, the percentage of men who felt current laws were too strict was 12.5%, compared to 3.1% for women. Similar gender differences were found in every demographic grouping across all environmental categories.

The Environment or the Economy; Level of Sensitivity to Private Property

Despite political rhetoric claiming hardship to the economy if environmental protections are strengthened, West Virginians believe that a healthy economy depends on a healthy environment. Over 65% felt that environmental protection and economic development are always compatible or compatible most of the time (see Table 5). When one must be given

Table 7–4:

Percentage of West Virginians who Believe Current Environmental Protection Laws in the State are too Restrictive, Fine As They Are, or Not Restrictive Enough, by Selected Demographic Categories [a]

Issue	U.S.	All	Age			Income		Gender		Political Party			Education		
			18–34	34–54	55+	>$30K	<$30K	Men	Women	Dem	Rep	Ind	<12	12	>12
Water Pollution															
Too Restrictive	3	1.6	1.6	1.9	1.2	2.6	0.8	2.3	1.1	1.1	3.0	0.5	0.7	2.3	1.4
Fine	13	26.3	23.8	24.1	30.6	27.2	24.7	33.5	21.0	21.7	34.8	23.9	26.6	27.9	24.5
Not Enough	79	62.2	68.0	62.5	57.5	61.0	64.5	55.8	67.0	69.3	51.3	65.0	65.6	61.4	62.4
River Protection															
Too Restrictive		3.0	2.3	3.0	3.4	3.5	2.5	4.0	2.2	3.3	3.8	1.0	2.6	2.8	3.2
Fine		31.3	30.9	28.5	38.9	33.6	28.5	35.0	28.7	28.7	35.6	31.0	32.5	31.8	30.0
Not Enough		55.6	60.9	55.6	51.4	53.1	60.6	53.5	57.1	60.8	48.3	57.4	61.0	55.23	55.0
Air Pollution															
Too Restrictive	5	3.4	3.1	1.9	5.8	4.0	3.3	4.8	2.7	3.3	4.9	2.5	4.6	3.4	3.0
Fine	18	35.9	30.9	40.0	35.2	45.6	30.3	45.5	28.8	32.5	40.5	36.3	24.0	36.9	34.3
Not Enough	72	50.4	58.2	46.6	48.6	45.8	55.9	41.9	57.1	56.6	42.3	51.3	63.0	50.7	46.2
Timber Harvesting															
Too Restrictive		3.6	3.5	2.7	.6	4.2	3.3	5.0	2.6	2.6	6.7	2.0	2.6	3.4	4.2
Fine		37.0	44.5	36.2	32.1	39.2	34.6	38.3	36.1	37.1	39.7	34.0	34.4	35.9	36.3
Not Enough		42.1	41.0	42.5	42.5	38.7	46.4	45.5	39.6	45.2	33.3	48.7	50.0	42.0	40.2
Coal Mining															
Too Restrictive		4.4	4.3	4.1	4.9	6.1	2.9	5.0	4.0	3.1	6.7	4.1	3.9	5.1	4.2
Fine		36.9	39.8	40.6	30.6	42.5	30.9	42.3	33.0	34.9	40.5	35.5	30.5	36.6	39.7
Not Enough		41.0	43.0	39.5	41.3	35.7	48.0	41.0	41.1	46.5	33.0	43.2	52.6	40.0	38.1

Continued on Next Page

Table 7–4:

— Continued from page 118 —

Percentage of West Virginians who Believe Current Environmental Protection Laws in the State are too Restrictive, Fine As They Are, or Not Restrictive Enough, by Selected Demographic Categories [a]

Issue	U.S.	All	Age			Income		Gender		Political Party			Education		
			18–34	34–54	55+	>$30K	<$30K	Men	Women	Dem	Rep	Ind	<12	12	>12
Endangered Species															
Too Restrictive	11	5.8	2.7	6.3	7.7	7.0	4.7	8.5	3.8	5.0	8.4	2.7	5.2	5.6	6.2
Fine	31	45.6	44.9	46.0	45.6	50.5	41.0	50.5	42.0	45.4	48.7	41.1	39.6	46.2	46.9
Not Enough	51	35.7	45.3	34.8	29.1	30.3	41.6	33.3	37.4	28.2	28.8	42.1	44.2	35.5	33.5
Wild or Natural Areas															
Too Restrictive	7	3.3	3.5	3.6	2.8	3.3	3.3	5.3	1.8	3.1	4.5	2.5	2.6	3.4	3.5
Fine	27	52.0	49.6	52.6	53.2	57.5	46.8	56.5	48.7	48.5	58.1	50.3	52.0	52.7	51.5
Not Enough	59	34.1	42.6	32.9	28.8	30.1	39.2	31.5	36.0	38.2	25.5	39.6	35.7	35.2	33.3
Wetland Areas															
Too Restrictive	8	7.1	3.5	7.4	9.5	9.4	5.4	12.5	3.1	5.9	12.0	2.5	4.6	7.6	7.6
Fine	24	41.0	42.2	42.2	38.8	42.5	39.2	45.0	38.1	38.4	44.6	42.1	40.3	42.5	40.0
Not Enough	53	32.3	39.5	31.0	28.1	30.0	35.5	32.5	32.1	37.5	22.1	36.6	37.0	31.8	31.6

priority over the other, over twice as many West Virginians (60.2%) said the environment should come first, compared to 30.0% who favored the economy, as shown in Table 6. These findings are similar to the results of recent national polls. Significant difference again existed between demographic groups, with women, young people, lower income groups, rural dwellers, and people with lower education more likely to favor the environment over development.

Table 7–5:

Degree to which West Virginians Believe Environmental Protection and Economic Development Go Hand In Hand

Response Category	%
Always	22.2
Most of the time	43.0
Sometimes	30.2
almost never	3.3
Don't know	.9

From the above findings alone, it might be concluded that a majority of West Virginians advocate laws and regulations that have the potential to inflict financial costs on property owners, whether they be businesses or individuals. To determine if this was true, the survey asked if three types of property owners—private individuals, small businesses, and large businesses or corporations—should be compensated for environmental laws and regulations that reduce the value of their property. Reflecting national opinion, 79% indicated that private land owners should be compensated, and 70.8% said small business should be compensated for reductions in the value of their property.

We believe these findings illustrate an important matter of principle held by West Virginians. Since stronger environmental laws and regulations, a goal clearly held by a large majority of West Virginians, result in benefits enjoyed by everyone—not just the individual or small business landowner who must make the sacrifices—West Virginians believe that everyone should help to shoulder the costs. State citizens want stronger environmental protection, but they also want the costs associated with those protections to be shared equally.

West Virginians are far less sympathetic toward large businesses and corporations on this issue. The slightly larger percentage (49.3%) believed

Table 7–6:

Percentage of West Virginians Who Report a Preference for Economic Development and Environmental Protection

Demographic Characteristic	% Indicating Economic Development More Important	% Indicating Environmental Protection More Important	t–test (p)
Household repair for money/exchange	9.7	48.3	
Overall	30 (U.S. = 17)	60 (U.S. = 64)	
Gender			
Male	31	56	
Female	28	61	
Education			
No High School Diploma	25	62	
High School Graduate	32	58	
Attended College	29	58	
Age			
18–34	23	70	
35–54	33	56	***
55+	30	54	
Income			*
More than $30,000	31	54	
Less than $30,000	28	62	
Political Party			
Democrat	28	61	
Republican	36	48	***
Independent or other	23	68	

*   Significant differences exist between groups at the .10 level
** Significant differences exist between groups at the .05 level
*** Significant differences exist between groups at the .01 level

that large businesses and corporations should not be compensated for laws and regulations that reduce the value of their property, compared to 46.4% who felt they should. Again, significant differences existed between demographic groups, with women indicating far less willingness to compensate all forms of landowners. Baby boomers (ages 35–54) and political independents also indicated less willingness to compensate large businesses.

This finding suggests that a deeply rooted resentment of corporate power still exists within the state. Acutely aware of the environmental degradation which often results in order to maximize corporate profits, West

Virginians apparently are not particularly interested in compensating those corporations for mitigating degradation. They may feel that corporations are not paying for the full environmental costs of their activities, and therefore should not be compensated when society limits those costs. Marginalized groups, often the recipients of an inequitable share of toxic and hazardous waste externalities produced by corporations, are the least sympathetic to compensating them for the claim of regulatory taking.

While it may be unrealistic to expect that compensation can be made available to all injured property owners, it seems safe to conclude that West Virginians would advocate at least partial compensation for some landowners under special circumstances. If these monies are not available, the results suggest that West Virginians would deem the needs of society and the environment more important than the needs of specific individuals. Thus, the hardships property owners incur are costs the public is willing to compensate—but frequently prepared to overrule-in the name of environmental protection.

Discussion of the Findings

Overall, West Virginians are deeply concerned about environmental issues. This concern takes on a unique form compared to the U.S. population in that it is decidedly blue-collar and working-class in character. Environmental activism in West Virginia is led by the rural working-class poor, women, and older residents. Our expectation that urban residents and in-migrants—with their higher levels of affluence and education—would hold more pro-environmental attitudes — was roundly contradicted by the findings.

Reasons for the working-class nature of the West Virginia's environmental movement are deep rooted and complex. One reason might be found in the fact that since many state residents still live in rural areas, environmental conditions have an intimate impact on the their lives. The livelihoods of a growing number of people are directly dependent upon the environmental health of the state. This is evident in the upsurge of renewable resource-based industries, namely tourism and wood products. Many West Virginians also remain highly dependent upon hunting and fishing for both recreation and as a significant source of their families' protein intake. As such, environmental threats to these activities such as water pollution and loss of open space are viewed with trepidation.

The problem with this explanation is that even though other rural regions of the U.S. are also highly resource dependent, they do not exhibit the same degree of environmental concern and activism exhibited by West

Virginians. In addition, while hunting and fishing are male-dominated activities, it is women who demonstrate a much higher level of concern about the environment.

An alternative explanation might be that the magnitude of environmental problems in West Virginia is greater than in the U.S. as a whole, leading to higher levels of concern and activism. Evidence of this is found in some of the state's most prominent environmental problems. To illustrate, mountain-top coal removal levels the landscape in southern parts of the state, toxic waste disposal and air pollution engulf the Kanawha Valley, suburban subdivisions and poultry facilities sprawl across the Eastern Panhandle, acid mine drainage etches the northern counties, and sewage overloads inadequate treatment facilities in many rural communities. Beyond these visible problems, however, it's difficult to argue that environmental degradation in West Virginia is any worse than other areas of the country. The air and water are generally cleaner, living is less crowded, unpopulated forested landscapes grace the horizon, and open space is easily accessible even to urban residents.

We suggest that the fundamental reason underlying West Virginian's inordinately high environmental concern can be found in the state's industrial history and the long-standing animosity rural residents hold towards extractive industry—primarily coal—and government support of those industries. As these industries have been historically associated with various social injustices, the source of West Virginians' environmental concern may arise out of resentment of the environmental injustices committed by these industries. As there is little doubt that the impacts of environmental damage fall disproportionately on those sectors of society least able to defend themselves due to poverty and political powerlessness (Bryant and Mohai 1992; Bullard 1990), it should not be surprising that resentment is highest among those sectors of the population.

Bryant (1995) defines "environmental justice" as:

> ...Those cultural norm and values, rules, regulations, behaviors, policies, and decisions to support sustainable communities, where people can interact with confidence that their environment is safe, nurturing, and productive...Environmental justice is supported by decent paying and safe jobs; quality schools and recreation; decent housing and adequate health care; democratic decision-making and personal empowerment; and communities free of violence, drugs and poverty. These are communities where both cultural and biological diversity are respected and highly revered and where distributed justice prevails.

Nationwide, environmental justice is a minority movement within the broad environmental movement. In West Virginia, however, the unique historical relationship between citizens on one hand and the industry/government establishment on the other, has elevated the importance of environmental justice issues. This history warrants further explanation.

Industrial Exploitation and Public Resentment

According to Harry M. Caudill (1983), West Virginians' collective resentment of corporate power and government began with the feudalism that bound many of the state's European immigrants to their lower-class status, and survived the trans-Atlantic journey in the form of indentured servitude in colonial America. For those who eventually escaped to the frontier of Western Virginia, old folkways lingered in the isolations of the hills, sustaining over multiple generations a certain deference to, and skepticism of, power. Government, rather than being a tool of democratic expression and progress, was seen as the enforcer of upper class control of land, capital and labor.

The great misfortune of Appalachia, Caudill tells us, is that its environmental capital attracted the very forces the mountaineer most feared, bringing their interlude of freedom to an end. With the arrival of coal and timber barons by the middle of the eighteenth century, the story of West Virginia became one of exploitation by "outlanders."

Hollenhorst and Salstrom (1994) have argued that the state's resource extractive industries, aided and encouraged at every turn by the policies of state government, had three residual effects on the West Virginia psyche. First and most obvious was the irony of the citizen's persistent poverty amid an abundance of natural resources. That is, while West Virginia's natural resources helped make the United States the world's wealthiest nation, West Virginians continued to be ranked at the bottom in personal income, employment, education, and health. Boosters have from the start promised that extraction and export of raw materials would make the state wealthy, but it remains, in the words of John Alexander Williams (1976) "one of the poorer states, a hewer of wood and a supplier of energy to its richer neighbors."

Second, abundant resources, combined with weak laws and lax enforcement, provided the opportunity for relatively unrestrained corporate exploitation by absentee owners who controlled most of the state's resources. The resulting abuse by lumber, mining and railroad companies—aided and abetted by state policy—occupies a central place in West Virginia history. The oral history of many West Virginia families, for example, is replete with stories of company towns and price rigging in company stores and company-owned housing. In these towns, corporations imposed the very type of indentured servitude West Virginians' earlier ancestors sought to escape (Schwab, 1994).

The third effect was the destruction of the state's wilderness and the landscape-scale degradation of its natural ecosystems. Virtually every acre of the state has been altered by human activity, mainly agriculture, logging, mining, and urbanization. In this regulatory vacuum, virtually all of the state's primary forest was cleared, rivers and streams suffered wide-scale damage, and much of the state's fish and wildlife were decimated. Loss of these subsistence resources increased rural residents' dependence on jobs in company towns. The findings suggest that West Virginians continue to be troubled by environmental conditions in the state, and that they perceive state policies to be concerned primarily with subsidizing exploitation at the expense of the health of natural systems and human communities.

Understanding this history does much to explain the higher level of environmental concern and activism among the state's marginalized groups: the poor, the elderly, rural residents, and women. In most of the U.S., the environmental movement has been championed by a middle and upper-middle class group interested in protecting biodiversity and wild nature. The reverse is true in West Virginia, where the concern and activism (if not environmental group membership) is highest among rural poor affected directly by threats to health and livelihood.

We contend that the reasons for this reversal are two fold. First, it is these marginalized groups who historically have been most directly and profoundly affected by the environmental damages caused by resource-extractive industries. These groups have been exposed to disproportionately high levels of pollution by toxics emitted from stacks, discharge pipes, or leaking landfills. Poor and minority communities are usually the places where companies and bureaucrats choose to site manufacturing facilities, sewage treatment plants, incinerators, and landfills.

The second and less obvious reason is the relatively weak environmental attitudes held by the states middle and upper classes. This may be the result of the what Caudill (1983) describes as the historical complicity of the state's middle and upper class in the environmental exploitation of the state, negating their potential to become environmental advocates and leaders. Caudill often notes that exploitation of West Virginia's resources by out-of-state corporations required the presence of a middle-class "fifth column" of state residents content to subvert the civic and economic well-being of their own communities for personal gain. He argues that by co-opting the assistance of this collaborative middle class, the state's resource industries effectively robbed the state of the very leadership most capable of speaking for the public interest. In other states, as the middle-class marshaled around progressive-era reforms such as worker's rights and conservation, West Virginia's middle class was collaborating with industry to maintain social and environmental exploitations viewed as abhorrent to their counterparts in other states. Thus, a tradition of middle-class advocacy for environmental issues does not exist within the state.

Yet while West Virginia's marginalized population exhibit the highest levels of concern and activism, it is interesting that they are less willing than the all U.S. citizens to impose tougher environmental laws. Again, explanation can be found in: (1) the historical deference West Virginians hold towards power, and (2) a lingering distrust rural West Virginians hold towards government. Rather than seeing government as a means of insuring equity and rectifying injustice, West Virginians may still view government skeptically as the unstoppable instrument of upper class control of land, capital and labor.

Who Do They Serve? The Role of Legislators and Bureaucrats

One of the most notable findings documented by this study is the gulf that exists between the apparent attitudes and preferences of citizens for more rigorous environmental protections, and the laws and regulations promulgated by the legislature and government agencies. Why this gap? The reason may be that compared to citizen groups, state agencies and corporations bring substantial resources to the legislative and regulatory process. Citizen groups may constantly confront a decision-making process dominated by technocrats working within the iron triangle of elected officials, bureaucracies, and corporations. Lacking comparable resources, these groups usually do not have access to technically trained professionals who can hold their own, except in the few instances when alliances between the academic community, environmental groups, and/or the media are able to force the issue onto the agenda of the legislature and the state bureaucracy. This is especially true in poor, rural communities. This may serve to explain why the body of environmental law and regulations bear little resemblance to the wishes of the state citizenry.

The findings of this study are an example of the impact the environmental movement may gain in state politics. In future elections, there is an indication that environmental concerns will be on the minds of voters as they decide who to send to the Governor's Office, the Legislature, county commissions, and city halls around the state. No political campaign, of course, is decided on one issue alone. It is clear, however, that environmental concerns weigh heavily on the minds of a large majority of the state's voting population. While the one-third who consider themselves environmentalists falls short of a majority, most elections are decided by margins much smaller than this, suggesting the potential for environmentalists to play a role in future elections.

Environmental concerns are more likely to cause voters to disqualify a candidate than be attracted to one (Times Mirror 1992). While many candidates can obviously benefit from a favorable environmental image, it is probably more important that candidates avoid earning a negative image. Moreover, supporting more rigorous environmental laws and regulations, while being sensitive to the property rights of individuals and small business, will likely meet with voter approval. At the same time, failure to assure protection of property rights may also undermine a candidate's environmental message, as may have occurred during the last gubernatorial election. Professionals within the state's natural resource and regulatory agencies may also benefit from these findings. Unfortunately, the relationship between agency officials and the public has been an adversarial one. Agencies are constantly defending themselves in hearings and in lawsuits brought by citizen groups and corporate interests. As a result, these agencies have adopted defensive postures, restricting interactions with the public to formal hearings limited on the technical merits of a proposal.

We believe that a means must be found to channel this conflict in constructive directions. Key to this approach is the willingness of government agencies to set aside biases and preconceived expectations and to listen to public expectations. The call to involve people more directly and meaningfully in state environmental policy can be beneficial from two directions (Hollenhorst and Salstrom 1994). First, there is persistent impression among citizens that the state's natural resource and regulatory agencies are more closely allied with industry than with the public interest. The public is therefore increasingly suspicious of decisions that conceal trade-offs and alternatives. Previously, public distrust was reserved for industry; now it is also focused on public officials.

Secondly, there is growing belief among both agency professionals and the public that there can be no real environmental protection without democratic, participatory processes. That is, more equitable and thereby more acceptable decisions result, if the public is engaged more meaningfully and effectively in the process. In this way, agency technocrats can learn from people in the affected communities who possess detailed knowledge of local human and natural systems and the impact of projects on those systems. In this context, officials are no longer the sole decision-makers, but rather facilitators of a decision process in which involvement of broad publics is fundamental. A recent example of this approach is the Division of

Environmental Protection's efforts to create a system of local community watershed associations.

Courting Irrelevance: West Virginia's Environmental Movement

Enduring movements for social change arise out of deeply felt injustices left unredressed by society over long periods of time. Abolition, women's suffrage, organized labor, and the civil rights movements are examples of social justice movements that appeared on the state and national stage after long decades of struggle, and have fundamentally changed the character of our society. Until recently, environmental issues have been largely small in the rhetoric of these movements.

The conservation movement of the early 20th century also has deep roots. At the philosophical center of the movement is the idea of utilitarian conservation, which holds that the best way to insure a healthy environment is through the "wise use" of resources. Nature is viewed essentially as a collection of parts that can be engineered to realize human benefits over sustained periods of time. Championed by politicians, bureaucrats, and natural resource professionals, the utilitarian conservation ideology has dominated public policy, both in West Virginia and the nation, for over a century. Concerned primarily with providing a sustained flow of materials, the movement paid scant attention to either the equitable distribution of natural resources, or the negative impacts of their extraction, processing, use, or disposal.

From the start, utilitarian conservation has been challenged by the amateur tradition of preservationism and the scientific tradition of conservation biology, which collectively formed the two major arms of the modern environmental movement. Rejecting the purely economic values of utilitarian conservation, these groups focus instead on the protection of wild nature and biodiversity for aesthetic, emotional, cultural, and ecological reasons. Demonstrating this commitment by launching huge campaigns dedicated to preserving wilderness and habitat for wildlife, these groups have in the past several decades successfully moved dialogue away from the utilitarian agenda.

The environmental movement begins the philosophical merging of the social justice and conservation movements through its profound sense of fairness—belief that all forms of life are interdependent and that all species have an inherent right to survive and flourish. Environmentalism extends the equity argument by assuming the role of protector for species that cannot defend themselves.

Decidedly more inclusive than utilitarian conservation, environmentalism—with its explicit commitment to preserving biological diversity—has nonetheless been criticized from within and from outside for its lack of cultural diversity (Dowey 1992). There is very little racial or cultural diversity in the environmental movement, either in its volunteer ranks or its political and educational activities. As with the national organizations focused on protecting natural habitats, West Virginia's environmental community has not addressed the protection of ecosystems where the poor and people of color are disproportionately exposed to environmental hazards. For instance, the statewide and national issues commanding the attentions of the state's environmental community focus largely on protecting biodiversity, wildlands, and natural ecosystems, and thus are not particularly relevant to local communities with toxic and hazardous waste problems. The result is that the agenda of the state's mainline environmental groups is out of step with the needs and concerns of most citizens.

From this perspective, a serious criticism of the West Virginia environmental community is its failure to address the environmental concerns of low income, working class, and rural citizens. To do so would require a significant philosophical shift that embraces both an environmental and a social justice ethic. Combining social justice concerns within a broader environmental agenda would strengthen the political power of both movements. The beginnings of such a coalescence appears to be happening. Most recently, collaboration between the construction trades unions, local citizens, and the environmental community stalled and possibly defeated construction of the proposed Apple Grove Pulp Mill in Mason county. Their success is attributable to their ability to shed light on the backroom decision-processes employed within the decision-making triangle.

Why have the state's environmental organizations generally failed to embrace the concerns of marginalized groups? One reason might be the perception that the interests of these groups are reactive, self-serving and transitory. Concern may only surface in marginalized groups when an environmental threat impacts a community directly. Once the threat is fended off, concern and support for environmental issues within that community disappears. Building an environmental organization on this type of reactive and episodic support would appear extremely difficult. Instead, environmental groups tend to appeal to middle-class environmentalists whose interests are more enduring and independent of specific threats.

Conclusions

In West Virginia, as in the U.S., growing concern for the environment is often stereotyped as the luxury of the affluent, well-educated, urban, young people, women, and in-migrants. This view holds that the environment is an "amenity," mostly of recreation or aesthetic value, for the middle and upper classes. With the exception of women, democrats and independents, who as expected showed high levels of environmental concern and activism, the results of this study lend little support for this hypothesis. Concern and activism were found to be highest among the state's traditionally marginalized groups: rural residents, households making less than $30,000/year, people with lower levels of education, older people, non-professionals, and non-voters. While concern over 14 specific environmental issues was uniformly higher than found in national surveys, concern is highest with local health related issues such as illegal dumping; pollution of lakes, rivers and streams, and; toxic and hazardous waste.

The working-class character of this environmental concern is attributable to two factors. First, the state's rural poor and working class have historically resented the resource extractive industries whom they view as the source of the environmental problems plaguing their communities. Second, extractive industries impose an unjustifiable share of environmental degradations upon marginalized and powerless groups, namely, West Virginia's rural and working class poor. Hence, environmental degradation and public distrust are based on historical economic processes somewhat unique to West Virginia.

A significant gap exists between the environmental concerns of most West Virginians on one side, and the policies of the legislature and state government on the other. Whether true or not, the perception persists that the interest of the legislature is more allied with industry than the public interest. Public distrust formerly reserved for industry now is also aimed at bureaucratic support of those industries. Closing this gap requires an inclusive bureaucratic commitment and participatory democratic process in the development of future environmental policy.

Finally, the results of this study serve as a wake-up call for the West Virginia environmental community. Advocating equitable distribution of environmental protection as part of a broadened environmental agenda builds upon, and is compatible with, traditional efforts to protect wildlife and preserve ecosystems. Combining the moral and ethical foundations of the social justice community with the considerable organizational and advocacy skills of the environmental justice community would significantly advance efforts to protect West Virginia's human and natural ecosystems.

Public Policy Recommendations

The results of this study suggest the presence, in West Virginia, of an enduring source of support for a more inclusive form of environmental advocacy. Establishing such partnerships can build on the vitality and morality of the social justice movement, and the resources, strategies, and tactics that have recently propelled environmental issues into the forefront of state policy. Such partnerships might include:

(1) Building public awareness, through educational efforts, of the effects of disproportionate exposure to toxics and hazardous waste;

(2) Establishing programs to facilitate local community defense against environmental despoliation;

(3) Encouraging public advocacy to ensure that government at all levels fulfills the duty to protect all groups equally from environmental threats;

(4) Developing programs to increase interaction between environmental groups and marginalized sectors of society, and;

(5) Actualization of the diversification of boards, staff, membership, and volunteers to reflect the particular concerns of the state's marginalized (e.g., the poor, ethnic minorities, and women's concerns) citizens.

References

Bloom, David E. 1995. "International Public Opinion on the Environment." Science, 269:358.

Bradshaw, Ted and Edward Blakely, 1981. *Resources of Recent Migrants to Rural Areas for Economic Development: Policy Implications.* Berkeley: Division of Agricultural Sciences, University of California.

Bullard, R.D. 1990. *Dumping in Dixie: Race, Class, and Environmental Quality.* Boulder, CO: Westview Press.

Buttel, Frederick H. 1979. "Age of Environmental Concern: A Multivariate Analysis." *Youth and Society* 10:237–56.

Bryant, Bunyan I. 1995. "Issues and Potential Policies and Solutions for Environmental Justice: An Overview" In Bunyan I. Bryant (ed) *Environmental Justice: Issues, Policies, and Solutions.* Washington D.C.: Island Press.

Bryant, Bunyan I. and Paul Mohai (eds.). 1992. *Race and the Incidence of Environmental Hazards: A time for Discourse.* Boulder, CO: Westview Press.

Caudill, Harry M. 1983. *Theirs be the Power.* Lexington KY: University Press of Kentucky.

Christenson, James A. 1978. "Individual Versus Public Rights: Implications of Support for Landuse Planning and Control." *Journal of Environmental Education* 9:50–57.

Dowie, M. 1992. "American Environmentalism: A Movement Courting Irrelevance." *World Policy Journal* Spring:67–92.

Fortmann, Louise and Jonathon Kusel, 1990. "New Voices, Old Beliefs: Forest Environmentalism among New and Long–Standing Rural Residents." *Rural Sociology* 55(2):214–232.

Foster, Christa and Michael Wadsworth. 1997. *1996 West Virginia Social Indicator Study Methodology Report: Sample Design, Questionnaire, and Technical Forms.* Morgantown, WV: West Virginia University Survey Research Center.

Hays, Samuel P. 1987. *Beauty, Health, and Permanence.* New York: Cambridge University Press.

Hollenhorst, Steve, and Paul Salstrom. 1994. "Keeping the Wild in Wonderful West Virginia." *The West Virginia Public Affairs Reporter* 11(3):2–12.

Honnold, Julie A. 1984. "Age and Environmental Concern: Some Specification of Effects." *Journal of Environmental Education* 16:4–9.

Inglehart, Ronald. 1977. *The Silent Revolution: Changing Values and Political Styles among Western Publics.* Princeton: Princeton University Press.

Inglehart, Ronald. 1990. *Culture Shift in Advanced Industrial Society.* Princeton: Princeton University Press.

Kunagy, C.L., C.R. Humphrey, and G. Firebaugh. 1994. "Surging Environmentalism: Changing Public Opinion or Changing Public?" *Social Science Quarterly,* 75(4):804–819.

Lowe, George D. and Thomas K. Pinhey. 1982. "Rural-urban differences in support for environmental protection." *Rural Sociology* 47(1):114–128.

Milbrath, Lester W. 1989. *Envisioning a Sustainable Society: Learning Our Way Out.* Albany: State University of New York Press.

Mitchell, Robert C., Angela G. Mertig, and Riley E. Dunlap. 1992. "Twenty Years of Environmental Mobilization: Trends Among National Organizations." In Riley E. Dunlap and Angela G. Mertig, eds., *American Environmentalism: The U.S. Environmental Movement, 1970–1990.* Philadelphia, PA: Taylor and Francis.

Mohai, Paul, and Ben W. Twight. 1987. "Age and Environmentalism: An Elaboration of the Buttel Model using National Survey Evidence." *Social Science Quarterly* 68:798–815.

Olsen, Marvin E., Dora G. Lodwick, and Riley E. Dunlap. 1992. *Viewing the World Ecologically.* Boulder, CO: Westview Press.

Rickson, Roy E. and Patti Stabler. 1985. "Community Responses to Non-Point Pollution from Agriculture." *Journal of Environmental Management* 20:281–293.

Sahmdahl, Diane M., and Robert Robertson. 1989. "Social Determinants of Environmental Concern." *Environment and Behavior* 21:57–81.

Schwab, Jim. 1994. Deeper Shades of Green: the Rise of Blue-Collar Minority *Environmentalism in America.* San Francisco: Sierra Club Books.

Sofranko, Andrew J. and James D. Williams. 1980. "Characteristics of Migrants and Residents." In Andrew. J. Sofranko and James D. Williams (eds), *Rebirth of Rural America: Rural Migration in the Midwest.* Ames, IA: North Central Center for Rural Development.

Times Mirror Magazines. 1992. "Natural Resource Conservation: Where Environmentalism is Headed in the 1990's: The *Times Mirror Magazines* National Environmental forum Survey." Conducted by the Roper Organization.

Van Liere, Kent D. and Riley E. Dunlap. 1980. "The Social Bases of Environmental Concern: A Review of Hypotheses, Explanations and Empirical Evidence." *Public Opinion Quarterly* 44:181–197.

Williams, John Alexander. 1976. *West Virginia: A Bicentennial History.* New York: W.W. Norton & Company.

Appendix A

West Virginia Social Indicator Survey Methodology
1993–1997

Introduction

The West Virginia Social Indicators Survey (WVSIS) is an omnibus study assessing the quality of life in West Virginia and is administered annually by the West Virginia University Survey Research Center (WVUSRC). This survey is designed to gather current information about the social and economic conditions of West Virginians and monitor change in the quality of their lives over time. The study was initiated during 1992–93 with a survey administered annually since its inception. The study is quite similar to a number of state and national surveys that are intended to gather information about the public perceptions, quality of life, and economic conditions of people residing within their respective regions. This section presents a detailed account of the methodological design and data collection strategies employed by the West Virginia Social Indicators Survey (WVSIS) during the years 1993–1997.

Questionnaire Design and Item Selection

The WVSIS is designed to meet the diverse needs of public agencies, policy planners, administrators, and researchers. The instrument design and item selection for the WVSIS is structured to accommodate these various needs in two specific ways. First, a set of "core" questions is developed with the intention of repeating these questions in subsequent years, thereby providing a basis of comparison over time. The core items, asked of all respondents each year, include basic demographic information on households and individuals within West Virginia as well as various quality of life indicators on economic and political participation, residential mobility, and community satisfaction. Questions are selected to provide information of most use for policy and planning at the state and local levels and to provide maximum comparability with other state and national social indicator data.

Items from preceding years are brought forward with some modifications. Some questions are removed from one year to the next because they are not found to be of use to researchers or policy analysts; such questions, in effect, become too expensive to maintain on the questionnaire. Those agencies purchasing space on the survey, hereafter referred to as subscribers, are charged a fee based on the number of items they submit and the number of respondent interviews requested. Subscribers work collaboratively with the WVUSRC staff to align the questions with their specific needs.

Each year, the items are entered into a questionnaire format and pretested with a minimum of 50 respondents to improve the clarity and fit of questions included on the questionnaire. Pretests are completed by professional interviewers at the WVUSRC and conducted by telephone with residents of West Virginia. Pre-test interviewers are instructed to be particularly cognizant of problems in wording, item ordering, and skip patterns. Following the pre-tests, a meeting is held with the interviewers to go over the instrument item-by-item and to discuss reactions to the questionnaire. This process reveals any problems in the wording of subscribers' questions, which are generally modified upon being reported to the subcribers.

Sampling Design

Each year, the sample is drawn from a population consisting of noninstitutionalized persons residing in the State of West Virginia and living in households with telephones during the survey period. Persons under 18 years of age, persons in custodial institutions, persons on military bases, transient visitors to the state, and persons without telephones are excluded from the sampling universe. The survey sample is designed to be used both as a sample of individuals drawn from the population of individuals and a sample of households. Household data are obtained from the respondents in the sample who provide information on other household members.

The WVSIS employs a Random Digit Dialing (RDD) sampling technique. This technique has been carefully evaluated for its validity and found to produce results of comparable quality and representativeness to conventional sampling procedures but at a significantly lower cost. The basic logic of an RDD sampling technique is straightforward. Within each three-digit exchange in the survey area, four-digit suffixes are selected randomly from all possible four-digit numbers. Every number, including unassigned, unlisted, previously assigned, and newly assigned numbers has an equal probability of inclusion in the sample. An equal number of four-digit suffixes is selected for each prefix, ensuring that these numbers are good in proportion to the population. This procedure overcomes the problems inherent in obtaining telephone numbers from directories: directories introduce bias into the sample because they are often compiled twelve or more months before interviewing takes place and exclude unlisted numbers.

Samples are purchased from Survey Sampling, Inc., an independent firm specializing in RDD samples for regional or national samples. Samples consist of a set of replicates (iterations), each of which contain 250 numbers. Survey Sampling, Inc. removed numbers they identified as being businesses or located in out-of-range telephone banks. Each of the replicates, being a random sample of West Virginians, provided the flexibility of drawing the sample to a close once the desired sample target was reached. Subscribers were given the option of having their questions asked of half the sample or the full sample. The telephone numbers generated by Survey Sampling, Inc. were printed on labels and affixed to call disposition sheets.

Selection of Respondents from Households

Since the WVSIS is a representative sample of the population of West Virginia, it would not be acceptable to interview the first person to answer the phone. To overcome biases associated with interview selection, studies commonly rely on a random selection table that selects a respondent based on the number of adults residing in the household (see, e.g., Kish 1965). A fairly new alternative approach selects a respondent living in the household who celebrated the most recent birthday.[1] Once the study is introduced to the person initially answering the phone, a request is made to speak with the adult who has most recently celebrated a birthday. The advantage of this approach is that it alleviates the awkward need to immediately list all persons in the household and randomly select adults from among them while still maintaining a random selection process. Typically, respondents are selected using the birthday method, although during 1996, a comparison between the birthday and the Kish method was undertaken. Findings from this comparison revealed that the Kish method introduced less bias into the respondent selection process.[2]

---

1 *For a complete discussion of this approach in relation to other techniques, refer to Paul Lavrakas,* Telephone Survey Methods: Sampling, Selection, and Supervision. *Newbury Park: Sage, 1988, pages 86–97.*

2 *Bruce Keith and Laura Carter. 1996. "Choice of Selection Technique and Nonresponse Error: A Comparison of the Birthday and Kish Methods." West Virginia University Survey Research Center.*

After identifying the designated respondent, interviewers are instructed to complete the interview only with the person selected by the corresponding selection method. If the person is not available to conduct the interview at the time of the initial contact, an alternative time is scheduled for a return call. While this procedure ensures that all adults in each household would have an equal probability of selection, the probability of a person being included in the sample when they live in a household with several adults present is less than if they are the only adult present. To illustrate, a household with only one adult present would have a 1/1 chance of being selected as the respondent while one of four adults would have a 1/4 probability of selection. To adjust for this bias, a weighting procedure was employed to ensure respondents had an equal probability of selection.

Sample Response Rates by Year

Table 1 below presents response rates for the five annual studies. Rates for this geographical region have previously been found to average around 54.9 percent.[3] In an effort to increase final response rates during 1995, households that had previously refused to participate were called back at the end of the study. Typically, one gatekeeper may initially refuse to participate for various reasons while another, if he or she had been reached, may have agreed to participate in the study. This effort increased response rates by nine percent and was subsequently maintained for surveys conducted after 1995.

Table A–1:
Response Rates from West Virginia Social Indicator Surveys by Year

Year	Response Rate (%)[4]	Number of Completions
1993	54	1,882
1994	52	2,166
1995	69	919
1996	68	922
1997	70	948

---

3 *A Survey Researcher's View of the United States. 1990. Survey Sampling Inc.*

4 *All completions divided by all eligibles. Non–eligibles included gatekeeper refusals, gatekeeper callbacks, unavailable during study, language, physical and mental barriers, answering machines, no eligibles in household, and "already participated."*

Interviewer Training, Supervision, and Quality Control

Interviewers are identified through paid advertisements in a local newspaper situated in Morgantown, WV and from persons who have participated as interviewers at the WVUSRC during previous studies. Typically, over 30 persons apply for the positions with an average of 15 persons eventually being hired as interviewers. Training for the interviewers involves two phases. During the first phase of training, potential interviewers are introduced to telephone interviewing through the use of the University of Michigan's Institute for Social Research training manuals.[5] This phase of general interviewing techniques involves eight (8) hours of training in which trainees are introduced to information on acceptable interviewing styles, handling difficult respondents and questions, and they are required to complete two practice telephone interviews with WVUSRC staff. During the second training phase, prospective interviewers become familiar with the WVSIS questionnaire. Each interviewer is introduced to the questionnaire and is given survey specific training. Following training, several pre-test interviews are administered to examine the questionnaire for errors, wording difficulties, and overall clarity. Following this pre-test, WVUSRC staff work closely with the interviewers to identify any problems inherent in the instrument or difficulties interviewers may experience.

All interviewing is conducted at the WVUSRC in soundproof booths. A monitoring system is maintained so that the project supervisors can listen in on the interviews as they occur, as a quality control measure, to ensure that they are conducted in the desired manner. WVUSRC project supervisors are accessible to the interviewers so that any questions that arise are handled immediately. Project supervisors carefully edited all interviews daily so that any errors can be immediately brought to the attention of the interviewers. If answers are incomplete or recorded incorrectly, interviewers are asked to call the respondent back for clarification.

Processing Completed Interviews: Data Entry, Cleaning, and Management

Each call disposition sheet is given an identification number ranging from 0001 through N for the sample based on the number of desired respondents. Completed or partial interviews are entered into personal computers using the EPI-INFO software package, a program available as

5 *Pamela J. Guenzel, Tracy R. Berckmans, and Charles F. Cannell. 1983.* General Interviewing Techniques. *Institute for Social Research. Ann Arbor: University of Michigan.*

shareware through the National Centers for Disease Control. Backups are created and continuously updated to ensure that no data are lost. Consistency checks in the form of frequency outputs of all variables are examined to identify any errors; identifiable errors are checked with the original questionnaire with corrections subsequently made to the data set. In addition, a thorough question-by-question check of ten percent of the completed questionnaires is undertaken to assess the reliability rate between the original responses and the data entry. Typically the reliability checks reveal less than a one percent error rate

An ASCII data set is constructed and uploaded to an account on West Virginia University's CMS/VM mainframe computer system. Programs using both SAS and SPSSx are created to manage the data. Subscribers are given a data set that is accessible using either one of these two statistical packages. Once a data set is constructed, frequency distributions are generated for each variable in the data set as a final check for any errors and unacceptable values. Missing value codes are subsequently assigned to all variables in the data set. Final versions of each of the WVSIS data sets are stored in an SPSSx system file and archived by the WVUSRC for future use.

Representativeness of the Survey and WVSIS Weights

The accuracy of the surveys is assessed through a comparison of selected characteristics of survey respondents with data on the West Virginia population from the U.S. Census. An accurate representation of the state's population can be made with some weighted adjustments to sex and age characteristics of the respondents. Table 2 presents the representativeness of the sample by age and sex of respondents using the weighted adjustments.

The first column of percentages in Table 2 contains a breakdown of the state's population into various age intervals, sex categories, and geographical regions as was presented by the U.S. Census of West Virginia. Due to concern about the extent to which the sample data approximate the distribution of persons in the state, some adjustments are necessary to pull the sample estimates into line with their respective proportions in West Virginia. The WVSIS samples do approximate the actual age intervals found in the state population. However, some differences were identified in the youngest age interval leading to an underestimation of the younger respondents. In addition, women were overrepresented in the sample; not an uncommon finding in this type of survey. The regions represent regional education service agencies (RESA) for the state of West Virginia. Counties associated with the eight regional districts are displayed in Figure A-3. To

Table A–2:
Representativeness of Sample by Age, Sex, And Region
(Percent Distribution by Selected Category for Persons
18 Years of Age and Older)

Demographic Category	1990 Cenus	1993 WVSIS	1994 WVSIS	1995 WVSIS	1996 WVSIS	1997 WVSIS
Age of Respondent						
18 – 24	13.3%	13.3	13.5	13.6	14.1	12.8
25 – 34	19.4%	19.4	19.4	19.3	19.1	17.1
35 – 44	20.1%	20.1	20.0	20.1	20.5	20.4
45 – 54	14.2%	14.2	14.2	14.3	14.2	16.7
55 – 64	13.0%	13.0	12.9	12.9	13.1	12.9
Over 65	20.0%	20.0	20.0	19.9	19.0	20.0
Sex of Respondent						
Male	48.0%	48.8	48.1	46.8	46.9	47.1
Female	52.0%	51.2	51.9	53.2	53.1	52.9
Region of State Residence						
District 1					12.9	12.4
District 2					15.4	13.9
District 3					15.6	16.3
District 4					7.8	8.0
District 5					9.3	9.2
District 6					9.6	9.3
District 7					19.3	20.1
District 8					10.2	10.8

account for these discrepancies, minor adjustments were made through weighting procedures. Of these three factors, the regional distribution of the unweighted data most closely resembled that of the actual population.

Weights, when applied to adjust for these differences, produce estimates nearly identical to those found in the state population. Two weights are calculated for each annual survey. One weight is constructed for analyses that employ the household as the unit of analysis. This weight contains adjustments for age, sex, and regional biases to ensure that the sample is representative of households in West Virginia. A second weight is constructed for analyses of individuals, 18 years of age and older who reside in households within West Virginia. In addition to the sex, age, and regional adjustment constructed for the household weight, the weight for individuals corrects for the different probabilities of selection based on the number of adults living in a household. Figures presented in Table 2 are weighted for individuals.

Figure A–3:
Regional Education Service Agencies in West Virginia

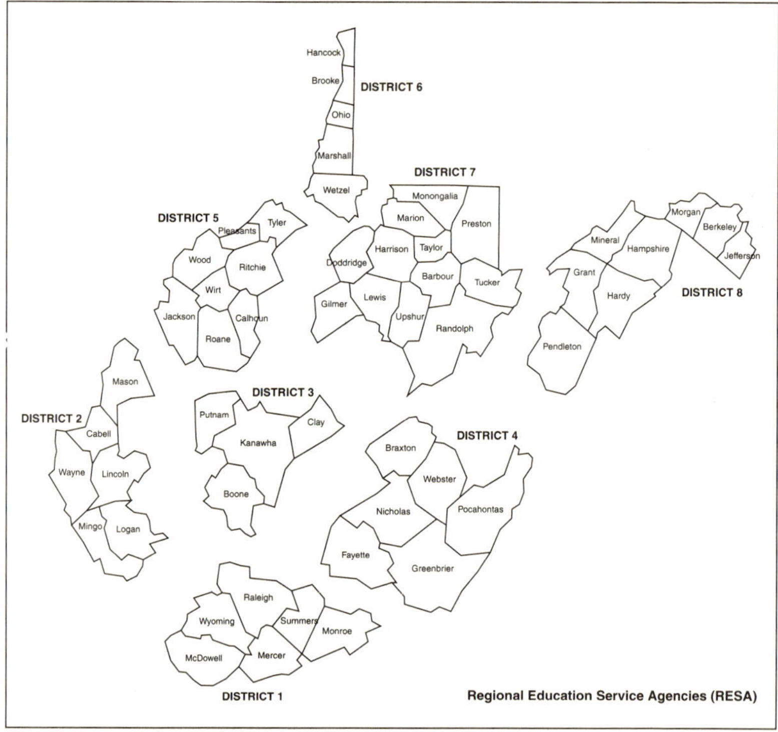

Estimates of Sampling Error

The WVSIS sample is a simple random sample of households within West Virginia with telephones. As a result, estimates of the sampling error are straightforward. Exact sampling errors, based on the size of the sample employed, are computed using a standard formula for the 95% confidence level:

$$1.96 \sqrt{\frac{pq}{N}}$$

where p equals the expected proportion selecting the answer and q equals 1-p. N is the sample size. To illustrate, if the true proportion of the population which is female is equal to 52% and 48 percent is male, an estimate for the sampling error can be computed whereby p=.52 and q=.48. The estimate of the sampling error can be computed and will vary depending on the size of the sample used, i.e., whether a user is employing a full-sample, a half-sample, a quarter-sample, or some other size based on a subset of the sample. For a sample of 922 respondents, the estimate of the sampling error would be plus or minus 3.3%. For a full sample of 922 respondents, we can be 95% confident that the true proportion of females in the state of West Virginia is .52 plus or minus .033. While this may appear to be making a great deal out of the obvious due to our knowledge of the U.S. Census count, we often do not have knowledge about other population characteristics such as the proportion of households having one or more members experience an injury. Consequently, estimates of the sampling error become necessary to draw inferences to the actual state population with some known degree of confidence.

Appendix B

West Virginia Social Indicator Survey
1997 Questionnaire

SUMMARY TABLE FOR PERSONS IN HOUSEHOLD   ID#

Person #1

Relation	Sex	Age	Marital Status	Years of Schooling	Highest Degree
Respondent Spouse/Partner Child/Step Parent Sibling Relative Boarder Other	Male Female		Married Widowed Divorced Separated Married, Apart Never Married		High School/GED Business/Technical Associate Bachelor Master Doctorate Professional

Person #2

Relation	Sex	Age	Marital Status	Years of Schooling	Highest Degree
Respondent Spouse/Partner Child/Step Parent Sibling Relative Boarder Other	Male Female		Married Widowed Divorced Separated Married, Apart Never Married		High School/GED Business/Technical Associate Bachelor Master Doctorate Professional

Person #3

Relation	Sex	Age	Marital Status	Years of Schooling	Highest Degree
Respondent Spouse/Partner Child/Step Parent Sibling Relative Boarder Other	Male Female		Married Widowed Divorced Separated Married, Apart Never Married		High School/GED Business/Technical Associate Bachelor Master Doctorate Professional

Person #4

Relation	Sex	Age	Marital Status	Years of Schooling	Highest Degree
Respondent Spouse/Partner Child/Step Parent Sibling Relative Boarder Other	Male Female		Married Widowed Divorced Separated Married, Apart Never Married		High School/GED Business/Technical Associate Bachelor Master Doctorate Professional

Person #5

Relation	Sex	Age	Marital Status	Years of Schooling	Highest Degree
Respondent Spouse/Partner Child/Step Parent Sibling Relative Boarder Other	Male Female		Married Widowed Divorced Separated Married, Apart Never Married		High School/GED Business/Technical Associate Bachelor Master Doctorate Professional

Page 3

Summary Table For Persons in Household (Cont)

Person #6

Relation	Sex	Age	Marital Status	Years of Schooling	Highest Degree
Respondent	Male		Married		High School/GED
Spouse/Partner	Female		Widowed		Business/Technical
Child/Step			Divorced		Associate
Parent			Separated		Bachelor
Sibling			Married, Apart		Master
Relative			Never Married		Doctorate
Boarder					Professional
Other					

Person #7

Relation	Sex	Age	Marital Status	Years of Schooling	Highest Degree
Respondent	Male		Married		High School/GED
Spouse/Partner	Female		Widowed		Business/Technical
Child/Step			Divorced		Associate
Parent			Separated		Bachelor
Sibling			Married, Apart		Master
Relative			Never Married		Doctorate
Boarder					Professional
Other					

Person #8

Relation	Sex	Age	Marital Status	Years of Schooling	Highest Degree
Respondent	Male		Married		High School/GED
Spouse/Partner	Female		Widowed		Business/Technical
Child/Step			Divorced		Associate
Parent			Separated		Bachelor
Sibling			Married, Apart		Master
Relative			Never Married		Doctorate
Boarder					Professional
Other					

Person #9

Relation	Sex	Age	Marital Status	Years of Schooling	Highest Degree
Respondent	Male		Married		High School/GED
Spouse/Partner	Female		Widowed		Business/Technical
Child/Step			Divorced		Associate
Parent			Separated		Bachelor
Sibling			Married, Apart		Master
Relative			Never Married		Doctorate
Boarder					Professional
Other					

Person #10

Relation	Sex	Age	Marital Status	Years of Schooling	Highest Degree
Respondent	Male		Married		High School/GED
Spouse/Partner	Female		Widowed		Business/Technical
Child/Step			Divorced		Associate
Parent			Separated		Bachelor
Sibling			Married, Apart		Master
Relative			Never Married		Doctorate
Boarder					Professional
Other					

Page 4

1997 WVSIS

IDNUM

We are interested in talking to people about a variety of things. First, I would like to ask you a few questions about your community.

C11. In what county do you live? ___________________________

| County | Region |

C12. Were you born in _____________ county? *[IWER: INSERT COUNTY NAME]*

    Yes   [SKIP TO C13]
    No
    Don't Know
    Missing
    Refused

C12A. Were you born in West Virginia, another state, or a foreign country?

    West Virginia
    Another state
    Foreign country
    Don't Know
    Missing
    Refused

C13. Do you live in open country or in a town or city?

                                          Open country
                                          Town/City
                                          Don't Know
                                          Missing
                                          Refused

C14. What is your Zip   Code?...
        [IWER: DON'T KNOW=77777, MISSING=88888, REFUSED=99999]

Zip Code

Next, we are interested in knowing how you feel about your financial situation.

C15. Has the income your household has earned in the past year allowed you to meet your basic needs?

    Yes   [SKIP TO C16]
    No
    Don't Know   [SKIP TO C16]
    Missing   [SKIP TO C16]
    Refused   [SKIP TO C16]

C15A. Which basic needs <u>have not</u> been met? *[IWER: PROBE FOR 2, ACCEPT ONLY 2]*

| Basic Need 1 | Basic Need 2 |

[IWER: DON'T KNOW=777, MISSING=888, REFUSED=999]

We are also interested in the type of work you normally do.

C16. How would you classify your work situation last week? Were you................*[IWER: READ ALL RESPONSES BELOW AND IF R SAYS MORE THAN 1 CATEGORY, ASK, "WHICH OF THESE IS YOUR PRIMARY WORK SITUATION"]*

> Working
> With a job, but not currently at work
> With a job, but temporarily laid off
> Looking for work   [SKIP TO C23]
> Not Looking for work   [SKIP TO C23]
> Keeping house   [SKIP TO C23]
> Going to school   [SKIP TO C23]
> Unable to work due to disability   [SKIP TO C23]
> Unable to work for other reasons or
> Retired
> Don't Know   [SKIP TO C23]
> Missing   [SKIP TO C23]
> Refused   [SKIP TO C23]

C17. What **(is/was)** your job title or what type of work **(do/did)** you do on your job?
> *[IWER: ACCEPT ONLY 1 JOB TITLE]*

____

____

C18. What **(are/were)** the most important activities or duties at this job? *[IWER: PROBE FOR 2]*

____

____

C19. What type of business or industry **(is/was)** that? *[IWER: ACCEPT ONLY 1]*

____

Occupation	Industry

[IWER: DON'T KNOW=7777. MISSING=8888, REFUSED=9999]

C20. Are you currently a member of a labor union?   Yes
> No   [SKIP TO C21]
> Don't Know   [SKIP TO C21]
> Missing   [SKIP TO C21]
> Refused   [SKIP TO C21]

C20A. What kind of work is represented by that union?

____

Type of Work-Union

[IWER: DON'T KNOW=777, MISSING=888, REFUSED=999]

[IF R IS NOT CURRENTLY EMPLOYED SKIP TO C23]

C21. How many hours do you normally work at your current job during an average week?

Hours __________   Minutes __________

Total Hours

[IWER: DON'T KNOW=777, MISSING=888, REFUSED=999]

C22. How long have you worked at your current job?

Years __________   Months __________

Total Months

[IWER: DON'T KNOW=7777, MISSING=8888, REFUSED=9999]

[IF R LIVES ALONE, SKIP TO EN28, PAGE8]

Now we have some questions about the primary income earner in your household.

C23. In your household, who is the primary income earner? *[IWER: DO NOT READ THE CATEGORIES]*

Self   [SKIP TO EN28, PAGE 8]
Spouse/Partner
Son/Step
Daughter/Step
Mother/Step
Father/Step
Sister/Step
Brother/Step
Share Equally
Other (Specify) ______________

Don't Know   [SKIP TO EN28 PAGE 8]
Missing   [SKIP TO EN28 PAGE 8]
Refused   [SKIP TO EN28 PAGE 8]

[IWER: IF THERE ARE 2 PRIMARY INCOME EARNERS AND ONE OF THEM IS RESPONDENT, GET THE FOLLOWING INFORMATION ON THE OTHER. IF THE RESPONDENT IS NOT ONE OF THE PRIMARY INCOME EARNERS, GET FOLLOWING INFORMATION ON THE PRIMARY INCOME EARNER THAT HAS HAD THE MOST RECENT BIRTHDAY]

C24. Last week was your (__________)..........*[IWER: READ <u>ALL</u> RESPONSES BELOW AND IF R SAYS MORE THAN 1 CATEGORY, ASK "WHICH OF THESE IS (<u>HIS/HER</u>) <u>PRIMARY</u> WORK SITUATION?"]*

Working
With a job, but not currently at work
With a job, but temporarily laid off
Looking for work   [SKIP TO EN28, PAGE 8]
Keeping house   [SKIP TO EN28, PAGE 8]
Going to school   [SKIP TO EN28, PAGE 8]
Unable to work due to disability   [SKIP TO EN28, PAGE 8]
Unable to work for other reasons or   [SKIP TO EN28, PAGE 8]
Retired
Don't Know   [SKIP TO EN28, PAGE 8]
Missing   [SKIP TO EN28, PAGE 8]
Refused   [SKIP TO EN28, PAGE 8]

C25. What (**is/was**) your ___________'s job title or what type of work (**does/did**) (**he/she**) do on (**his/her**) job?
[IWER: ACCEPT ONLY 1 JOB TITLE]

C26. What (**are/were**) the most important activities or duties at this job? *[PROBE FOR 2]*

C27. What type of business or industry is that? *[IWER: ACCEPT ONLY 1]*___________________________

Occupation	Industry

[IWER: DON'T KNOW=7777, MISSING=8888, REFUSED=9999]

Now we would like to know a little about the air in your community.

EN28. Please rate the air in your community from 1 to 5 where 1 is not at all polluted and 5 is extremely polluted.

　　not at all polluted　　　　DK
　　　　　　　　　　　　　　　Mis
　　　　　　　　　　　　　　　Ref

　　extremely polluted

EN29A. Is there a routine source of information available concerning air quality in your area, such as on radio or TV or in the newspaper?

　　Yes　　　　　　　　　　DK [SKIP TO EN30]
　　No [SKIP TO EN30]　　　Mis [SKIP TO EN30]
　　　　　　　　　　　　　　Ref [SKIP TO EN30]

EN29B. How often is that information available?　　　Daily　　　　　DK
　　　　　　　　　　　　　　　　　　　　　　　　　Weekly　　　　Mis
　　　　　　　　　　　　　　　　　　　　　　　　　Monthly　　　Ref
　　　　　　　　　　　　　　　　　　　　　　　　　Bi-Weekly

EN29C. Would you like that information
provided more often?　　　　　　　　Yes [SKIP TO EN31]　　　DK [SKIP TO EN31]
　　　　　　　　　　　　　　　　　　No [SKIP TO EN31]　　　Mis [SKIP TO EN31]
　　　　　　　　　　　　　　　　　　　　　　　　　　　　　Ref [SKIP TO EN31]

EN30. Would you like to have a routine source of information about air quality in your　　　Yes　　　DK
area?　　　　　　　　　　　　　　　　　　　　　　　　　　　　　　　　　　　　　No　　　Mis
　　　Ref

EN31. How many members of your household have been told by a medical doctor that they have:

EN31A1. Asthma   If 0 go to B1

EN31A2. What are their ages?

Person 1	Person 2	Person 3	Person 4	Person 5

EN31A3. Does that (______) person smoke?

Person 1	Person 2	Person 3	Person 4	Person 5
Yes	Yes	Yes	Yes	Yes
No	No	No	No	No
DK	DK	DK	DK	DK
Mis	Mis	Mis	Mis	Mis
Ref	Ref	Ref	Ref	Ref

EN31B1. Chronic Bronchitis   If 0 go to C1

EN31B2. What are their ages?

Person 1	Person 2	Person 3	Person 4	Person 5

EN31B3. Does that (______) person smoke?

Person 1	Person 2	Person 3	Person 4	Person 5
Yes	Yes	Yes	Yes	Yes
No	No	No	No	No
DK	DK	DK	DK	DK
Mis	Mis	Mis	Mis	Mis
Ref	Ref	Ref	Ref	Ref

EN31C1. Emphysema   If 0 go to EN32

EN31C2. What are their ages?

Person 1	Person 2	Person 3	Person 4	Person 5

EN31C3. Does that (______) person smoke?

Person 1	Person 2	Person 3	Person 4	Person 5
Yes	Yes	Yes	Yes	Yes
No	No	No	No	No
DK	DK	DK	DK	DK
Mis	Mis	Mis	Mis	Mis
Ref	Ref	Ref	Ref	Ref

EN32. What is the primary source of heat in your home?

Gas (natural or propane)   DK
Electric   Mis
Wood   Ref
Kerosene
Coal
Oil
Heat Pump
Solar
None of the above/None

EN33. Thinking about some specific areas, how do you feel about the current environmental protection laws and regulations in West Virginia?

For _____________ *[READ THE FIRST ITEM]*, are the present laws Too Restrictive, Not Restrictive Enough, or Fine As They Are?

What about _____________ *[READ NEXT ITEM]*?

	Too Restrictive	Fine As They Are	Not Restrictive Enough	DK	Mis	Ref
a. air pollution						
b. river protection						
c. wild or natural areas						
d. coal mining						
e. endangered species						
f. timber harvesting						
g. wetland areas						
h. water pollution						

EN34. Are you aware that the U.S. Environmental Protection Agency has proposed a regulatory change to improve air quality by making power plants and factories reduce their air emissions?

Yes
No [SKIP TO HC35]
DK
Mis
Ref

EN34A. How supportive are you of these changes? Are you Extremely Supportive, Somewhat Supportive, Neutral, Not Very Supportive, or Not At All Supportive?

Extremely supportive
Somewhat supportive
Neutral
Not very supportive
Not at all supportive
DK
Mis
Ref

Now I would like to ask you some questions about your current health coverage.

HC35. Do you currently have any kind of health care coverage, including private health insurance, prepaid plans such as HMO's, or goverment plans such as Medicare or Medicaid?

- Yes
- No [GO TO HC41]
- DK
- Mis
- Ref

HC36. I am going to read you a list of types of health insurance. Please tell me whether or not you have coverage from each type.

	Yes	No	DK	Mis	Ref
a. Medicare Part A					
b. Medicare Part B					
c. Medicaid or Medical Assistance					
d. Military or VA					
e. A fee-for-service plan					
f. A HMO or Health Maintenance Organization					
g. A PPO or Preferred Provider Organization					
h. Medigap, the Medicare supplemental					
i. Long-term care for nursing home care					

[If R says no to all categories, ask, "What kind of coverage plan do you have?"]

Open-ended Health Insurance Code

HC37. Does (**do any of**) your health plan(s) help pay for prescription drugs?

Yes   No   DK   MIS   REF

HC38. In the past year has (**have any of**) your health plan(s) denied or refused to pay for any kind of treatment or service that your doctor recommended for you, <u>not</u> including the emergency room?

Yes   No   DK   MIS   REF

HC39. On a scale of 1 to 5 where 1 is very easy and 5 is very difficult, how understandable are the forms, notices, and procedures for your health plan(s)?

- Very Easy
-
-
-
- Very Difficult

- DK
- Mis
- Ref

HC40. Overall, how satisfied are you with your health plan(s)? Please use a scale of 1 to 5 where 1 is extremely satisfied and 5 is not at all satisfied.

- Extremely satisfied
-
-
-
- Not at all satisfied   **[IWER: ALL RESPONSES SKIP TO SC42]**

- DK
- Mis
- Ref

HC41. How long has it been since you had health care coverage? **[DON'T READ CATEGORIES]**

- Within the past 6 months (0 to 6 months)
- 6 to 12 months ago
- 1 to 2 years ago
- 2 to 5 years ago
- 5 or more years ago
- DK
- Mis
- Ref

Now we have some questions in a different topic.

SC42. Other than traffic court, have you been involved with a case in a WV court in the <u>last four years</u> in any of the following ways....

Have you....	Yes	No	DK	Mis	Ref
a. Been a witness in a case?......................	⬭	⬭	⬭	⬭	⬭
b. Been a juror in a case?.........................	⬭	⬭	⬭	⬭	⬭
c. Been involved in a criminal case?...........	⬭	⬭ go to D	⬭ go to D	⬭ go to D	⬭ go to D
Were you the defendant?.................	⬭	⬭	⬭	⬭	⬭
d. Been involved in a civil case?...............	⬭	⬭ go to E	⬭ go to E	⬭ go to E	⬭ go to E
Were you the plaintiff?.....................	⬭	⬭	⬭	⬭	⬭
Were you the defendant?.................	⬭	⬭	⬭	⬭	⬭
e. Ever observed a proceeding?.................	⬭	⬭	⬭	⬭	⬭
f. Ever been an attorney in court?.............	⬭	⬭	⬭	⬭	⬭

[IWER: IF R LIVES ALONE GO TO SC44]

SC43. Has anyone else in your household been involved in a WV court case in any of those ways in the <u>last four years</u>? *[IWER: <u>ANY OF THE WAYS IN THE ABOVE QUESTIONS</u>]*

    ⬭ **Yes**   ⬭ **No**   ⬭ **DK**   ⬭ **Mis**   ⬭ **Ref**

SC44. Have you ever been employed in either the WV court system or the criminal justice system?

    ⬭ **Yes**   ⬭ **No**   ⬭ **DK**   ⬭ **Mis**   ⬭ **Ref**

SC45. Do you consider the WV courts to be affordable for ordinary people?

    ⬭ **Yes**   ⬭ **No**   ⬭ **DK**   ⬭ **Mis**   ⬭ **Ref**

SC46. On a scale of 1 to 5 where 1 is extremely easy and 5 is extremely difficult, how understandable are the WV courts?

Extremely Easy	Easy	Neutral	Difficult	Extremely Difficult	DK	MIS	REF
⬭	⬭	⬭	⬭	⬭	⬭	⬭	⬭

Please tell me how much you agree or disagree with the following statements:

	SA	A	N	D	SD	DK	MIS	REF
SC47. People get the justice they deserve. Do you strongly agree, agree, neutral, disagree, or strongly disagree?...............................	⬭	⬭	⬭	⬭	⬭	⬭	⬭	⬭
SC48. What about the statement: West Virginia courts treat people equally.......................	⬭	⬭	⬭	⬭	⬭	⬭	⬭	⬭
SC49. The courts have a positive reputation in my area...	⬭	⬭	⬭	⬭	⬭	⬭	⬭	⬭
SC50. The justice system works...........................	⬭	⬭	⬭	⬭	⬭	⬭	⬭	⬭

SC51. How much confidence do you have in the decisions of WV courts? Are you extremely confident, somewhat confident, not very confident, or not at all confident?

    EC   ⬭ SC   ⬭ NVC   ⬭ NAAC   ⬭ **Don't Know**   ⬭ **Missing**   ⬭ **Refused**

Now, I have some questions that may be somewhat sensitive. Please remember that all your answers are completely confidential and we appreciate your honesty.

SJ52. I am going to read some statements about various groups teaching in <u>public high schools</u>.
    Please tell me how much you agree or disagree with each statement.
    The first statement is I object to Blacks or African-Americans teaching in <u>public high schools</u>.

    Do you Strongly Agree, Agree, are Neutral, Disagree, or Strongly Disagree?

    What about the statement:
    I object to *(_______) [Insert Next Group]* teaching in <u>public high schools</u>?

	SA	A	N	D	SD	DK	Mis	Ref
a. Blacks or African-Americans	(1)	(2)	(3)	(4)	(5)	(7)	(8)	(9)
b. Hispanics or Latin-Americans	(1)	(2)	(3)	(4)	(5)	(7)	(8)	(9)
c. Asians or Asian-Americans	(1)	(2)	(3)	(4)	(5)	(7)	(8)	(9)
d. People with obvious and permanent physical disabilities	(1)	(2)	(3)	(4)	(5)	(7)	(8)	(9)
e. Gay men	(1)	(2)	(3)	(4)	(5)	(7)	(8)	(9)
f. Gay women or lesbians	(1)	(2)	(3)	(4)	(5)	(7)	(8)	(9)
g. People who believe that whites are racially superior to other races	(1)	(2)	(3)	(4)	(5)	(7)	(8)	(9)
h. Women in general	(1)	(2)	(3)	(4)	(5)	(7)	(8)	(9)
i. Men in general	(1)	(2)	(3)	(4)	(5)	(7)	(8)	(9)

SJ53. I am going to read some statements about various groups teaching in <u>public colleges</u> or <u>universities</u>.
    Please tell me how much you agree or disagree with each statement.
    The first statement is I object to Blacks or African-Americans teaching in <u>public colleges</u> or <u>universities</u>.

    Do you Strongly Agree, Agree, are Neutral, Disagree, or Strongly Disagree?

    What about the statement:
    I object to *(_______) [Insert Next Group]* teaching in <u>public colleges</u> or <u>universities</u>?

	SA	A	N	D	SD	DK	Mis	Ref
a. Blacks or African-Americans	(1)	(2)	(3)	(4)	(5)	(7)	(8)	(9)
b. Hispanics or Latin-Americans	(1)	(2)	(3)	(4)	(5)	(7)	(8)	(9)
c. Asians or Asian-Americans	(1)	(2)	(3)	(4)	(5)	(7)	(8)	(9)
d. People with obvious and permanent physical disabilities	(1)	(2)	(3)	(4)	(5)	(7)	(8)	(9)
e. Gay men	(1)	(2)	(3)	(4)	(5)	(7)	(8)	(9)
f. Gay women or lesbians	(1)	(2)	(3)	(4)	(5)	(7)	(8)	(9)
g. People who believe that whites are racially superior to other races	(1)	(2)	(3)	(4)	(5)	(7)	(8)	(9)
h. Women in general	(1)	(2)	(3)	(4)	(5)	(7)	(8)	(9)
i. Men in general	(1)	(2)	(3)	(4)	(5)	(7)	(8)	(9)

SJ54. At what point in most people's lives do you think the following events happen? This could be at any age, or never. What do you think is the typical or average age that. . .

AGE

a. most females begin to go out on dates?

b. most males begin to go out on dates?

c. most females have their first sexual encounter?

d. most males have their first sexual encounter?

e. most females begin to drink alcohol?

f. most males begin to drink alcohol?

g. most females begin to experiment with drugs?

h. most males begin to experiment with drugs?

SJ55. We have 5 ideas for strategies to help young people in college deal with peer pressures. Please tell me which **one** you think is best for each situation. Which strategy do you think is best for colleges to use to help young people deal with sexual activity?
The strategies are: Education programs to increase awareness of dangers, more rules to restrict activity, counseling to enhance self esteem, tighter security to enforce rules, or more family support in the college's policies.

	Education Programs	More Rules	Counseling	Tighter Security	Family Support	Dk	Mis	Ref
a. Which strategy do you think is best for colleges to use to help young people deal with sexual activity?								
b. What is the best strategy for colleges to helping students deal with drinking?								
c. What is the most effective strategy for colleges to deter students from using drugs?								

Before we close, I have just a few remaining questions. We are interested in the political participation of West Virginians.

C56. First of all, do you consider yourself a Democrat, a Republican, an Independent, or something else?

Democrat   ⃝   ⃝ Don't Know   ⃝ Missing   ⃝ Refused

Republican   ⃝

Independent   ⃝

Something else (Specify) ____

In the last four years, have you...

	Yes	No	Dk	Miss	Ref
C57. Voted?	⃝	⃝	⃝	⃝	⃝
C58. Given money to help someone try to win an election?	⃝	⃝	⃝	⃝	⃝
C59. Worked in a political campaign?	⃝	⃝	⃝	⃝	⃝
C60. Written letters to elected officials, Senators or Members of Congress, Mayors, etc.?	⃝	⃝	⃝	⃝	⃝
C61. Signed a petition?	⃝	⃝	⃝	⃝	⃝
C62. Participated in a strike?	⃝	⃝	⃝	⃝	⃝
C63. Worked with others in your community to solve some local problem?	⃝	⃝	⃝	⃝	⃝

CRACE. Of what race do you consider yourself? *[DO NOT READ CATEGORIES]*

White/Caucasian.. ⃝   ⃝ Don't Know   ⃝ Missing   ⃝ Refused
Chicano/Mexican/Hispanic/Latino (of any race).. ⃝
Black/African American (non-Hispanic)............... ⃝
American Indian/Native American/Alaskan Native ⃝
Asian/Pacific Islander.. ⃝

Other race (Specify) ____

CINC1.　Is your total household income more than $30,000 or less than $30,000 a year?

　　　　$30,000 or more　　　　　[SKIP TO CINC2]
　　　　Less than $30,000　　　　[SKIP TO CINC3]
　　　　Don't Know　　　　　　　[SKIP TO C64]
　　　　Missing　　　　　　　　　[SKIP TO C64]
　　　　Refused　　　　　　　　　[SKIP TO C64]

CINC2.　I am going to mention a number of categories. When I mention the category which describes your total household income in the last 12 months, please stop me.

　　　　$30,000 to less than $40,000
　　　　$40,000 to less than $50,000
　　　　$50,000 to less than $60,000
　　　　$60,000 to less than $70,000
　　　　$70,000 to less than $80,000
　　　　$80,000 or more
　　　　Don't Know
　　　　Missing
　　　　Refused

[SKIP TO C64]

CINC3.　I am going to mention a number of categories. When I mention the category which describes your total household income in the last 12 months, please stop me.

　　　　Less than $5,000
　　　　$5,000 to less than $10,000
　　　　$10,000 to less than $15,000
　　　　$15,000 to less than $20,000
　　　　$20,000 to less than $25,000
　　　　$25,000 to less than $30,000
　　　　Don't Know
　　　　Missing
　　　　Refused

C64.　Is any of your total household income supported by public assistance?

　　　　Yes
　　　　No　　　　　　　　[SKIP TO CLOSING STATEMENT]
　　　　Don't Know　　　　[SKIP TO CLOSING STATEMENT]
　　　　Missing　　　　　　[SKIP TO CLOSING STATEMENT]
　　　　Refused　　　　　　[SKIP TO CLOSING STATEMENT]

C65.　Approximately what proportion or percentage of your household income would you say comes from public assistance?

　　　　% of income

　　　　[DON'T KNOW=777, MISSING=888, REFUSED=999]

Those are all the questions I have for you. Thank you very much for your time and cooperation.

Have a good __________.

Appendix C

West Virginia Social Indicator Survey
1996 Questionnaire

We are interested in talking to people about a variety of things. First, I want to ask a few questions about your community.

C11.	In what county do you live?____

REGION

C12.	Were you born in ___________ county? [IWER: INSERT COUNTY NAME]
	Yes .... [SKIP TO C13] □1
	No .... □2
						Don't Know □7
						Missing □8
						Refused □9

C12A.	Were you born in West Virginia, another state, or a foreign country?
	West Virginia .... □1
	Another state .... □2
	Foreign country .... □3
						Don't Know □7
						Missing □8
						Refused □9

C13.	Do you live in open country or in a town or city?
	Open country .... □1
	Town/City .... □2
						Don't Know □7
						Missing □8
						Refused □9

C14.	What is your Zip Code? .... ZIP CODE
						Don't Know □77777
						Missing □88888
						Refused □99999

Next, we are interested in knowing how you feel about your financial situation.

C15.	Has the income your household has earned during the past year allowed you to meet your basic needs?
	Yes .... [SKIP TO C16] □1
	No .... □2
						Don't Know [SKIP TO C16] □7
						Missing [SKIP TO C16] □8
						Refused [SKIP TO C16] □9

C15A.   Which basic needs <u>have not</u> been met? [IWER: PROBE FOR 2, ACCEPT ONLY 2]

Don't Know ☐ 777
Missing ☐ 888
Refused ☐ 999

We are also interested in the type of work you normally do.

C16.   How would you classify your work situation last week? Were you ... [IWER: READ <u>ALL</u> RESPONSES BELOW AND IF R SAYS MORE THAN 1 CATEGORY, ASK, "WHICH OF THESE IS YOUR <u>PRIMARY WORK SITUATION</u>"]

Working ... ☐ 1
With a job, but not currently at work ... ☐ 2
With a job, but temporarily laid off ... ☐ 3
Looking for work ... [SKIP TO C23] ☐ 4
Keeping house ... [SKIP TO C23] ☐ 5
Going to school ... [SKIP TO C23] ☐ 6
Unable to work due to disability ... [SKIP TO C23] ☐ 7
Unable to work for other reasons or ... [SKIP TO C23] ☐ 8
Retired ... ☐ 9

Don't Know [SKIP TO C23] ☐ 77
Missing [SKIP TO C23] ☐ 88
Refused [SKIP TO C23] ☐ 99

C17.   What **(is/was)** your job title or what type of work **(do/did)** you do on your job? [IWER: ACCEPT ONLY 1 JOB TITLE]

C18.   What **(are/were)** the most important activities or duties at this job? [PROBE FOR 2]

C19.   What type of business or industry **(is/was)** that? [IWER: ACCEPT ONLY 1]

OCCUPATION ☐☐☐   **INDUSTRY** ☐☐☐

Don't Know ☐ 7777
Missing ☐ 8888
Refused ☐ 9999

C20.   Are you currently a member of a labor union?

Yes .... ☐1
No .... [SKIP TO C21] ☐2
Don't Know [SKIP TO C21] ☐7
Missing [SKIP TO C21] ☐8
Refused [SKIP TO C21] ☐9

C20A.   What kind of work is represented by that union?

☐☐

Don't Know ☐777
Missing ☐888
Refused ☐999

[IF R IS NOT CURRENTLY EMPLOYED SKIP TO C23]

C21.   How many hours do you normally work at your current job during an average week?

HOURS ☐☐ **MINUTES** ☐☐

TOTAL HOURS ☐☐☐

Don't Know ☐777
Missing ☐888
Refused ☐999

C22.   How long have you worked at your current job? .... **YEARS** ☐☐ **MONTHS** ☐☐

TOTAL MONTHS ☐☐☐

Don't Know ☐7777
Missing ☐8888
Refused ☐9999

[IF R LIVES ALONE, SKIP TO H28, PAGE 5]

Now we have some questions about the primary income earner in your household.

C23.   In your household, who is the primary income earner? [IWER: DO NOT READ CATEGORIES]

Self .... [SKIP TO H28 PAGE 5] ☐1
Spouse .... ☐2
Son/ Step .... ☐3
Daughter/ Step .... ☐4
Mother/ Step .... ☐5
Father / Step .... ☐6
Sister/ Step .... ☐7
Brother/ Step .... ☐8
Other (Specify)____
Don't Know [SKIP TO H28 PAGE 5] ☐77
Missing [SKIP TO H28 PAGE 5] ☐88
Refused [SKIP TO H28 PAGE 5] ☐99

[IWER: IF THERE ARE 2 PRIMARY INCOME EARNERS AND ONE OF THEM IS RESPONDENT, GET FOLLOWING INFORMATION ON THE OTHER. IF RESPONDENT IS NOT ONE OF THE PRIMARY INCOME EARNERS, GET FOLLOWING INFORMATION ON THE PRIMARY INCOME EARNER THAT HAS HAD THE MOST RECENT BIRTHDAY.

C24.   Last week was your (________) .... [IWER: READ ALL RESPONSES BELOW AND IF R SAYS MORE THAN 1 CATEGORY, ASK "WHICH OF THESE IS (HIS/HER) PRIMARY WORK SITUATION?"]

Working .... ☐1
With a job, but not currently at work .... ☐2
With a job, but temporarily laid off .... ☐3
Looking for work .... ☐4
Keeping house .... [SKIP TO H28, PAGE 5] ☐5
Going to school .... [SKIP TO H28, PAGE 5] ☐6
Unable to work due to disability .... [SKIP TO H28, PAGE 5] ☐7
Unable to work for other reasons or .... [SKIP TO H28, PAGE 5] ☐8
Retired .... ☐9

Don't Know [SKIP TO H28, PAGE 5] ☐77
Missing [SKIP TO H28, PAGE 5] ☐88
Refused [SKIP TO H28, PAGE 5] ☐99

C25.   What **(is/was)** your __________'s job title or what type of work **(does/did)** **(he/she)** do on **(his/her)** job? [IWER: ACCEPT ONLY 1 JOB TITLE]
____

____

C26.   What **(are/were)** the most important activities or duties at this job? [PROBE FOR 2]
____

____

C27.   What type of business or industry is that? [IWER: ACCEPT ONLY 1]________________
____

OCCUPATION ☐☐☐   INDUSTRY ☐☐☐

Don't Know ☐7777
Missing ☐8888
Refused ☐9999

Now we would like to know a little bit about your health.

H28.   Do you have <u>any</u> kind of health insurance coverage, including private health insurance, prepaid plans such as HMOs, or government plans such as Medicare or Medicaid?

    Yes .... ☐1
    No .... [SKIP TO H30] ☐2
    Don't Know ☐7
    Missing ☐8
    Refused ☐9

H29.   Was there a time in the past twelve months when you were without health insurance coverage?

    Yes .... ☐1
    No .... ☐2
    Don't Know ☐7
    Missing ☐8
    Refused ☐9

[IWER: IF NO CHILDREN LIVING IN HOUSEHOLD, SKIP TO H32, PAGE 6]

H30.   Do you have children living in your household who have health coverage through Medicaid?

    Yes .... ☐1
    No .... ☐2
    Don't Know ☐7
    Missing ☐8
    Refused ☐9

H31A.   Was there a time in the past twelve months when a child living in your household was without health insurance?

    Yes .... ☐1
    No .... [SKIP TO H32] ☐2
    Don't Know ☐7
    Missing ☐8
    Refused ☐9

H31B.   How many children in your household were without health insurance coverage in the past twelve months?

    ☐ # children
    Don't Know ☐77
    Missing ☐88
    Refused ☐99

H32. In general, would you say your health is Excellent, Very Good, Good, Fair, or Poor?

  Excellent .... ☐ 1
  Very Good .... ☐ 2
  Good .... ☐ 3
  Fair .... ☐ 4
  Poor .... ☐ 5
                Don't Know ☐ 7
                 Missing ☐ 8
                 Refused ☐ 9

H33A. On how many days in an average week do you participate in physical activities <u>as exercise</u> such as ~~walking~~, jogging, dancing, aerobics, yard work or on-the-job activities, for at least 30 minutes per day?

            ☐ # of days [IF 0 DAYS, SKIP TO H33D, PAGE 7]

        Don't Know [SKIP TO H33D, PAGE 7] ☐ 77
        Missing [SKIP TO H33D, PAGE 7] ☐ 88
        Refused [SKIP TO H33D, PAGE 7] ☐ 99

H33B. In what kinds of exercise or physical activities do you participate? [PROBE FOR 3]

____

____

____

H33C. For how long have you been exercising? [IWER: DO NOT READ CATEGORIES]

  Less than 6 months .... [SKIP TO H34, PAGE 7] ☐ 1
  6 months to 1 year .... [SKIP TO H34 ,PAGE 7] ☐ 2
  More than 1 year .... [SKIP TO H34, PAGE 7] ☐ 3
        Don't Know [SKIP TO H34, PAGE 7] ☐ 7
        Missing [SKIP TO H34, PAGE 7] ☐ 8
        Refused [SKIP TO H34, PAGE 7] ☐ 9

H33D.   Have you thought about beginning an exercise program?

Yes .... ☐ 1

No .... [SKIP TO H34] ☐ 2

Don't Know   [SKIP TO H34] ☐ 7

Missing   [SKIP TO H34] ☐ 8

Refused   [SKIP TO H34] ☐ 9

H33E.   When do you plan to begin?   [IWER: DO NOT READ CATEGORIES]

Within the next week (Immediately) .... ☐ 1

Within the next month .... ☐ 2

Within the next 6 months .... ☐ 3

More than 6 months .... ☐ 4

Don't Know ☐ 7

Missing ☐ 8

Refused ☐ 9

H34.   About how many hours of TV did you watch yesterday? [IWER: DO NOT READ CATEGORIES]

None .... ☐ 1

1-3 .... ☐ 2

4-6 .... ☐ 3

7-9 .... ☐ 4

10 or more .... ☐ 5

Watched but can't recall number of hours .... ☐ 6

Don't Know ☐ 7

Missing ☐ 8

Refused ☐ 9

H35A.   Have you ever lost any permanent teeth to <u>tooth decay</u> or <u>gum disease</u>?

Yes .... ☐ 1

No .... [SKIP TO H36] ☐ 2

Don't Know   [SKIP TO H36] ☐ 7

Missing   [SKIP TO H36] ☐ 8

Refused   [SKIP TO H36] ☐ 9

H35B.   How many teeth have you lost to tooth decay or gum disease? [IWER: DO NOT READ CATEGORIES]

One .... ☐ 1

Two .... ☐ 2

Three or more .... ☐ 3

Don't Know ☐ 7

Missing ☐ 8

Refused ☐ 9

H36.   Please tell me how much you agree with the statement: My health is my responsibility. Do you Strongly Agree, Agree, Are Neutral, Disagree, or Strongly Disagree?

- **Strongly Agree** ☐1
- **Agree** ☐2
- **Neutral** ☐3
- **Disagree** ☐4
- **Strongly Disagree** ☐5

Don't Know ☐7
Missing ☐8
Refused ☐9

H37.   What about the statement: There is <u>not</u> much I can do to reduce my risk of <u>heart disease</u>. Do you Strongly Agree, Agree, Are Neutral, Disagree, or Strongly Disagree?

- **Strongly Agree** ☐1
- **Agree** ☐2
- **Neutral** ☐3
- **Disagree** ☐4
- **Strongly Disagree** ☐5

Don't Know ☐7
Missing ☐8
Refused ☐9

H38.   And what about the statement: There is <u>not</u> much I can do to reduce my risk of <u>cancer</u>. Do you Strongly Agree, Agree, Are Neutral, Disagree, or Strongly Disagree?

- **Strongly Agree** ☐1
- **Agree** ☐2
- **Neutral** ☐3
- **Disagree** ☐4
- **Strongly Disagree** ☐5

Don't Know ☐7
Missing ☐8
Refused ☐9

H39.   Do you drink milk?

- **Yes** ☐1
- **No** [SKIP TO H40, PAGE 9] ☐2

Don't Know [SKIP TO H40, PAGE 9] ☐7
Missing [SKIP TO H40, PAGE 9] ☐8
Refused [SKIP TO H40, PAGE 9] ☐9

H39a.   What kind of milk do you drink? [IWER: DO NOT READ CATEGORIES]

- **Whole/Vitamin D/Regular milk** ☐1
- **2% milk** ☐2
- **1% milk** ☐3
- **Half-percent milk** ☐4
- **Skim/non-fat milk** ☐5
- **Another type** (specify _______________) ☐6

Don't Know ☐7
Missing ☐8
Refused ☐9

H40.   In the past year have you (or any other members of your household) participated in any health promotion activities, such as a health fair or wellness program, in the community or place of employment?

Yes . . . . [GO TO H41] ☐ 1

No . . . . [SKIP TO ED42, PAGE 10] ☐ 2

H41.   [IWER: READ EACH COLUMN HEADING FOR EACH ROW ITEM.]

	A	B	C
	Have you **(or any other members of** **your household)** **participated in:**	**Who was the <u>main</u> sponsor?** **Was it a:** School (S); Local Health Dept (LHD); Community Group (CG); Private Business (PB); Local Coalition (LC); Hospital (H); Primary Care Center (PCC) or something else? (Oth)	**[IWER: DO NOT READ IF R LIVES ALONE]** **How many household members participated in the event ?**
1	**a Health Fair or Screening** **Yes** . . . . (GO TO 1B) ☐ 1 **No** . . . . . (GO TO 2A) ☐ 2	1 ☐ S 2 ☐ LHD 3 ☐ CG 4 ☐ PB 5 ☐ LC 6 ☐ H 7 ☐ PCC 8 ☐ Oth:_________________ (GO TO 1C)	☐☐ Number of Participants (GO TO 2A)
2	**a Fun Run or Walk** **Yes** . . . . (GO TO 2B) ☐ 1 **No** . . . . . (GO TO 3A) ☐ 2	1 ☐ S 2 ☐ LHD 3 ☐ CG 4 ☐ PB 5 ☐ LC 6 ☐ H 7 ☐ PCC 8 ☐ Oth:_________________ (GO TO 2C)	☐☐ Number of Participants (GO TO 3A)
3	**an Informational Session** **Yes** . . . . (GO TO 3B) ☐ 1 **No** . . . . . (GO TO 4A) ☐ 2	1 ☐ S 2 ☐ LHD 3 ☐ CG 4 ☐ PB 5 ☐ LC 6 ☐ H 7 ☐ PCC 8 ☐ Oth:_________________ (GO TO 3C)	☐☐ Number of Participants (GO TO 4A)
4	**Volunteering** **Yes** . . . . (GO TO 4B) ☐ 1 **No** . . . . . (GO TO 5A) ☐ 2	1 ☐ S 2 ☐ LHD 3 ☐ CG 4 ☐ PB 5 ☐ LC 6 ☐ H 7 ☐ PCC 8 ☐ Oth:_________________ (GO TO 4C)	☐☐ Number of Participants (GO TO 5A)
5	**an Immunization Program** **Yes** . . . . (GO TO 5B) ☐ 1 **No** . . . . . (GO TO 6A) ☐ 2	1 ☐ S 2 ☐ LHD 3 ☐ CG 4 ☐ PB 5 ☐ LC 6 ☐ H 7 ☐ PCC 8 ☐ Oth:_________________ (GO TO 5C)	☐☐ Number of Participants (GO TO 6A)
6	**Another Health Promotion Event** (spec__________) **Yes** . . . . (GO TO 6B) ☐ 1 **No** . . . (GO TO ED42) ☐ 2	1 ☐ S 2 ☐ LHD 3 ☐ CG 4 ☐ PB 5 ☐ LC 6 ☐ H 7 ☐ PCC 8 ☐ Oth:_________________ (GO TO 6C)	☐☐ Number of Participants (GO TO ED42)

Now we would like to know some things about higher education in West Virginia.

ED42.   I am going to read you some items that people think about when choosing a school in higher education. This could include a college, university, or technical school.

For each item, please tell me whether you think it is Extremely Important, Very Important, Somewhat Important, Not Very Important, or Not at all Important when someone is choosing an institution of higher education.

Let's start with _____ [READ FIRST ITEM]. Do you think this is Extremely Important, Very Important, Somewhat Important, Not Very Important, or Not at all Important for someone choosing a school in higher education.

What about _____ [READ NEXT ITEM]?

	EI	VI	SI	NVI	NAI	DK	MIS	REF
cost or affordability	☐1	☐2	☐3	☐4	☐5	☐7	☐8	☐9
the availability of financial aid	☐1	☐2	☐3	☐4	☐5	☐7	☐8	☐9
the availability of scholarships	☐1	☐2	☐3	☐4	☐5	☐7	☐8	☐9
high quality faculty	☐1	☐2	☐3	☐4	☐5	☐7	☐8	☐9
recommendations by family, friends, and co-workers	☐1	☐2	☐3	☐4	☐5	☐7	☐8	☐9
the availability of a particular major	☐1	☐2	☐3	☐4	☐5	☐7	☐8	☐9
high quality libraries	☐1	☐2	☐3	☐4	☐5	☐7	☐8	☐9
individual contact with instructors	☐1	☐2	☐3	☐4	☐5	☐7	☐8	☐9
availability of job placement programs	☐1	☐2	☐3	☐4	☐5	☐7	☐8	☐9
outside of the classroom activities, such as recreational, cultural, or wellness programs	☐1	☐2	☐3	☐4	☐5	☐7	☐8	☐9

ED43.   In general, what are the most important things that determine a school's Academic Reputation or Prestige? These could be some of the items we just talked about or something else. [IWER: PROBE FOR 3 SUBSTANTIVE CHARACTERISTICS.]

____

____

____

ED44A.   Are you (or any of the other members of your household) <u>currently</u> attending a college, university, or technical school?
Yes .... [GO TO ED44B] ☐ 1
No .... [SKIP TO ED45, PAGE 10] ☐ 2
Don't Know [SKIP TO ED45, PAGE 10] ☐ 7
Missing [SKIP TO ED45, PAGE 10] ☐ 8
Refused [SKIP TO ED45, PAGE 10] ☐ 9

[IF RESPONDENT LIVES ALONE, GO TO ED44C]

ED44B.   Would that be you or someone else in the household?

Self .... ☐ 1

Other .... ☐ 2

Both respondent and another .... ☐ 3

Don't Know ☐ 7

Missing ☐ 8

Refused ☐ 9

[IWER: IF BOTH RESPONDENT AND ANOTHER ATTENDING, ASK FOR RESPONDENT]

ED44C.   What type of school are **(you/they)** attending?

4 year college or university .... ☐ 1

2 year community college .... ☐ 2

Technical or vocational school .... ☐ 3

Don't Know ☐ 7

Missing ☐ 8

Refused ☐ 9

ED45.   Are you (or any of the other members of your household) <u>considering</u> beginning attendance at a college, university, or technical school sometime in the next three years?

Yes .... [GO TO ED46A] ☐ 1

No .... [SKIP TO ED47, PAGE 12] ☐ 2

Don't Know [SKIP TO ED47, PAGE 12] ☐ 7

Missing [SKIP TO ED47, PAGE 12] ☐ 8

Refused [SKIP TO ED47, PAGE 12] ☐ 9

[IF RESPONDENT LIVES ALONE, GO TO ED46B]

ED46A.   Would that be you or someone else in the household?

Self .... ☐ 1

Other .... ☐ 2

Both respondent and another .... ☐ 3

Don't Know ☐ 7

Missing ☐ 8

Refused ☐ 9

[IWER: IF BOTH RESPONDENT AND ANOTHER ARE CONSIDERING, ASK FOR RESPONDENT]

ED46B.   What type of school are **(you /they)** considering?

4 year college or university .... ☐ 1

2 year community college .... ☐ 2

Technical or vocational school .... ☐ 3

Don't Know ☐ 7

Missing ☐ 8

Refused ☐ 9

ED46C.   When do **(you / they)** plan to begin or enroll in school?

In the next six months .... ☐ 1

Between 6 months and 1 year .... ☐ 2

Between 1 year and 2 years .... ☐ 3

'n more than 2 years .... ☐ 4

Don't Know ☐ 7

Missing ☐ 8

Refused ☐ 9

ED47.   Now I'm going to read you some items having to do with what higher education should be able to do. Again, this could include a college, university, or technical school.

For each item, please tell me whether you think it is Extremely Important, Very Important, Somewhat Important, Not Very Important, or Not at all Important to get from higher education.

Let's start with _____ [READ FIRST ITEM] Do you think this is Extremely Important, Very Important, Somewhat Important, Not Very Important, or Not at all Important for higher education to be able to do for students.

What about _____ [READ NEXT ITEM]?

	EI	VI	SI	NVI	NAI		DK	MIS	REF
Providing degrees that get students good jobs	☐ 1	☐ 2	☐ 3	☐ 4	☐ 5		☐ 7	☐ 8	☐ 9
Providing education that teaches critical thinking and life-long learning	☐ 1	☐ 2	☐ 3	☐ 4	☐ 5		☐ 7	☐ 8	☐ 9
Equipping students with better job skills in their careers	☐ 1	☐ 2	☐ 3	☐ 4	☐ 5		☐ 7	☐ 8	☐ 9
Students gaining an appreciation of the diversity of people and cultures	☐ 1	☐ 2	☐ 3	☐ 4	☐ 5		☐ 7	☐ 8	☐ 9
Students gaining an appreciation of ideas and concepts	☐ 1	☐ 2	☐ 3	☐ 4	☐ 5		☐ 7	☐ 8	☐ 9

Now we have some questions on a different topic.

EN48. I am going to read you a list of items. Please tell me whether or not you have recycled each item at home in the <u>past two weeks</u>. In the past 2 weeks, have you recycled:

		Yes	No		DK	MIS	REF
a.	paper?	☐1	☐2		☐7	☐8	☐9
b.	newspaper?	☐1	☐2		☐7	☐8	☐9
c.	cardboard?	☐1	☐2		☐7	☐8	☐9
d.	aluminum, including cans?	☐1	☐2		☐7	☐8	☐9
e.	glass?	☐1	☐2		☐7	☐8	☐9
f.	plastic?	☐1	☐2		☐7	☐8	☐9
e.	Have you composted yard waste or household organics?	☐1	☐2		☐7	☐8	☐9

EN49. In your area, are recyclable goods picked up at curbside?

Yes .... ☐1
No .... ☐2
Don't Know ☐7
Missing ☐8
Refused ☐9

EN50. Overall, how satisfied are you with the level of convenience for recycling in your area? Are you Very Satisfied, Mostly Satisfied, Somewhat Satisfied, Not Very Satisfied, or Not At All Satisfied?

Very Satisfied .... ☐1
Mostly Satisfied .... ☐2
Somewhat Satisfied .... ☐3
Not Very Satisfied .... ☐4
Not At All Satisfied .... ☐5
Don't Know ☐7
Missing ☐8
Refused ☐9

EN51. Do you consider yourself an Active Environmentalist?

Yes .... ☐1
No .... ☐2
Don't Know ☐7
Missing ☐8
Refused ☐9

EN52.   How serious are each of the following issues having to do with environmental conservation?

Let's start with _____ [READ FIRST ITEM], is this issue Extremely Serious, Very Serious, Somewhat Serious, Not Very Serious, or Not At All Serious?

What about _____ [READ NEXT ITEM] is this issue Extremely Serious, Very Serious, Somewhat Serious, Not Very Serious, or Not At All Serious?

	ES	VS	SS	NVS	NAS	DK	MIS	REF
a. pollution from toxic waste sites	1	2	3	4	5	7	8	9
b. global warming or the 'greenhouse effect'	1	2	3	4	5	7	8	9
c. coal mine subsidence	1	2	3	4	5	7	8	9
d. not enough landfill space for garbage and trash	1	2	3	4	5	7	8	9
e. loss of wetland areas	1	2	3	4	5	7	8	9
f. acid mine drainage from coal mines	1	2	3	4	5	7	8	9
g. extinction of endangered species	1	2	3	4	5	7	8	9
h. shortage of good drinking water	1	2	3	4	5	7	8	9
i. loss of open space or natural areas to development	1	2	3	4	5	7	8	9
j. pollution of lakes, rivers, streams, and coastal waters	1	2	3	4	5	7	8	9
k. improper logging	1	2	3	4	5	7	8	9
l. air pollution	1	2	3	4	5	7	8	9
m. damage to the ozone layer of the atmosphere	1	2	3	4	5	7	8	9
n. illegal dumping	1	2	3	4	5	7	8	9

EN53.   To what degree do you think environmental protection and economic development can go hand in hand: Always, Most of the Time, Sometimes, Almost Never, or Never?

Always 1

Most of the Time 2

Sometimes 3

Almost Never 4

Never 5

Don't Know 7

Missing 8

Refused 9

EN54.   Which do you believe is generally more important: Economic Development or Environmental Protection?

Economic Development .... ☐1
Environmental Protection .... ☐2
Depends on the circumstances [DO NOT READ] .... ☐3

Don't Know ☐7
Missing ☐8
Refused ☐9

EN55.   Now I am going to read you a list of some state-wide issues, starting with _____ [READ FIRST ITEM] -- is that issue one in which you are Very Concerned, Somewhat Concerned, Neutral, Not Very Concerned, or Not At All Concerned?
How about _____ [READ NEXT ITEM] are you Very Concerned, Somewhat Concerned, Neutral, Not Very Concerned, or Not at all Concerned?

	VC	SC	N	NVC	NAC	DK	MIS	REF
a. Crime	☐1	☐2	☐3	☐4	☐5	☐7	☐8	☐9
b. Education	☐1	☐2	☐3	☐4	☐5	☐7	☐8	☐9
c. Drugs	☐1	☐2	☐3	☐4	☐5	☐7	☐8	☐9
d. Inflation	☐1	☐2	☐3	☐4	☐5	☐7	☐8	☐9
↑ e. Jobs	☐1	☐2	☐3	☐4	☐5	☐7	☐8	☐9
f. Roads	☐1	☐2	☐3	☐4	☐5	☐7	☐8	☐9
g. the Environment	☐1	☐2	☐3	☐4	☐5	☐7	☐8	☐9
h. Health Care	☐1	☐2	☐3	☐4	☐5	☐7	☐8	☐9
i. Taxes	☐1	☐2	☐3	☐4	☐5	☐7	☐8	☐9
j. the Economy	☐1	☐2	☐3	☐4	☐5	☐7	☐8	☐9

EN56.   Thinking about some specific areas, how do you feel about the current environmental protection laws and regulations in West Virginia?
For _____ [READ FIRST ITEM], are the present laws Too Restrictive, Not Restrictive Enough, or Fine As They Are?
What about _____ [READ NEXT ITEM]?

	Too R	Fine	NotRE	DK	MIS	REF
a. air pollution	☐1	☐2	☐3	☐7	☐8	☐9
b. river protection	☐1	☐2	☐3	☐7	☐8	☐9
c. wild or natural areas	☐1	☐2	☐3	☐7	☐8	☐9
↑ d. coal mining	☐1	☐2	☐3	☐7	☐8	☐9
e. endangered species	☐1	☐2	☐3	☐7	☐8	☐9
f. timber harvesting	☐1	☐2	☐3	☐7	☐8	☐9
g. wetlands areas	☐1	☐2	☐3	☐7	☐8	☐9
h. water pollution	☐1	☐2	☐3	☐7	☐8	☐9

EN57.   If environmental laws and regulations restrict how <u>private individuals</u> can use their land, do you think the government should be required to compensate those people for the lost value of the land? [IWER: DO NOT READ CATEGORIES]

Yes ☐1
No ☐2
Doesn't matter ☐3
It depends on the circumstances ☐4
Don't Know ☐7
Missing ☐8
Refused ☐9

EN58.   If environmental laws and regulations restrict how <u>small businesses</u> can use their land, do you think the government should be required to compensate those small businesses for the lost value of the land? [IWER: DO NOT READ CATEGORIES]

Yes ☐1
No ☐2
Doesn't matter ☐3
It depends on the circumstances ☐4
Don't Know ☐7
Missing ☐8
Refused ☐9

EN59.   If environmental laws and regulations restrict how <u>large businesses or corporations</u> can use their land, do you think the government should be required to compensate those businesses and corporations for the lost value of the land? [IWER: DO NOT READ CATEGORIES]

Yes ☐1
No ☐2
Doesn't matter ☐3
It depends on the circumstances ☐4
Don't Know ☐7
Missing ☐8
Refused ☐9

Before we close, I have just a few remaining questions:

We are interested in the political participation of West Virginians.

C60.　　First of all, do you consider yourself a Democrat, a Republican, an Independent, or something else?

Democrat .... ☐1
Republican .... ☐2
Independent .... ☐3
Something else (Specify)_______________________________________

Don't Know ☐77
Missing ☐88
Refused ☐99

In the last four years, have you ...		Yes	No	DK	Mis	Ref
C61.	Voted?	☐1	☐2	☐7	☐8	☐9
C62.	Given money to help someone try to win an election?	☐1	☐2	☐7	☐8	☐9
C63.	Worked in a political campaign?	☐1	☐2	☐7	☐8	☐9
C64.	Written letters to elected officials, Senators or Members of Congress, Mayors, etc.?	☐1	☐2	☐7	☐8	☐9
C65.	Signed a petition?	☐1	☐2	☐7	☐8	☐9
C66.	Participated in a strike?	☐1	☐2	☐7	☐8	☐9
C67.	Worked with others in your community to solve some local problem?	☐1	☐2	☐7	☐8	☐9

CRACE.　　Of what race do you consider yourself? [DO NOT READ CATEGORIES]

White/Caucasian .... ☐1
Chicano/Mexican/Hispanic/Latino (of any race) .... ☐2
Black/African American (non-Hispanic) .... ☐3
American Indian/Native American .... ☐4
Asian .... ☐5
Other race (Specify) _______________________________________

Don't Know ☐77
Missing ☐88
Refused ☐99

CINC1.　　Is your total household income more than $30,000 or less than $30,000 a year?

$30,000 or more .... [SKIP TO CINC2, PAGE 18] ☐1
Less than $30,000 .... [SKIP TO CINC3, PAGE 18] ☐2
Don't Know [SKIP TO C68] ☐7
Missing [SKIP TO C68] ☐8
Refused [SKIP TO C68] ☐9

CINC2. I am going to mention a number of income categories. When I mention the category which describes your total household income in the last 12 months, please stop me.

$30,000 to less than $40,000 .... ☐ 1
$40,000 to less than $50,000 .... ☐ 2
$50,000 to less than $60,000 .... ☐ 3
$60,000 to less than $70,000 .... ☐ 4
$70,000 to less than $80,000 .... ☐ 5
$80,000 or more .... ☐ 6
Don't Know ☐ 7
Missing ☐ 8
Refused ☐ 9

[SKIP TO C68]

CINC3. I am going to mention a number of income categories. When I mention the category which describes your total household income in the last 12 months, please stop me.

Less than $5,000 .... ☐ 1
$5,000 to less than $10,000 .... ☐ 2
$10,000 to less than $15,000 .... ☐ 3
$15,000 to less than $20,000 .... ☐ 4
$20,000 to less than $25,000 .... ☐ 5
$25,000 to less than $30,000 .... ☐ 6
Don't Know ☐ 7
Missing ☐ 8
Refused ☐ 9

C68. Is any of your total household income supported by public assistance?
Yes .... ☐ 1
No .... [SKIP TO CLOSING STATEMENT] ☐ 2
Don't Know ☐ 7
Missing ☐ 8
Refused ☐ 9

C69. Approximately what proportion or percentage of your household income would you say comes from public assistance?

☐ %

Don't Know ☐ 777
Missing ☐ 888
Refused ☐ 999

Those are all the questions I have for you. Thank you very much for your time and cooperation.
Have a good __________.

Appendix D

West Virginia Social Indicator Survey
1995 Questionnaire

A.   First, I would like to know how many people live in your household, including yourself, and excluding temporary visitors? Now I would like to know a little about each of these (repeat number) people.

Let's start with you.

B.   [IWER: RECORD RELATIONSHIP AS "RESPONDENT"]

C.   [IWER: RECORD RESPONDENT'S SEX -- ASK IF UNSURE]

D.   What was your age on your last birthday?

E.   Are you married, widowed, divorced, separated, married, but apart, or never married?

F.   How many years of schooling have you completed?

G.   Do you have a high school diploma or GED Certificate?

[IWER: REPEAT A1 THROUGH G1 FOR EACH ADDITIONAL PERSON IN THE HOUSEHOLD, AND RECORD THE INFORMATION IN THE APPROPRIATE SPACE]

[IF NO MORE IN THE HOUSEHOLD SKIP TO PAGE 1 C11]

A1. Now, how about the next person in your household?

B1. How is this person related you?

C1. [IWER: RECORD SEX OF HOUSEHOLD MEMBER. IF NOT CLEAR, ASK WHETHER PERSON IS A MALE OR FEMALE]

D1. What was (his/her) age on (his/her) last birthday?

E1. Is (he/she) married, widowed, divorced, separated, married, but apart, or never married?

F1. How many years of schooling has (he/she) completed?

G1. Does (he/she) have a high school diploma or GED Certificate?

SUMMARY TABLE FOR PERSONS IN HOUSEHOLD

A	B	C	D	E	F	G
	Relation to Respondent			Marital Status		
Person	Respondent / Spouse / Child/Step / Parent / Sibling / Relative / Boarder / Other	Sex	Age	Married / Widowed / Divorced / Separated / Married, Apart / Never Married	Years of Schooling	High School Diploma
1	1 2 3 4 5 6 7 8	M F	____	1 2 3 4 5 6	________	Yes No
2	1 2 3 4 5 6 7 8	M F	____	1 2 3 4 5 6	________	Yes No
3	1 2 3 4 5 6 7 8	M F	____	1 2 3 4 5 6	________	Yes No
4	1 2 3 4 5 6 7 8	M F	____	1 2 3 4 5 6	________	Yes No
5	1 2 3 4 5 6 7 8	M F	____	1 2 3 4 5 6	________	Yes No
6	1 2 3 4 5 6 7 8	M F	____	1 2 3 4 5 6	________	Yes No
7	1 2 3 4 5 6 7 8	M F	____	1 2 3 4 5 6	________	Yes No
8	1 2 3 4 5 6 7 8	M F	____	1 2 3 4 5 6	________	Yes No
9	1 2 3 4 5 6 7 8	M F	____	1 2 3 4 5 6	________	Yes No
10	1 2 3 4 5 6 7 8	M F	____	1 2 3 4 5 6	________	Yes No

We are interested in talking to people about a variety of things. First, I want to ask a few questions about your community.

C11.   In what county do you live?____ ☐☐

REGION ☐☐

C12.   Were you born in ____________ county? [IWER: INSERT COUNTY NAME]

Yes .... [SKIP TO C13] ☐ 1

No .... ☐ 2

Don't Know ☐ 7

Missing ☐ 8

Refused ☐ 9

C12A.   Were you born in West Virginia, another state, or a foreign country?

West Virginia .... ☐ 1

Another state .... ☐ 2

Foreign country .... ☐ 3

Don't Know ☐ 7

Missing ☐ 8

Refused ☐ 9

C13.   Do you live in open country or in a town or city?

Open country .... ☐ 1

Town/City .... ☐ 2

Don't Know ☐ 7

Missing ☐ 8

Refused ☐ 9

C14.   What is your Zip Code? .... ZIP CODE ☐☐☐☐☐

Don't Know ☐ 77777

Missing ☐ 88888

Refused ☐ 99999

Next, we are interested in knowing how you feel about your financial situation.

C15.   Has the income your household has earned during the past year allowed you to meet your basic needs?

        Yes .... [SKIP TO C16] ☐ 1

        No .... ☐ 2

        Don't Know [SKIP TO C16] ☐ 7

        Missing [SKIP TO C16] ☐ 8

        Refused [SKIP TO C16] ☐ 9

C15A.   Which basic needs <u>have not</u> been met? [IWER: PROBE FOR 2, ACCEPT ONLY 2]

____

____

        Don't Know ☐ 777

        Missing ☐ 888

        Refused ☐ 999

We are also interested in the type of work you normally do.

C16.   How would you classify your work situation last week? Were you ... [IWER: READ ALL RESPONSES BELOW AND IF R SAYS MORE THAN 1 CATEGORY, ASK, "WHICH OF THESE IS YOUR PRIMARY WORK SITUATION"]

        Working .... ☐ 1

        With a job, but not currently at work .... ☐ 2

        With a job, but temporarily laid off .... ☐ 3

        Looking for work .... [SKIP TO C24] ☐ 4

        Keeping house .... [SKIP TO C24] ☐ 5

        Going to school .... [SKIP TO C24] ☐ 6

        Unable to work due to disability .... [SKIP TO C24] ☐ 7

        Unable to work for other reasons or .... [SKIP TO C24] ☐ 8

        Retired .... ☐ 9

        Don't Know [SKIP TO C24] ☐ 77

        Missing [SKIP TO C24] ☐ 88

        Refused [SKIP TO C24] ☐ 99

C17.   What <u>(is/was)</u> your job title or what type of work <u>(do/did)</u> you do on your job? [IWER: ACCEPT ONLY 1 JOB TITLE]____

____

C18. What **(are/were)** the most important activities or duties at this job?
[PROBE FOR 2]

C19. What type of business or industry **(is/was)** that? **[IWER: ACCEPT ONLY 1]**

OCCUPATION ⬚⬚⬚ INDUSTRY ⬚⬚⬚

Don't Know ☐ 7777
Missing ☐ 8888
Refused ☐ 9999

C20. Are you currently a member of a labor union?

Yes .... ☐ 1
No .... **[SKIP TO C21]** ☐ 2
Don't Know **[SKIP TO C21]** ☐ 7
Missing **[SKIP TO C21]** ☐ 8
Refused **[SKIP TO C21]** ☐ 9

C20A. What kind of work is represented by that union?

⬚⬚

Don't Know ☐ 777
Missing ☐ 888
Refused ☐ 999

[IF NOT CURRENTLY EMPLOYED SKIP TO C24]

C21. How many hours do you normally work at your current job during an average week?

HOURS ⬚⬚ MINUTES ⬚⬚

TOTAL HOURS ⬚⬚⬚

Don't Know ☐ 777
Missing ☐ 888
Refused ☐ 999

C22.　　How long have you worked at your current job? .... YEARS ☐☐ MONTHS ☐☐

TOTAL MONTHS ☐☐☐

Don't Know ☐ 7777
Missing ☐ 8888
Refused ☐ 9999

C23.　　Do you think the income you currently earn matches the skills and training you have?

Yes .... [SKIP TO C24] ☐ 1
No .... ☐ 2
Don't Know [SKIP TO C24] ☐ 7
Missing [SKIP TO C24] ☐ 8
Refused [SKIP TO C24] ☐ 9

C23A.　　Why do you say so? [PROBE FOR 2]_______________________________________

____

____

Don't Know ☐ 77
Missing ☐ 88
Refused ☐ 99

Now we have some questions about the primary income earner in your household.

C24.　　In your household, who is the primary income earner? [IWER: DO NOT READ CATEGORIES]

Self .... [SKIP TO EC29 PAGE 6] ☐ 1
Spouse .... ☐ 2
Son/ Step .... ☐ 3
Daughter/ Step .... ☐ 4
Mother/ Step .... ☐ 5
Father / Step .... ☐ 6
Sister/ Step .... ☐ 7
Brother/ Step .... ☐ 8
Other (Specify)____

Don't Know [SKIP TO EC29 PAGE 6] ☐ 77
Missing [SKIP TO EC29 PAGE 6] ☐ 88
Refused [SKIP TO EC29 PAGE 6] ☐ 99

C25. Last week was your (_____) ....[IWER: READ ALL RESPONSES BELOW AND IF R SAYS MORE
THAN 1 CATEGORY, ASK "WHICH OF THESE IS (HIS/HER) PRIMARY WORK SITUATION?"]

Working	☐ 1
With a job, but not currently at work	☐ 2
With a job, but temporarily laid off	☐ 3
Looking for work	☐ 4
Keeping house	[SKIP TO EC29] ☐ 5
Going to school	[SKIP TO EC29] ☐ 6
Unable to work due to disability	[SKIP TO EC29] ☐ 7
Unable to work for other reasons or	[SKIP TO EC29] ☐ 8
Retired	☐ 9
Don't Know [SKIP TO EC29]	☐ 77
Missing [SKIP TO EC29]	☐ 88
Refused [SKIP TO EC29]	☐ 99

C26. What (is/was) your _______ job title or what type of work (does/did) (he/she) do on (his/her) job?
[IWER: ACCEPT ONLY 1 JOB TITLE]____

____

C27. What (are/were) the most important activities or duties at this job?
[PROBE FOR 2]____

____

C28. What type of business or industry is that? [IWER: ACCEPT ONLY 1]_______________________

____

OCCUPATION ☐☐☐ INDUSTRY ☐☐☐

Don't Know ☐ 7777

Missing ☐ 8888

Refused ☐ 9999

The next questions concern <u>other</u> work you or someone in your household may do.

I'm going to read a list of <u>extra</u> work some people do to help them get by. You might be doing one or more of these things to save yourself some money, earn extra money, or in exchange or trade for something else.

In the past 12 months, have you or any member of your household done any of the following things to save money, earn extra money, or in exchange for something else? Please do not include doing something as part of your main occupation, purely for recreation, as a hobby, or as part of regular household chores. In the last 12 months.....

[IWER: CHECK THE SPECIFIC CATEGORY FOR EACH TYPE OF ACTIVITY RESPONDENT INDICATED THEY OR SOMEONE IN THE HOUSEHOLD PERFORMED. PROBE FOR MULTIPLE REASONS. IF NO ONE IN HOUSEHOLD PERFORMED ACTIVITY, MARK NO AND CONTINUE.]

		No	Save Money	Earn Extra Money	Exchange
EC29.	Did someone in your household do household repair or handiwork such as plumbing, roofing, painting, wall papering, car, truck, or appliance repair?				
EC30.	Did someone in your household cut wood, gather coal, do yard work, or landscaping?				
EC31.	Did someone in your household hunt, fish, or trap game or rattlesnakes?				
EC32.	In the last 12 months, did someone in your household raise farm animals (eggs, frying chickens, sheep) or grow fresh produce (berries, ginseng or other foods)?				
EC33.	Did someone in your household raise non- -farm animals (dogs, cats, gamecocks, rabbits)?				
EC34.	Did someone in your household make hand made crafts or do sewing or knitting?				
EC35.	Did someone in your household provide personal service such as child care, nursing, or housework?				
EC36.	In the last 12 months, did someone in your household do bookkeeping, financial work, typing, or word processing?				

EC37.   Considering all of the money that came into your household during the last 12 months, would you say that more than 50% or less than 50% came from the activities mentioned above?

More .... [SKIP TO EC39] ☐ 1

Less .... ☐ 2

Don't Know [SKIP TO CC40] ☐ 7

Missing [SKIP TO CC40] ☐ 8

Refused [SKIP TO CC40] ☐ 9

EC38.   We are interested in knowing more precisely <u>how much</u> of your household income during the past 12 months has come from these extra activities. Would you say that between 0 and 10% of your income has come from these activities, between 10 and 20%, between 20 and 30%, between 30 and 40%, or between 40 and 50%?

0%-10% .... ☐ 1

10%-20% .... ☐ 2

20%-30% .... ☐ 3

30%-40% .... ☐ 4

40%-50% .... ☐ 5

Don't Know ☐ 7

Missing ☐ 8

Refused ☐ 9

EC39.   We are interested in knowing more precisely <u>how much</u> of your household income during the past 12 months has come from these extra activities. Would you say that between 50 and 60% of your income has come from these activities, between 60 and 70%, between 70 and 80%, between 80 and 90%, or between 90 and 100%?

50%-60% .... ☐ 1

60%-70% .... ☐ 2

70%-80% .... ☐ 3

80%-90% .... ☐ 4

90%-100% .... ☐ 5

Don't Know ☐ 7

Missing ☐ 8

Refused ☐ 9

GO TO CC40 BELOW. OTHERWISE, SKIP TO HARV47 PAGE 10]

[IWER: IF THE RESPONDENT HAS INDICATED THAT HE/SHE HAS A CHILD UNDER THE AGE OF 13, GO TO CC40 BELOW. OTHERWISE, SKIP TO HARV47 PAGE 10]

CC40.　You mentioned that the youngest child in your household is (_____) years of age. The next few questions concern child care arrangements for this child. Excluding time at school, but including time at pre-school programs, does someone other than a household member take care of this child for five or more hours per week?

　　　Yes .... ☐ 1
　　　No .... [SKIP TO HARV47 PAGE 10] ☐ 2
　　　　　　　　　　　　　　　　　　　　　　　　　　　Don't Know ☐ 7
　　　　　　　　　　　　　　　　　　　　　　　　　　　　　Missing ☐ 8
　　　　　　　　　　　　　　　　　　　　　　　　　　　　　Refused ☐ 9

CC41.　Is this child cared for in the home, at someone else's home, at a child care center, at a nursery school or preschool, or does (he/she) participate in an after school program? [IWER: IF CHILD IS CARED FOR IN MULTIPLE PLACES, ASK WHERE CHILD SPENDS THE MOST TIME]

　　　At home .... ☐ 1
　　　Someone else's home .... ☐ 2
　　　Child Care center .... [SKIP TO CC43] ☐ 3
　　　Nursery school or preschool .... [SKIP TO CC43] ☐ 4
　　　After school program .... [SKIP TO CC43] ☐ 5
　　　　　　　　　　　　　　　　　　　　　　　　　　　Don't Know ☐ 7
　　　　　　　　　　　　　　　　　　　　　　　　　　　　　Missing ☐ 8
　　　　　　　　　　　　　　　　　　　　　　　　　　　　　Refused ☐ 9

CC42.　In this child care setting, is this child cared for by a relative, a non-relative, or does (he/she) care for (him/her)self?

　　　Relative .... ☐ 1
　　　Non-relative .... ☐ 2
　　　Self .... ☐ 3
　　　　　　　　　　　　　　　　　　　　　　　　　　　Don't Know ☐ 7
　　　　　　　　　　　　　　　　　　　　　　　　　　　　　Missing ☐ 8
　　　　　　　　　　　　　　　　　　　　　　　　　　　　　Refused ☐ 9

CC43.　How many hours per week does this child usually spend in this main child care arrangement? [IWER: IF RESPONDENT ANSWERS IN TERMS OF HOURS PER DAY OR HOURS PER MONTH, RECORD FULL RESPONSE AND CONTINUE]

　　　　　　　　　　　　　　　　HOURS ☐☐ MINUTES ☐☐

　　　　　　　　　　　　　　　　TOTAL HOURS ☐☐☐

　　　　　　　　　　　　　　　　　Don't Know ☐ 777

Missing ☐ 888
Refused ☐ 999

CC44.   How much does your household pay per week for this child care arrangement? [IWER: IF RESPONDENT ANSWERS IN TERMS OF PAY PER HOUR, PAY PER DAY, OR PAY PER MONTH, RECORD FULL RESPONSE AND CONTINUE]

$ ☐

Don't Know ☐ 777
Missing ☐ 888
Refused ☐ 999

[IWER: IF THE RESPONDENT HAS INDICATED THAT HE/SHE HAS MORE THAN ONE CHILD UNDER THE AGE OF 13, GO TO CC45 BELOW. OTHERWISE, SKIP TO HARV47]

CC45.   Including the youngest child, how many children in your household receive some type of care from someone other than a household member for 5 or more hours per week? (THIS INCLUDES TIME SPENT IN PRE-SCHOOL PROGRAMS OR AFTER-SCHOOL PROGRAMS, BUT NOT REGULAR SCHOOL TIME.)

☐

Don't Know ☐ 777
Missing ☐ 888
Refused ☐ 999

[IWER: IF MORE THAN 1, GO TO CC46 BELOW. OTHERWISE, SKIP TO HARV47]

CC46.   How much does your household pay <u>per week</u> for <u>all</u> types of care used by <u>all</u> of these children? [IWER: IF RESPONDENT ANSWERS IN TERMS OF PAY PER DAY OR PAY PER MONTH, RECORD FULL RESPONSE AND CONTINUE]

$ ☐

Don't Know ☐ 777
Missing ☐ 888
Refused ☐ 999

Now I have some questions on another topic.

West Virginia is known for its forests, and many people in the state spend time outdoors hunting, cutting firewood, gathering edible plants such as ramps and mushrooms, and collecting plants to sell such as ginseng, yellowroot, grape vines, and mosses. We are interested in learning whether you or members of your household have participated in some of these activities in the past year.

HARV47.   In the past year, have you or any members of your household hunted?

Yes . . . . □ 1

No . . . . [SKIP TO HARV49] □ 2

Don't Know [SKIP TO HARV49] □ 7

Missing [SKIP TO HARV49] □ 8

Refused [SKIP TO HARV49] □ 9

HARV48.   What kinds of animals were hunted? How many were killed? Who in your household participated in this activity? [IWER: CIRCLE ANIMAL AND ASK SERIES OF QUESTIONS FOR EACH. PROBE ONCE FOR A/O]

	Number Killed	Participants
Deer		
Turkey		
Squirrel		
Rabbit		
Grouse		
Bear		
Pheasant		
Raccoon		
Other (________)		

HARV49.   In the past year, have you or any members of your household gathered wild foods such as mushrooms, ramps, nuts, berries, or others?

Yes . . . . □ 1

No . . . . [SKIP TO HARV51] □ 2

Don't Know [SKIP TO HARV51] □ 7

Missing [SKIP TO HARV51] □ 8

Refused [SKIP TO HARV51] □ 9

HARV50.   What kinds of foods were harvested? Approximately how much was harvested? Who in your
            household participated in this activity? [IWER: CIRCLE FOOD AND ASK SERIES OF
            QUESTIONS FOR EACH. PROBE ONCE FOR A/O]

	Amount Harvested	Participants
Ramps		
Mushrooms		
Blackberries		
Blueberries		
Walnuts		
Other (________)		
Other (________)		

HARV51.   In the past year, have you or any members of your household gathered plants or plant materials to
            sell for the floral trade, such as mosses, grapevines, pine boughs, orchids, or others?

Yes . . . . □ 1

No . . . . [SKIP TO HARV53] □ 2

Don't Know [SKIP TO HARV53] □ 7

Missing [SKIP TO HARV53] □ 8

Refused [SKIP TO HARV53] □ 9

HARV52.   What kind of plants were harvested? About how much was harvested? Who in your household
               participated in this activity? [IWER: CIRCLE PLANT AND ASK SERIES OF QUESTIONS FOR
               EACH. PROBE ONCE FOR A/O]

	Amount Harvested	Participants
Grape Vines		
Camphor Vine		
Mosses		
Ladyslipper Orchids		
Other (______)		
Other (______)		

HARV53.   In the past year, have you or any members of your household dug wild roots or herbs to sell?
               Yes . . . . ☐ 1
               No . . . . [SKIP TO EX55] ☐ 2
                                                           Don't Know [SKIP TO EX55] ☐ 7
                                                              Missing [SKIP TO EX55] ☐ 8
                                                              Refused [SKIP TO EX55] ☐ 9

HARV54.   What kind of roots or herbs were gathered? Approximately how much was harvested? Who in your
           household participated in this activity? [IWER: CIRCLE HERB AND ASK SERIES OF
           QUESTIONS FOR EACH. PROBE ONCE FOR A/O]

	Amount Harvested	Participants
Ginseng		
Yellowroot or Goldenseal		
Black Cohosh		
Blue Cohosh		
Mayapple		
Slippery Elm Bark		
Wild Ginger		
Bloodroot		
Hydrangea		
Wild Yam		
Virginia Snake Root		
Ninebark		
Other (_______)		
Other (_______)		

Next, I'd like to ask you some questions about exercise and physical activity.

EX55.   Do you participate in any physical activities or exercises such as walking, dancing, gardening, or stair
         climbing?

Yes	☐ 1
No .... [SKIP TO EX57]	☐ 2
Don't Know [SKIP TO EX57]	☐ 7
Missing [SKIP TO EX57]	☐ 8
Refused [SKIP TO EX57]	☐ 9

EX56. Do you <u>REGULARLY</u> participate in physical activities, that is, for at least 20 minutes at a time, 3 or more times per week?

Yes . . . . [SKIP TO EX68 PAGE 18] ☐ 1

No . . . . ☐ 2

Don't Know ☐ 7

Missing ☐ 8

Refused ☐ 9

EX57. Was there ever a time in your <u>adult</u> life when you considered yourself a regular exerciser?

Yes . . . . ☐ 1

No . . . . [SKIP TO EX60] ☐ 2

Don't Know [SKIP TO EX60] ☐ 7

Missing [SKIP TO EX60] ☐ 8

Refused [SKIP TO EX60] ☐ 9

EX58. What was your approximate age at the time you were <u>most recently</u> a regular exerciser? [IWER: IF THE RESPONDENT GIVES A RANGE ENTER EACH AGE IN A BOX BELOW. IF THE RESPONDENT GIVES ONE AGE, ENTER THE ONE RESPONSE IN BOTH BOXES AND CONTINUE]

Don't Know ☐ 777

Missing ☐ 888

Refused ☐ 999

EX59. What caused you to <u>stop</u> exercising or being active on a regular basis? [IWER: PROBE FOR TWO <u>MAIN</u> RESPONSES. ACCEPT <u>ONLY</u> TWO RESPONSES]

____

____

Don't Know ☐ 777

Missing ☐ 888

Refused ☐ 999

EX60. Many things can interfere with regular participation in physical activity or exercise. What are the <u>MAIN</u> reasons that you do not <u>currently</u> exercise regularly? [IWER: PROBE FOR TWO <u>MAIN</u> RESPONSES. ACCEPT <u>ONLY</u> TWO RESPONSES]

____

____

Don't Know ☐ 777
Missing ☐ 888
Refused ☐ 999

EX61. People have different motivations for exercising. What would personally motivate you to exercise or to be physically active on a regular basis? [IWER: PROBE FOR TWO <u>MAIN</u> RESPONSES. ACCEPT <u>ONLY</u> TWO RESPONSES]

____

____

Don't Know ☐ 777
Missing ☐ 888
Refused ☐ 999

EX62. If you made the decision to begin exercising regularly, do you feel the people who are most important to you would support your effort?

Yes . . . . ☐ 1
No . . . . ☐ 2
Don't Know ☐ 7
Missing ☐ 8
Refused ☐ 9

EX63. Next, I will be reading some statements concerning physical activity. Please tell me whether you strongly agree, agree, disagree, or strongly disagree with each statement.

a. Regular physical activity helps control weight.

Strongly agree . . . . ☐ 1
Agree . . . . ☐ 2
Disagree . . . . ☐ 3
Strongly disagree . . . . ☐ 4
Don't Know ☐ 7
Missing ☐ 8
Refused ☐ 9

b.   Regular physical activity helps reduce stress.

        Strongly agree ☐ 1

        Agree ☐ 2

        Disagree ☐ 3

        Strongly disagree ☐ 4

        Don't Know ☐ 7

        Missing ☐ 8

        Refused ☐ 9

c.   Regular physical activity helps prevent heart disease.

        Strongly agree ☐ 1

        Agree ☐ 2

        Disagree ☐ 3

        Strongly disagree ☐ 4

        Don't Know ☐ 7

        Missing ☐ 8

        Refused ☐ 9

d.   Regular physical activity makes you feel more energetic.

        Strongly agree ☐ 1

        Agree ☐ 2

        Disagree ☐ 3

        Strongly disagree ☐ 4

        Don't Know ☐ 7

        Missing ☐ 8

        Refused ☐ 9

e.   Regular physical activity helps strengthen bones.

        Strongly agree ☐ 1

        Agree ☐ 2

        Disagree ☐ 3

        Strongly disagree ☐ 4

        Don't Know ☐ 7

        Missing ☐ 8

        Refused ☐ 9

f.   I am more productive when I exercise.

          Strongly agree .... □ 1

          Agree .... □ 2

          Disagree .... □ 3

          Strongly disagree .... □ 4

                                                                                    Don't Know □ 7

                                                                                       Missing □ 8

                                                                                      Refused □ 9

g.   I feel better about myself when I exercise.

          Strongly agree .... □ 1

          Agree .... □ 2

          Disagree .... □ 3

          Strongly disagree .... □ 4

                                                                                    Don't Know □ 7

                                                                                       Missing □ 8

                                                                                      Refused □ 9

h.   I am confident that if I decided to exercise regularly, I would.

          Strongly agree .... □ 1

          Agree .... □ 2

          Disagree .... □ 3

          Strongly disagree .... □ 4

                                                                                    Don't Know □ 7

                                                                                       Missing □ 8

                                                                                      Refused □ 9

EX64.   Different people enjoy different kinds of physical activities. What are some particular physical activities
         that you are not currently involved with that you would like to <u>become</u> involved with?
         [IWER: PROBE FOR TWO <u>MAIN</u> RESPONSES. ACCEPT <u>ONLY</u> TWO RESPONSES]

         ____

         ____

                                                                                    Don't Know □ 77

                                                                                       Missing □ 88

                                                                                      Refused □ 99

EX65.   Would you prefer to participate in group physical activities or those physical activities that you can do alone?

    Group .... □ 1
    Alone .... □ 2
                                                                      Don't Know □ 7
                                                                        Missing □ 8
                                                                        Refused □ 9

[IWER: IF ONE PERSON IN HOUSEHOLD, SKIP TO EX67]

EX66.   Would you prefer to engage in physical activities that your family can do together?

    Yes .... □ 1
    No .... □ 2
                                                                      Don't Know □ 7
                                                                        Missing □ 8
                                                                        Refused □ 9

EX67.   If exercise facilities or classes were available near where you live or work, would you use them?

    Yes .... □ 1
    No .... □ 2
    Already do .... □ 3
                                                                      Don't Know □ 7
                                                                        Missing □ 8
                                                                        Refused □ 9

EX68.   Has your doctor, nurse, or other health care provider recommended that you participate regularly in physical activity?

    Yes .... □ 1
    No .... [SKIP TO EX70] □ 2
                                                                Don't Know [SKIP TO EX70] □ 7
                                                                  Missing [SKIP TO EX70] □ 8
                                                                  Refused [SKIP TO EX70] □ 9

EX69.   Have you participated in regular exercise <u>in response</u> to this recommendation from your doctor, nurse, or other health care provider?

    Yes .... □ 1
    No .... □ 2
                                                                      Don't Know □ 7
                                                                        Missing □ 8
                                                                        Refused □ 9

EX70.   What is your height without shoes?

FEET ☐☐ INCHES ☐☐

TOTAL INCHES ☐☐☐

Don't Know ☐ 777
Missing ☐ 888
Refused ☐ 999

EX71.   What is your weight without shoes?

POUNDS ☐☐☐

Don't Know ☐ 777
Missing ☐ 888
Refused ☐ 999

Before we close, I have just a few remaining questions:
We are interested in the political participation of West Virginians.

C72.   First of all, do you consider yourself a Democrat, a Republican, an Independent, or something else?

Democrat .... ☐ 1

Republican .... ☐ 2

Independent .... ☐ 3

Something else (Specify)____

Don't Know ☐ 77
Missing ☐ 88
Refused ☐ 99

In the last four years, have you ...	Yes	No	DK	Mis	Ref
C73. Voted?	☐ 1	☐ 2	☐ 7	☐ 8	☐ 9
C74. Given money to help someone try to win an election?	☐ 1	☐ 2	☐ 7	☐ 8	☐ 9
C75. Worked in a political campaign?	☐ 1	☐ 2	☐ 7	☐ 8	☐ 9
C76. Written letters to elected officials, Senators or Members of Congress, Mayors, etc.?	☐ 1	☐ 2	☐ 7	☐ 8	☐ 9
C77. Signed a petition?	☐ 1	☐ 2	☐ 7	☐ 8	☐ 9
C78. Participated in a strike?	☐ 1	☐ 2	☐ 7	☐ 8	☐ 9
C79. Worked with others in your community to solve some local problem?	☐ 1	☐ 2	☐ 7	☐ 8	☐ 9

CRACE. Of what race do you consider yourself? **[DO NOT READ CATEGORIES]**

    White/Caucasian .... ☐ 1

    Chicano/Mexican/Hispanic .... ☐ 2

    Black/African American .... ☐ 3

    American Indian/Native American .... ☐ 4

    Asian .... ☐ 5

    Other race (Specify) ____

Don't Know ☐ 77

Missing ☐ 88

Refused ☐ 99

CINC1. Is your total household income more than $30,000 or less than $30,000 a year?

    $30,000 or more .... **[GO TO CINC2]** ☐ 1

    Less than $30,000 .... **[GO TO CINC3]** ☐ 2

Don't Know **[SKIP TO C80]** ☐ 7

Missing **[SKIP TO C80]** ☐ 8

Refused **[SKIP TO C80]** ☐ 9

CINC2. I am going to mention a number of income categories. When I mention the category which describes your total household income in the last 12 months, please stop me.

    $30,000 to less than $40,000 .... ☐ 1

    $40,000 to less than $50,000 .... ☐ 2

    $50,000 to less than $60,000 .... ☐ 3

    $60,000 to less than $70,000 .... ☐ 4

    $70,000 to less than $80,000 .... ☐ 5

    $80,000 or more .... ☐ 6

Don't Know ☐ 7

Missing ☐ 8

Refused ☐ 9

[SKIP TO C80]

CINC3. I am going to mention a number of income categories. When I mention the category which describes your total household income in the last 12 months, please stop me.

    Less than $5,000 .... ☐ 1

    $5,000 to less than $10,000 .... ☐ 2

    $10,000 to less than $15,000 .... ☐ 3

    $15,000 to less than $20,000 .... ☐ 4

    $20,000 to less than $25,000 .... ☐ 5

    $25,000 to less than $30,000 .... ☐ 6

Don't Know ☐ 7

Missing ☐ 8

Refused ☐ 9

C80.   Is any of your total household income supported by public assistance?

       Yes .... ☐ 1

       No .... [SKIP TO CLOSING STATEMENT] ☐ 2

       Don't Know ☐ 7

       Missing ☐ 8

       Refused ☐ 9

C81.   Approximately what proportion or percentage of your household income would you say comes from public assistance?

       ☐ %

       Don't Know ☐ 777

       Missing ☐ 888

       Refused ☐ 999

Those are all the questions I have for you. Thank you very much for your time and cooperation.
Have a good ____________ .

| Appendix E |

West Virginia Social Indicator Survey
1994 Questionnaire

A.   First, I would like to know how many people live in your household, including yourself, and
     excluding temporary visitors? Now I would like to know a little about each of these (repeat
     number) people.
     Let's start with you. Could I have your first name?

B.   [IWER: RECORD RELATIONSHIP AS "RESPONDENT"]

C.   [IWER: RECORD RESPONDENTS SEX]

D.   What was your age on your last birthday?

E.   Are you married, widowed, divorced, separated, married, but apart, or never married?

F.   How many years of schooling have you completed?

G.   Do you have a high school diploma or GED Certificate?

[IWER: REPEAT A1 THROUGH G1 FOR EACH ADDITIONAL PERSON IN THE
HOUSEHOLD, AND RECORD THE INFORMATION IN THE
APPROPRIATE SPACE]

[IF NO MORE IN THE HOUSEHOLD SKIP TO PAGE 1 C1]

A1. What is the first name of the next person living in the household?

B1. How is this person related you?

C1. [IWER: RECORD SEX OF HOUSEHOLD MEMBER. IF NOT CLEAR, ASK
     WHETHER PERSON IS A MALE OR FEMALE]

D1. What was (his/her) age on (his/her) last birthday?

E1. Is (he/she) married, widowed, divorced, separated, married, but apart, or never married?

F1. How many years of schooling has (he/she) completed?

G1. Does (he/she) have a high school diploma or GED Certificate?

SUMMARY TABLE FOR PERSONS IN HOUSEHOLD

A	B	C	D	E	F	G
	Relation to Respondent			Marital Status		
Person	Respondent Spouse Child/Step Parent Sibling Relative Boarder Other	Sex	Age	Married Widowed Divorced Separated Married, Apart Never Married	Years of Schooling	High School Diploma
1	1 2 3 4 5 6 7 8	M F	_____	1 2 3 4 5 6	_______	Yes No
2	1 2 3 4 5 6 7 8	M F	_____	1 2 3 4 5 6	_______	Yes No
3	1 2 3 4 5 6 7 8	M F	_____	1 2 3 4 5 6	_______	Yes No
4	1 2 3 4 5 6 7 8	M F	_____	1 2 3 4 5 6	_______	Yes No
5	1 2 3 4 5 6 7 8	M F	_____	1 2 3 4 5 6	_______	Yes No
6	1 2 3 4 5 6 7 8	M F	_____	1 2 3 4 5 6	_______	Yes No
7	1 2 3 4 5 6 7 8	M F	_____	1 2 3 4 5 6	_______	Yes No
8	1 2 3 4 5 6 7 8	M F	_____	1 2 3 4 5 6	_______	Yes No
9	1 2 3 4 5 6 7 8	M F	_____	1 2 3 4 5 6	_______	Yes No
10	1 2 3 4 5 6 7 8	M F	_____	1 2 3 4 5 6	_______	Yes No

We are interested in talking to people about a variety of things. First, I want to ask a few questions about your community and what you think of it as a place to live.

C11.   In what county do you live?____

                                                            REGION

C12.   Were you born in ____________ county? [IWER: INSERT COUNTY NAME]

         Yes .... [SKIP TO C13] ☐ 1

         No .... ☐ 2

         Don't Know ☐ 7

         Missing ☐ 8

         Refused ☐ 9

C12A.   Were you born in West Virginia, another state, or a foreign country?

         West Virginia .... ☐ 1

         Another state .... ☐ 2

         Foreign country .... ☐ 3

         Don't Know ☐ 7

         Missing ☐ 8

         Refused ☐ 9

C13.   Do you live in open country or in a town?

         Open country .... [SKIP TO C14] ☐ 1

         Town .... ☐ 2

         Don't Know [SKIP TO C14] ☐ 7

         Missing [SKIP TO C14] ☐ 8

         Refused [SKIP TO C14] ☐ 9

C13A.   In what town or city do you live? _______________________ [SKIP TO C15]

         Don't Know ☐ 777

         Missing ☐ 888

         Refused ☐ 999

C14.   What town or city is closest to where you live?________________________

         Don't Know ☐ 777

         Missing ☐ 888

         Refused ☐ 999

C15. What is your Zip Code? .... ZIP CODE □□□□□

Don't Know □ 77777
Missing □ 88888
Refused □ 99999

We are interested in knowing how you feel about your financial situation.

C16. Has the income you have earned during the past year allowed you to meet your basic needs?

Yes .... [SKIP TO C17] □ 1
No .... □ 2
Don't Know [SKIP TO C17] □ 7
Missing [SKIP TO C17] □ 8
Refused [SKIP TO C17] □ 9

C16A. Which basic needs <u>have not</u> been met? [IWER: PROBE FOR 2]

____

____

Don't Know □ 777
Missing □ 888
Refused □ 999

We are also interested in the type of work you normally do.

C17. How would you classify your work situation last week? Were you ... [IWER: READ ALL RESPONSES BELOW AND IF R SAYS MORE THAN 1 CATEGORY, ASK, "WHICH OF THESE IS YOUR PRIMARY WORK SITUATION"]

Working .... □ 1
With a job, but not currently at work .... □ 2
With a job, but temporarily laid off .... □ 3
Looking for work .... [SKIP TO C23] □ 4
Keeping house .... [SKIP TO C23] □ 5
Going to school .... [SKIP TO C23] □ 6
Unable to work due to disability .... [SKIP TO C23] □ 7
Unable to work for other reasons or .... [SKIP TO C23] □ 8
Retired .... □ 9
Don't Know [SKIP TO C23] □ 77
Missing [SKIP TO C23] □ 88
Refused [SKIP TO C23] □ 99

C18. What (<u>is/was</u>) your job title or what type of work (<u>do/did</u>) you do on your job? [IWER: ACCEPT ONLY 1 JOB TITLE]

____

____

C19.   What **(are/were)** the most important activities or duties at this job?
            [PROBE FOR 2] ____

            ____

C20.   What type of business or industry **(is/was)** that? [IWER: ACCEPT ONLY 1] _______________

            ____

                                              OCCUPATION ☐☐☐ INDUSTRY ☐☐☐
                                                          Don't Know ☐ 7777
                                                             Missing ☐ 8888
                                                             Refused ☐ 9999

[IF NOT CURRENTLY EMPLOYED SKIP TO C23]

C21.   How many hours do you normally work at your current job during an average week?
                                                    HOURS ☐☐ MINUTES ☐☐
                                                    TOTAL HOURS ☐☐☐
                                                          Don't Know ☐ 777
                                                             Missing ☐ 888
                                                             Refused ☐ 999

C22.   How long have you worked at your current job? . . . . YEARS ☐☐ MONTHS ☐☐
                                                    TOTAL MONTHS ☐☐☐

                                                          Don't Know ☐ 7777
                                                             Missing ☐ 8888
                                                             Refused ☐ 9999

Now we have some questions about the primary income earner in your household.

C23.   In your household, who is the primary income earner? [IWER: DO NOT READ CATEGORIES]

    Self .... [SKIP TO C28] ☐ 1

    Spouse .... ☐ 2

    Son/ Step .... ☐ 3

    Daughter/ Step .... ☐ 4

    Mother/ Step .... ☐ 5

    Father / Step .... ☐ 6

    Sister/ Step .... ☐ 7

    Brother/ Step .... ☐ 8

    Other (Specify)____

                                              Don't Know [SKIP TO C28] ☐ 77

                                                Missing [SKIP TO C28] ☐ 88

                                                Refused [SKIP TO C28] ☐ 99

[IWER: IF THERE ARE 2 PRIMARY INCOME EARNERS AND ONE OF THEM IS RESPONDENT, GET
FOLLOWING INFORMATION ON THE OTHER. IF RESPONDENT IS NOT ONE OF THE PRIMARY INCOME
EARNERS, GET FOLLOWING INFORMATION ON THE PRIMARY INCOME EARNER THAT HAS HAD THE
MOST RECENT BIRTHDAY.

C24.   Last week was your (_____) ....[IWER: READ ALL RESPONSES BELOW AND IF R SAYS MORE
        THAN 1 CATEGORY, ASK "WHICH OF THESE IS YOUR PRIMARY WORK SITUATION?"]

    Working .... ☐ 1

    With a job, but not currently at work .... ☐ 2

    With a job, but temporarily laid off .... ☐ 3

    Looking for work .... [SKIP TO C28] ☐ 4

    Keeping house .... [SKIP TO C28] ☐ 5

    Going to school .... [SKIP TO C28] ☐ 6

    Unable to work due to disability .... [SKIP TO C28] ☐ 7

    Unable to work for other reasons or .... [SKIP TO C28] ☐ 8

    Retired .... ☐ 9

                                              Don't Know [SKIP TO C28] ☐ 77

                                                Missing [SKIP TO C28] ☐ 88

                                                Refused [SKIP TO C28] ☐ 99

C25.   What (is/was) your _______ job title or what type of work (does/did) (he/she) do on (his/her) job? [IWER:
        ACCEPT ONLY 1 JOB TITLE]____

C26.   What **(are/were)** the most important activities or duties at this job?
            [PROBE FOR 2]

____

C27.   What type of business or industry is that? [IWER: ACCEPT ONLY 1]_______________

____

                                        OCCUPATION ☐☐☐   INDUSTRY ☐☐☐
                                                             Don't Know ☐ 7777
                                                              Missing ☐ 8888
                                                              Refused ☐ 9999

C28.   How does your household pay for most of its medical expenses? [IWER: READ RESPONSE
            CATEGORIES and CHOOSE ONE ONLY]

            Medicaid . . . . ☐ 1
            Medicare . . . . ☐ 2
            Private Insurance . . . . ☐ 3
            Employer Insurance . . . . ☐ 4
            Worker's Compensation . . . . ☐ 5
            Out of Pocket . . . . ☐ 6
            Are You Unable to Pay, ... ☐ 7
            Or Is There Some Other Way . . . . ☐ 8
                                                              Don't Know ☐ 77
                                                               Missing ☐ 88
                                                               Refused ☐ 99

Each year, thousands of West Virginians are injured by falls, car crashes, fires, poisonings, drownings, assaults, and
other kinds of unexpected incidents. I would like to ask you about any injuries that you or other members of your
household may have experienced during the past year.

INJ29.   Has anyone who lives in your household experienced an accident or injury, and received medical
            attention for that injury during the past year?
            Yes . . . . ☐ 1
            No . . . . [SKIP TO INTRO TO MIN41, PAGE8] ☐ 2
                                                               Don't Know ☐ 7
                                                               Missing ☐ 8
                                                               Refused ☐ 9

INJ30.   How many times total did household members receive medical attention for different injuries last
            year?

                                                              Number ☐☐
                                                           Don't Know ☐ 77
                                                              Missing ☐ 88
                                                              Refused ☐ 99

[IF MORE THAN ONE INJURY ASK ABOUT THE MOST SERIOUS INJURY]. Now I would like to ask you some questions concerning **(this/the most serious)** injury.

[IF ONLY ONE PERSON IN THE HOUSEHOLD, SKIP TO INJ32]

INJ31.　How was **(the injured person/the most seriously injured person)** related to you?________________

Number Person is in Household Matrix (1-11) .... ☐☐

Don't Know ☐ 77

Missing ☐ 88

Refused ☐ 99

INJ32.　How did this injury happen? **[IWER: Get what caused the injury to happen, for example, fall, motor vehicle, PROBE FOR 2]**____

Injury Code ☐☐☐

Not an Injury **[SKIP TO INTRO TO MIN41]** ☐ 18

Don't Know ☐ 777

Missing ☐ 888

Refused ☐ 999

INJ33.　How did **(you/the injured person)** travel to receive medical care?

Ambulance (Ground or Helicopter) .... ☐ 1

Private Vehicle or Walked .... ☐ 2

Other .... ☐ 3

Don't Know ☐ 7

Missing ☐ 8

Refused ☐ 9

INJ34.　How many days, if any, did **(you/the person)** spend in the hospital as a result of this injury?

Number ☐☐☐

Don't Know ☐ 777

Missing ☐ 888

Refused ☐ 999

INJ35. What was the final outcome of the injury? Did **(you/the person)** recover completely, are **(you/they)** temporarily disabled, permanently disabled, or what?

Recover Completely .... □ 1
Temporarily Disabled .... □ 2
Permanently Disabled .... □ 3
Injured Person Died .... □ 4

Don't Know □ 7
Missing □ 8
Refused □ 9

INJ36. **(Were/Was) (you/the injured person)** treated at a doctor's office, a hospital emergency room, a primary care clinic, an urgent care center or some other place?

Doctor's Office .... □ 1
Emergency Room .... □ 2
Primary Care Clinic .... □ 3
Urgent Care Center .... □ 4
Other Place .... □ 5

Don't Know □ 7
Missing □ 8
Refused □ 9

INJ37. Did this injury occur during...

Working hours (getting paid/compensation) .... □ 1
Leisure time (recreation/fun/goofing off) .... [SKIP TO INTRO TO MIN41] □ 2
Travelling time/transport time .... [SKIP TO INTRO TO MIN41] □ 3
Private time (chores/activities) .... [SKIP TO INTRO TO MIN41] □ 4
School Hours/Training time .... [SKIP TO INTRO TO MIN41] □ 5
Other _______________________ .... [SKIP TO INTRO TO MIN41] □ 6

Don't Know □ 77
Missing □ 88
Refused □ 99

INJ38. How long had **(you/the person)** been working at the job where injured?___________________

Number of Months □□□
Don't Know □ 7777
Missing □ 8888
Refused □ 9999

INJ39.   Was a worker's compensation claim filed for this injury?

Yes . . . . ☐ 1

No . . . . ☐ 2

Don't Know ☐ 7

Missing ☐ 8

Refused ☐ 9

INJ40.   How many days of work did **(you/the person)** miss as a result of this injury?

0 days . . . . ☐ 1

1 day or less . . . . ☐ 2

2 - 6 days . . . . ☐ 3

7 - 13 days . . . . ☐ 4

2 - 4 weeks . . . . ☐ 5

Over a month . . . . ☐ 6

Never able to work again . . . . ☐ 7

Don't Know ☐ 77

Missing ☐ 88

Refused ☐ 99

We are also interested in talking with people about their experiences with and opinions about the mining industry in West Virginia.

MIN41.   In the last 10 years, have you ever worked in mining?

Yes . . . . [SKIP TO INTRO TO MIN43] ☐ 1

No . . . . ☐ 2

Don't Know ☐ 7

Missing ☐ 8

Refused ☐ 9

MIN42.   In the last 10 years, has anyone in your household ever worked in mining?

Yes . . . . ☐ 1

No . . . . [SKIP TO INTRO TO UNIV63, PAGE 13] ☐ 2

Don't Know ☐ 7

Missing ☐ 8

Refused ☐ 9

    Thinking about the person in your household with the most experience in mining, please
answer the following questions.

MIN43.   Was **(your/this person's)** work in the mines in West Virginia?

      Yes .... ☐ 1
      No .... [SKIP TO MIN45] ☐ 2
      Don't Know ☐ 7
      Missing ☐ 8
      Refused ☐ 9

MIN44.   In what county of West Virginia?_______________________________ ☐☐

      Don't Know ☐ 7
      Missing ☐ 8
      Refused ☐ 9

MIN45.   In what state did **(you/this person)** work in mining?_______________ ☐☐

      Don't Know ☐ 7
      Missing ☐ 8
      Refused ☐ 9

MIN46.   Was this work experience in unionized mines?

      Yes .... ☐ 1
      No .... ☐ 2
      Experienced work in both union and non-union mines .... ☐ 3
      Don't Know ☐ 7
      Missing ☐ 8
      Refused ☐ 9

MIN47.   **(Were/are) (you/this person)** a contracted/hourly employee, or a salaried worker?

      Contracted/Hourly .... ☐ 1
      Salaried .... ☐ 2
      Don't Know ☐ 7
      Missing ☐ 8
      Refused ☐ 9

MIN48. Was this experience in coal mining or some other kind of mining?

Coal mining . . . . □ 1

Some other kind of mining . . . . [SKIP TO INTRO TO UNIV63, PAGE13] □ 2

Don't Know □ 7

Missing □ 8

Refused □ 9

MIN49. Was any of this experience in small mines, that is, mines with fewer than 50 workers, including supervisory and hourly employees?

Yes . . . . □ 1

No . . . . [SKIP TO INTRO TO UNIV63, PAGE 13] □ 2

Don't Know □ 7

Missing □ 8

Refused □ 9

Now thinking of how small mines compare with large mines:

MIN50. Which do you feel is more dangerous, a large mine, a small mine, or is one no more dangerous than the other?

Large mines . . . . □ 1

Small mines . . . . □ 2

One is no more dangerous than the other . . . . □ 3

Don't Know □ 7

Missing □ 8

Refused □ 9

MIN51. Which do you feel is more likely to be unionized, a large mine, a small mine, or is one no more likely to be unionized than the other?

Large mines . . . . □ 1

Small mines . . . . □ 2

One is no more likely to be unionized than the other . . . . □ 3

Don't Know □ 7

Missing □ 8

Refused □ 9

MIN52. Which do you feel has more occupational health risks, a large mine, a small mine, or does one have no more occupational health risks than the other?

Large mines . . . . □ 1

Small mines . . . . □ 2

One has no more occupational health risks than the other . . . . □ 3

Don't Know □ 7

Missing □ 8

Refused □ 9

MIN53. Which do you feel has more safety violations, a large mine, a small mine, or does one have no more safety violations than the other?

   Large mines .... □ 1

   Small mines .... □ 2

   One has no more safety violations than the other .... □ 3

   Don't Know □ 7

   Missing □ 8

   Refused □ 9

MIN54. Which do you feel is more affected by changes in the economy, a large mine, a small mine, or is one no more affected by the economy than the other?

   Large mines .... □ 1

   Small mines .... □ 2

   One is no more affected by the economy than the other .... □ 3

   Don't Know □ 7

   Missing □ 8

   Refused □ 9

MIN55. Which do you feel is more prepared for an emergency, a large mine, a small mine, or is one no more prepared for an emergency than the other?

   Large mines .... □ 1

   Small mines .... □ 2

   One is no more prepared for an emergency than the other .... □ 3

   Don't Know □ 7

   Missing □ 8

   Refused □ 9

MIN56. Which do you feel provides more training, a large mine, a small mine, or does one provide no more training than the other?

   Large mines .... □ 1

   Small mines .... □ 2

   One provides no more training than the other .... □ 3

   Don't Know □ 7

   Missing □ 8

   Refused □ 9

MIN57. Which do you feel is managed with more concern for the well being of workers, a large mine, a small mine, or is one no more concerned with the well being of workers than others?

Large mines .... ☐ 1

Small mines .... ☐ 2

One is no more concerned with the well being of workers than the other .... ☐ 3

Don't Know ☐ 7

Missing ☐ 8

Refused ☐ 9

MIN58. Which do you feel is harder pressed to make a profit, a large mine, a small mine, or is one no more concerned with profit than the other?

Large mines .... ☐ 1

Small mines .... ☐ 2

One is no more concerned with profit than the other .... ☐ 3

Don't Know ☐ 7

Missing ☐ 8

Refused ☐ 9

MIN59. Which do you feel provides more job security, a large mine, a small mine, or does one provide no more job security than the other?

Large mines .... ☐ 1

Small mines .... ☐ 2

One provides no more job security than the other .... ☐ 3

Don't Know ☐ 7

Missing ☐ 8

Refused ☐ 9

MIN60. Overall, do you believe that small mines have a positive effect on West Virginia's economy, a negative effect, or do you think they do not affect the economy one way or the other?

Positive effect .... ☐ 1

Negative effect .... ☐ 2

Do not affect the economy one way or the other .... ☐ 3

Don't Know ☐ 7

Missing ☐ 8

Refused ☐ 9

MIN61.   Do you think that small mines have a positive effect on West Virginia's employment level, a negative
           effect, or do you think they do not affect employment one way or the other?
           Positive effect .... ☐ 1
           Negative effect .... ☐ 2
           Do not affect employment one way or the other .... ☐ 3
                                                                                 Don't Know ☐ 7
                                                                                   Missing ☐ 8
                                                                                  Refused ☐ 9

MIN62.   Do you think that small mines have a positive effect on West Virginia's industrial image, a negative
           effect, or do you think they do not affect the industrial image one way or the other?
           Positive effect .... ☐ 1
           Negative effect .... ☐ 2
           Do not affect industrial image one way or the other .... ☐ 3
                                                                                 Don't Know ☐ 7
                                                                                   Missing ☐ 8

Education has been and continues to be a real concern to people in the state of West Virginia. Before we close,
we'd like to take a few minutes to ask you a few questions about education in the state.

UNIV63.   How many members of your household have studied courses at a college or university?
                                                                          Number ☐☐☐
                                                                     Don't Know ☐ 777
                                                                       Missing ☐ 888
                                                                       Refused ☐ 999

IF 0, SKIP TO UNIV65

UNIV64.   How many members of your household have graduated from a four year college or university?
                                                                          Number ☐☐☐
                                                                     Don't Know ☐ 777
                                                                       Missing ☐ 888
                                                                       Refused ☐ 999

UNIV65. Do you believe that a college education contributes significantly to an individual's earning potential?

Yes .... ☐ 1

No .... ☐ 2

Don't Know ☐ 7

Missing ☐ 8

Refused ☐ 9

UNIV66. Do you think the state's colleges and universities are teaching knowledge and skills that are valued by the people of West Virginia?

Yes .... ☐ 1

No .... ☐ 2

Don't Know ☐ 7

Missing ☐ 8

Refused ☐ 9

UNIV67. Do you feel a need or an interest in furthering your own education?

Yes .... ☐ 1

No .... ☐ 2

Don't Know ☐ 7

Missing ☐ 8

Refused ☐ 9

Before we close, I have just a few remaining questions:

CRACE. Of what race do you consider yourself? [DO NOT READ CATEGORIES]

White/Caucasian .... ☐ 1

Chicano/Mexican/Hispanic .... ☐ 2

Black/African American .... ☐ 3

American Indian/Native American .... ☐ 4

Asian .... ☐ 5

Other race (Specify) ____

Don't Know ☐ 77

Missing ☐ 88

Refused ☐ 99

CINC1.   Is your total household income more than $30,000 or less than $30,000 a year?

$30,000 or more .... [GO TO CINC2] ☐ 1

Less than $30,000 .... [GO TO CINC3] ☐ 2

Don't Know [SKIP TO CLOSING STATEMENT] ☐ 7

Missing [SKIP TO CLOSING STATEMENT] ☐ 8

Refused [SKIP TO CLOSING STATEMENT] ☐ 9

CINC2.   Lastly, I am going to mention a number of income categories. When I mention the category which describes
                your total household income in the last 12 months, please stop me.

$30,000 to less than $40,000 .... ☐ 1

$40,000 to less than $50,000 .... ☐ 2

$50,000 to less than $60,000 .... ☐ 3

$60,000 to less than $70,000 .... ☐ 4

$70,000 to less than $80,000 .... ☐ 5

$80,000 or more .... ☐ 6

Don't Know ☐ 7

Missing ☐ 8

Refused ☐ 9

[SKIP TO CLOSING STATEMENT]

CINC3.   Lastly, I am going to mention a number of income categories. When I mention the category which describes
                your total household income in the last 12 months, please stop me.

Less than $5,000 .... ☐ 1

$5,000 to less than $10,000 .... ☐ 2

$10,000 to less than $15,000 .... ☐ 3

$15,000 to less than $20,000 .... ☐ 4

$20,000 to less than $25,000 .... ☐ 5

$25,000 to less than $30,000 .... ☐ 6

Don't Know ☐ 7

Missing ☐ 8

Refused ☐ 9

Those are all the questions I have for you. Thank you very much for your time and cooperation.
Have a good ____________.

Appendix F

West Virginia Social Indicator Survey
1993 Questionnaire

A.   First, I would like to know how many people live in your household, including yourself, and
      excluding temporary visitors? Now I would like to know a little about each of these (repeat
      number) people.
      Let's start with you. Could I have your first name?

B.   [IWER: RECORD RELATIONSHIP AS "RESPONDENT"]

C.   [IWER: RECORD RESPONDENTS SEX]

D.   What was your age on your last birthday?

E.   Are you married, widowed, divorced, separated, married, but apart, or never married?

F.   How many years of schooling have you completed?

G.   Do you have a high school diploma or GED Certificate?

        [IWER: REPEAT A1 THROUGH G1 FOR EACH ADDITIONAL PERSON IN THE
                    HOUSEHOLD, AND RECORD
        THE INFORMATION IN THE APPROPRIATE SPACE]

              [IF NO MORE IN THE HOUSEHOLD SKIP TO PAGE 1 Q12]

A1.   What is the first name of the next person living in the household?

B1.   How is this person related you?

C1.   [IWER: RECORD SEX OF HOUSEHOLD MEMBER. IF NOT CLEAR, ASK
      WHETHER PERSON IS A MALE OR FEMALE]

D1.   What was (his/her) age on (his/her) last birthday?

E1.   Is (he/she) married, widowed, divorced, separated, married, but apart, or never married?

F1.   How many years of schooling has (he/she) completed?

G1.   Does (he/she) have a high school diploma or GED Certificate?

SUMMARY TABLE FOR PERSONS IN HOUSEHOLD

A	B	C	D	E	F	G
	Relation to Respondent			Marital Status		
Persons in Household		Sex	Age		Years of Schooling	High School Diploma
1. ____________	1 2 3 4 5 6 7 8	M F	___	1 2 3 4 5 6	______	Yes No
2. ____________	1 2 3 4 5 6 7 8	M F	___	1 2 3 4 5 6	______	Yes No
3. ____________	1 2 3 4 5 6 7 8	M F	___	1 2 3 4 5 6	______	Yes No
4. ____________	1 2 3 4 5 6 7 8	M F	___	1 2 3 4 5 6	______	Yes No
5. ____________	1 2 3 4 5 6 7 8	M F	___	1 2 3 4 5 6	______	Yes No
6. ____________	1 2 3 4 5 6 7 8	M F	___	1 2 3 4 5 6	______	Yes No
7. ____________	1 2 3 4 5 6 7 8	M F	___	1 2 3 4 5 6	______	Yes No
8. ____________	1 2 3 4 5 6 7 8	M F	___	1 2 3 4 5 6	______	Yes No
9. ____________	1 2 3 4 5 6 7 8	M F	___	1 2 3 4 5 6	______	Yes No
10. ____________	1 2 3 4 5 6 7 8	M F	___	1 2 3 4 5 6	______	Yes No

We are interested in talking to people about a variety of things. First, I want to ask a few questions about your community and what you think of it as a place to live.

12.   In what county do you live?____ ☐☐

REGION ☐☐

13.   Were you born in ________ county? [IWER: INSERT COUNTY NAME]

Yes . . . . [SKIP TO Q14] ☐ 1

No . . . . ☐ 2

Don't Know ☐ 7

Refused ☐ 9

13A.   Were you born in West Virginia, another state, or a foreign country?

West Virginia . . . . ☐ 1

Another state . . . . ☐ 2

Foreign country . . . . ☐ 3

Don't Know ☐ 7

Refused ☐ 9

14.   How many total years have you lived in ___________ county?

YEARS ☐☐ MONTHS ☐☐

TOTAL YEARS ☐☐☐

Don't Know ☐ 777

Refused ☐ 999

15.   Do you live in open country, or in a town or city?

Open country . . . . [SKIP TO Q16] ☐ 1

Town or city . . . . ☐ 2

Don't Know [SKIP TO Q16] ☐ 7

Refused [SKIP TO Q16] ☐ 9

15A.   In what town or city do you live? [SKIP TO Q17]______________________________

Don't Know ☐ 777

Refused ☐ 999

16.   What town or city is closest to where you live?__________________________________

Don't Know ☐ 777

Refused ☐ 999

17.   What is your Zip Code? . . . . ZIP CODE ☐☐☐☐☐

                                                                        Don't Know ☐ 77777
                                                                        Refused ☐ 99999

18.   Where were you living two years ago?____________________________ CITY/TOWN
          [IWER: GET BOTH CITY AND STATE]   Don't Know ☐ 777
                                                                        Refused ☐ 999

                                                                        STATE ☐☐

                                                                        Don't Know ☐ 77
                                                                        Refused ☐ 99

19.   How do you feel about the quality of the **public** schools that the children in your area attend?
          Would you say the quality of the public schools is very good, fairly good, not very good, or not
          good at all?

          Very good . . . . ☐ 1
          Fairly good . . . . ☐ 2
          Not very good . . . . ☐ 3
          Not good at all . . . . ☐ 4

                                                                        Don't Know ☐ 7
                                                                        Refused ☐ 9

We are interested in knowing how you feel about your financial situation.

20.   Overall, how satisfied are you with your current financial situation? Would you say you are
          very satisfied, satisfied, dissatisfied, or very dissatisfied?

          Very satisfied . . . . ☐ 1
          Satisfied . . . . ☐ 2
          Dissatisfied . . . . ☐ 3
          Very dissatisfied . . . . ☐ 4

                                                                        Don't Know ☐ 7
                                                                        Refused ☐ 9

21.   Has the income you have earned during the past year allowed you to meet your basic needs?

          Yes . . . . [SKIP TO Q22] ☐ 1
          No . . . . ☐ 2
                                                             Don't Know [SKIP TO Q22] ☐ 7
                                                                Refused [SKIP TO Q22] ☐ 9

21A.   Which basic needs <u>have not</u> been met?   [IWER: PROBE FOR 2]

____

____

                                                                    Don't Know ☐ 777
                                                                       Refused ☐ 999

22.   Would you say you are better off, about the same, or worse financially this year than you were
              two years ago at this time?
              Better . . . . ☐ 1
              About the same . . . . ☐ 2
              Worse . . . . ☐ 3
                                                    Don't Know [SKIP TO Q24] ☐ 7
                                                       Refused [SKIP TO Q24] ☐ 9

23.   Why do you say so? [IWER: PROBE FOR 2 REASONS]_____________________________

____

                                                                    Don't Know ☐ 777
                                                                       Refused ☐ 999

Now I am going to ask you a few questions about the type of housing you live in.
24.   Which of the following comes closest to the type of housing unit you live in now?
              Do you live in: [IWER:READ LIST AND STOP WHEN R. SELECTS TYPE]
              A mobile home . . . . ☐ 1
              A detached single house . . . . ☐ 2
              A duplex . . . . ☐ 3
              A townhouse (row house) . . . . ☐ 4
              A condominium . . . . ☐ 5
              An apartment or . . . . ☐ 6
              Some other type of unit (Specify) _______________________________
                                                                    Don't Know ☐ 77
                                                                       Refused ☐ 99

25.   Do you, or does some member of your household, own your home outright, are you buying it
              or do you rent?
              Own . . . . [ASK Q25A] ☐ 1
              Buying it . . . . [ASK Q25A] ☐ 2
              Rent . . . . [SKIP TO Q25C] ☐ 3
                                                    Don't Know [SKIP TO VOL26] ☐ 7
                                                       Refused [SKIP TO VOL26] ☐ 9

25A.   How much do you pay on your home per month, including taxes and home owners

        insurance? . . . . $☐☐☐☐

                                                                            Don't Know ☐ 7777
                                                                            Refused ☐ 9999

25B.   How long ago did you buy your home? [SKIP TO VOL26] . . . .

                                                            YEARS ☐☐   MONTHS ☐☐

                                                            TOTAL YEARS ☐☐☐

                                                                            Don't Know ☐ 777
                                                                            Refused ☐ 999

25C.   How much is your rent per month? . . . . $☐☐☐☐

                                                                            Don't Know ☐ 7777
                                                                            Refused ☐ 9999

26.   In your housing unit, are you on a Municipal water supply, private well or what?
        Municipal water supply . . . . ☐ 1
        Private Well/Spring . . . . ☐ 2
        Other (Specify) ____

                                                                            Don't Know ☐ 7
                                                                            Refused ☐ 9

27.   Generally speaking, does a lack of transportation interfere with your or another household
        member's daily activities?
        Yes . . . . ☐ 1
        No . . . . [SKIP TO Q29] ☐ 2
                                                        Don't Know [SKIP TO Q29] ☐ 7
                                                        Refused [SKIP TO Q29] ☐ 9

28.   Does a lack of transportation prevent you or members of your household from getting to:
        [IWER: READ THE FOLLOWING ITEMS AND RECORD AN ANSWER FOR EACH

		Yes	No	DK	Ref
28A.	**Shopping Centers**	☐ 1	☐ 2	☐ 7	☐ 9
28B.	**Health Care facilities (such as a doctor's office)**	☐ 1	☐ 2	☐ 7	☐ 9
28C.	**Government activities**	☐ 1	☐ 2	☐ 7	☐ 9
28D.	**Recreational activities**	☐ 1	☐ 2	☐ 7	☐ 9
28E.	**A place of employment**	☐ 1	☐ 2	☐ 7	☐ 9

We are interested in the type of work you normally do.

29. How would you classify your work situation last week? Were you ... [IWER: READ ALL RESPONSES BELOW AND IF R SAYS MORE THAN 1 CATEGORY, ASK, "WHICH OF THESE IS YOUR PRIMARY WORK SITUATION"]

    Working .... [SKIP TO Q30] ☐ 1

    With a job, but not at work because of temporary illness,

        vacation, or strike .... [SKIP TO Q30] ☐ 2

    With a job, but temporarily laid off .... [SKIP TO Q30] ☐ 3

    Looking for work .... ☐ 4

    Keeping house .... ☐ 5

    Going to school .... ☐ 6

    Unable to work due to disability .... ☐ 7

    Retired or .... ☐ 8

    Unable to work for other reasons. [IWER: PROBE, "WHAT OTHER REASON WOULD THAT BE?"]____

                                       Don't Know [SKIP TO Q30] ☐ 77

                                          Refused [SKIP TO Q30] ☐ 99

29A. Did you ever work for as long as one year?

    Yes .... ☐ 1

    No .... [SKIP TO Q43] ☐ 2

                        Don't Know [SKIP TO Q43] ☐ 7

                          Refused [SKIP TO Q43] ☐ 9

30. What (is/was) your job title or what type of work (do/did) you do on your job? [IWER: ACCEPT ONLY 1 JOB TITLE]_________________________________

____

31. What (are/were) the most important activities or duties at this job?
[PROBE FOR 2]____

____

32. What type of business or industry (is/was) that? [IWER: ACCEPT ONLY 1]__________

____

                  OCCUPATION ☐☐☐   INDUSTRY ☐☐☐

                                   Don't Know ☐ 7777

                                   Refused ☐ 9999

33. **(Are/were)** you self-employed or employed by someone else?

        Self-employed ☐ 1

        Employed by someone else ☐ 2

        Don't Know ☐ 7

        Refused ☐ 9

[IF NOT CURRENTLY EMPLOYED SKIP TO Q43]

34. Do you think the income you currently earn matches the skills and training you have?

        Yes [SKIP TO Q35] ☐ 1

        No ☐ 2

        Don't Know [SKIP TO Q35] ☐ 7

        Refused [SKIP TO Q35] ☐ 9

34A. Why do you say so? **[PROBE FOR 2]** _______________________________________

____

        Don't Know ☐ 77

        Refused ☐ 99

35. How many hours do you normally work at your current job during an average week?

        HOURS ☐☐ **MINUTES** ☐☐

        TOTAL HOURS ☐☐☐

        Don't Know ☐ 777

        Refused ☐ 999

36. Approximately how many miles from your home do you travel to work in one direction? . . . .

        MILES ☐☐☐

        Don't Know ☐ 777

        Refused ☐ 999

37. Approximately how many minutes does it take you to get from your home to your job in one direction . . . .

        TOTAL MINUTES ☐☐☐

        Don't Know ☐ 777

        Refused ☐ 999

38.   What type of transportation do you generally use to get to your place of employment?

    Car/truck .... ☐ 1

    Motorcycle/Motorscooter .... ☐ 2

    Municipal bus .... ☐ 3

    Taxi .... ☐ 4

    Bicycle .... ☐ 5

    Walk .... ☐ 6

    Ride from other person .... ☐ 7

    Other (Specify)_______________________________________

    Don't Know ☐ 77

    Refused ☐ 99

39.   How many different jobs have you worked at over the last four years? ....

    NUMBER OF JOBS ☐☐

    Don't Know ☐ 77

    Refused ☐ 99

40.   How long have you worked at your current job? .... YEARS ☐☐ MONTHS ☐☐

    TOTAL MONTHS ☐☐☐

    Don't Know ☐ 7777

    Refused ☐ 9999

40A.   What was your job title or what type of work did you do just prior to your present work situation?

____

    OCCUPATION ☐☐☐ INDUSTRY ☐☐☐

    Don't Know ☐ 7777

    Refused ☐ 9999

[IWER: IF R HAS NEVER WORKED PRIOR TO NOW, SKIP TO Q41]

40B. How long had you worked continuously at the last job you held? . . . .

YEARS ☐☐ **MONTHS** ☐☐

TOTAL MONTHS ☐☐☐

Don't Know ☐ 7777
Refused ☐ 9999

41. How satisfied are you with your present job? Would you say you are very satisfied, satisfied, dissatisfied, or very dissatisfied?

Very Satisfied . . . . ☐ 1
Satisfied . . . . ☐ 2
Dissatisfied . . . . ☐ 3
Very Dissatisfied . . . . ☐ 4

Don't Know ☐ 7
Refused ☐ 9

42. Have you been unemployed for any period during the last twelve months?

Yes . . . . ☐ 1
No . . . . ☐ 2

Don't Know ☐ 7
Refused ☐ 9

43. Are you currently a member of a labor union?

Yes . . . . ☐ 1
No . . . . [SKIP TO NEXT PAGE] ☐ 2
Don't Know [SKIP TO NEXT PAGE] ☐ 7
Refused [SKIP TO NEXT PAGE] ☐ 9

43A. Which labor union would that be?

☐☐☐

Don't Know ☐ 777
Refused ☐ 999

IWER: CHOOSE ONE OF THE FOLLOWING LEAD-IN STATEMENTS!!!!

[IWER: IF R HAS ALREADY INDICATED THAT S/HE OWNS A SMALL BUSINESS]
We're interested in learning more about West Virginians who currently own a small business as well as those who plan to start a small business in the near future. You've indicated that you presently own a small business. **[SKIP TO 45]**

[IWER: IF R WORKING, BUT NOT A SMALL BUSINESS OWNER]
We're interested in learning more about West Virginians who currently own a small business as well as those who plan to start a small business. You've indicated that you ___ **[IWER: INSERT JOB TITLE]**. **[SKIP TO 44]**

[IWER: IF R NOT WORKING]
We're interested in learning more about West Virginians who currently own a small business as well as those who plan to start a small business. You've indicated that you are currently not working. **[SKIP TO 45]**

BUS44.   Do you also currently own a small business in West Virginia?

        Yes .... ☐ 1

        No .... ☐ 2

        Don't Know ☐ 7

        Refused ☐ 9

BUS45.   Do you *plan* to start a new small business in West Virginia within the next year?

        Yes .... ☐ 1

        No .... **[SKIP TO Q50]** ☐ 2

        Don't Know [SKIP TO Q50] ☐ 7

        Refused [SKIP TO Q50] ☐ 9

BUS46.   Are you looking for assistance in writing a business plan or in conducting a   feasibility study?

        Yes .... ☐ 1

        No .... ☐ 2

        Don't Know ☐ 7

        Refused ☐ 9

BUS47.   Have you ever heard of the Small Business Institute at West Virginia University in
           Morgantown?

                   Yes .... ☐ 1
                   No .... ☐ 2
                                                         Don't Know ☐ 7
                                                            Refused ☐ 9

BUS48.   Have you ever heard of the Small Business Administration?

                   Yes .... ☐ 1
                   No .... [SKIP TO Q50] ☐ 2
                                            Don't Know [SKIP TO Q50] ☐ 7
                                               Refused [SKIP TO Q50] ☐ 9

BUS49.   Have you ever contacted the Small Business Administration?

                   Yes .... ☐ 1
                   No .... ☐ 2
                                                         Don't Know ☐ 7
                                                            Refused ☐ 9

Now we have some questions about the primary income earner in your household.

50.   In your household, who is the primary income earner? [IWER: DO NOT READ
           CATEGORIES]

                   Self .... [SKIP TO Q59] ☐ 1
                   Spouse .... ☐ 2
                   Son/ Step .... ☐ 3
                   Daughter/ Step .... ☐ 4
                   Mother/ Step .... ☐ 5
                   Father / Step .... ☐ 6
                   Sister/ Step .... ☐ 7
                   Brother/ Step .... ☐ 8
                   Other (Specify)____
                                            Don't Know [SKIP TO Q59] ☐ 77
                                               Refused [SKIP TO Q59] ☐ 99

51.   Last week was your _______ working, with a job but not at work, unable to work due to disability, retired, or what?

      Working now .... [SKIP TO Q52] ☐ 1

      With a job, but not at work because of temporary illness,

      vacation, or strike .... [SKIP TO Q52] ☐ 2

      Unable to work due to disability .... ☐ 3

      Retired .... ☐ 4

      Unable to work for other reason (Specify)_______________________

                 Don't Know [SKIP TO Q52] ☐ 77

                 Refused [SKIP TO Q52] ☐ 99

51A.   Did your _________ ever work for as long as one year?

      Yes .... ☐ 1

      No .... [SKIP TO Q59] ☐ 2

               Don't Know [SKIP TO Q59] ☐ 7

                 Refused [SKIP TO Q59] ☐ 9

52.   What **(is/was)** your _______ job title or what type of work **(does/did)** **(he/she)** do on **(his/her)** job? [IWER: ACCEPT ONLY 1 JOB TITLE]_______________________

____

53.   What **(are/were)** the most important activities or duties at this job?
     [PROBE FOR 2]

____

54.   What type of business or industry is that? [IWER: ACCEPT ONLY 1]_______________________

____

                   OCCUPATION ☐☐☐ INDUSTRY ☐☐☐

                               Don't Know ☐ 7777

                               Refused ☐ 9999

55.　　　**(Is/was)** your _____ self-employed or employed by someone else?

    Self-employed .... ☐ 1

    Employed by someone else .... ☐ 2

    Don't Know ☐ 7

    Refused ☐ 9

[IF PRIMARY INCOME EARNER IS DISABLED, RETIRED, OR OTHER: SKIP TO Q59]

56.　　　How many hours does your _______ normally work at this job

during an average week? .... **HOURS** ☐☐　**MINUTES** ☐☐

TOTAL HOURS ☐☐☐

Don't Know ☐ 777

Refused ☐ 999

57.　　　Approximately how many miles from your home does your _______ travel to
work in one direction? .... **MILES** ☐☐☐

Don't Know ☐ 777

Refused ☐ 999

58.　　　How long has your _______ worked at this job? .... **YEARS** ☐☐　**MONTHS** ☐☐

TOTAL MONTHS ☐☐☐☐

Don't Know ☐ 7777

Refused ☐ 9999

[IWER: IF PRIMARY INCOME EARNER HAS WORKED AT JOB 12 OR MORE
MONTHS SKIP TO Q58C]

58A.　　What was your _______ job title or what type of work did your _______ do before this?
[IWER: ACCEPT ONLY 1 JOB TITLE]____

____

OCCUPATION ☐☐☐　**INDUSTRY** ☐☐☐

Don't Know ☐ 7777

Refused ☐ 9999

[IWER: IF PRIMARY INCOME EARNER HAS NEVER WORKED PRIOR TO NOW
SKIP TO Q59]

58B.   How long did **(he/she)** work continuously at the last job **(he/she)** held? . . . .

YEARS ☐☐   MONTHS ☐☐

TOTAL MONTHS ☐☐☐☐

Don't Know ☐ 7777

Refused ☐ 9999

58C.   How many different jobs has your _________ worked at

over the last four years? . . . .   NUMBER OF JOBS ☐☐

Don't Know ☐ 77

Refused ☐ 99

59.   Does anyone in your household have an employment package which includes:
              [IWER: READ LIST AND CHECK ANSWER FOR EACH ITEM]

		Yes	No	DK	Ref
59A.	**Paid vacation?**	☐1	☐2	☐7	☐9
59B.	**Paid sick leave?**	☐1	☐2	☐7	☐9
59C.	**Health insurance?**	☐1	☐2	☐7	☐9
59D.	**A retirement program?**	☐1	☐2	☐7	☐9
59E.	**Paid child care?**	☐1	☐2	☐7	☐9

[IWER: IF R HAS ALREADY INDICATED THAT S/HE WORKS AS A CHILD CARE PROVIDER]
We're interested in learning more about West Virginians who provide child care. You've indicated that you presently are a child care provider. [SKIP TO Q61]

[IWER: IF R NOT WORKING AS A CHILD CARE PROVIDER]
We're interested in learning more about West Virginians who provide child care. [SKIP TO Q60]

CCP1.   Are you **(also)** a childcare provider?

Yes . . . . ☐1

No . . . . [SKIP TO Q77 IF NO CHILDREN 0-5, SKIP TO Q83] ☐2

Don't Know ☐7

Refused ☐9

CCP2.   How do you see yourself as a child care provider, "in business" or "helping friends and family"?

  Business .... □ 1

  Friends/family .... □ 2

  Both .... □ 3

  Don't know □ 7

  Refused □ 9

CCP3.   How many children do you provide care for? .... Number ☐☐

  Don't know □ 77

  Refused □ 99

[IWER: IF NO CHILDREN 0-5 IN HOUSEHOLD, SKIP TO Q65]

CCP4.   When providing care for these children, do you have children from your own household who are with you?

  Yes .... □ 1

  No .... [SKIP TO Q65] □ 2

  Don't know □ 7

  Refused □ 9

CCP5.   How many children from your own household are with you? .... **Number** ☐☐

  Don't know □ 77

  Refused □ 99

CCP6.   About how many hours per week do you provide child care?_______________________

  Total Hours ☐☐

  Don't know □ 777

  Refused □ 999

CCP7.   How much do you receive per hour as pay for child care services? .... $☐☐

  Don't know □ 77

  Refused □ 99

[IWER: IF R DOES NOT RECEIVE PAY, SKIP TO Q69. IF PAY IS PER WEEK/MONTH, ASK FOR TOTAL WORK HOURS PER WEEK OR MONTH]

CCP8.   Is child care the only source of income for you and your household?

        Yes .... [SKIP TO Q69] ☐ 1

        No .... ☐ 2

        Don't know ☐ 7

        Refused ☐ 9

CCP9.   What percentage of your household's total income is supported by your work as

        a child care provider? .... ☐☐☐

        Don't know ☐ 777

        Refused ☐ 999

CCP10. Have you had training in child care?

        Yes .... ☐ 1

        No .... [SKIP TO Q71] ☐ 2

        Don't know [SKIP TO Q71] ☐ 7

        Refused [SKIP TO Q71] ☐ 9

CCP11. Where did you get your training? [IWER: ACCEPT ONLY 1]________________

        Don't know ☐ 77

        Refused ☐ 99

CCP12. Does anyone help you with your child care work?

        Yes .... ☐ 1

        No .... [SKIP TO Q73] ☐ 2

        Don't know [SKIP TO Q73] ☐ 7

        Refused [SKIP TO Q73] ☐ 9

CCP13. Do you pay them?

        Yes .... ☐ 1

        No .... ☐ 2

        R and other providers/ helpers are paid by someone else .... ☐ 3

        Don't know ☐ 7

        Refused ☐ 9

CCP14. Are you in need of anything to make your work as a child care provider run more smoothly?

        Yes .... ☐ 1

        No .... [SKIP TO Q75] ☐ 2

        Don't know [SKIP TO Q75] ☐ 7

        Refused [SKIP TO Q75] ☐ 9

CCP15.   What would that be? [PROBE FOR 2]

____

____

Don't know ☐ 77

Refused ☐ 99

CCP16.   Would you be interested in learning about tax laws in the child care business?

Yes .... ☐ 1

No .... ☐ 2

Don't know ☐ 7

Refused ☐ 9

CCP17.   Would you be interested in knowing about the state regulations for the child care business?

Yes .... ☐ 1

No .... ☐ 2

Don't know ☐ 7

Refused ☐ 9

[IF NO CHILDREN 0-5, SKIP TO Q83]

Now we have some questions about the **child(ren)** in your own household.

CCP18.   **(Do/does)** the **child(ren)** in your household have a child care provider?

Yes .... ☐ 1

No .... [SKIP TO Q81] ☐ 2

Don't know [SKIP TO Q81] ☐ 7

Refused [SKIP TO Q81] ☐ 9

CCP19.   How much do you pay this child care provider per hour? .... $ ☐☐ . ☐☐

Don't know ☐ 77

Refused ☐ 99

[IWER: IF PAY IS PER WEEK/MONTH, ASK FOR TOTAL WORK HOURS PER WEEK/MONTH]

CCP20.   Do you send your **child(ren)** to day care in someone else's home, day care in your own home, a day care center, or some other place?

Day care in someone else's home .... ☐ 1

Day care in your own home .... ☐ 2

Day care center .... ☐ 3

Other (specify)____

Don't know ☐ 77

Refused ☐ 99

CCP21.   How did you find your provider? [IWER: DO NOT READ CATEGORIES]
              RECORD ALL RESPONSES GIVEN

              Newspaper .... □ 1
              Referred by family/friend or acquaintance .... □ 2
              Church .... □ 3
              Resource & Referral agency .... □ 4
              Other (specify)____
                                                                    Don't know □ 77
                                                                      Refused □ 99

CCP22.   Has an employer ever provided you with any help in paying for child care?

              Yes .... □ 1
              No .... □ 2
                                                                     Don't know □ 7
                                                                       Refused □ 9

CCP23.   Has an employer ever provided you with any help in locating child care?

              Yes .... □ 1
              No .... □ 2
                                                                     Don't know □ 7

We are interested in the political participation of West Virginians.

60.   First of all, do you consider yourself a Democrat, a Republican, an Independent, or something
              else?

              Democrat .... □ 1
              Republican .... □ 2
              Independent .... □ 3
              Something else (Specify)_______________________________________
                                                                    Don't Know □ 77
                                                                      Refused □ 99

In the last four years, have you ...	Yes	No	DK	Ref
61. **Voted?**	☐ 1	☐ 2	☐ 7	☐ 9
62. **Given money to help someone try to win an election?**	☐ 1	☐ 2	☐ 7	☐ 9
63. **Worked in a political campaign?**	☐ 1	☐ 2	☐ 7	☐ 9
64. **Written letters to elected officials, Senators or Members of Congress, Mayors, etc.?**	☐ 1	☐ 2	☐ 7	☐ 9
65. **Signed a petition?**	☐ 1	☐ 2	☐ 7	☐ 9
66. **Participated in a strike?**	☐ 1	☐ 2	☐ 7	☐ 9
67. **Worked with others in your community to solve some local problem?**	☐ 1	☐ 2	☐ 7	☐ 9

We are especially interested in talking to people about the volunteer work they currently do.

VOL68.   Do you regularly volunteer time to some organization in your community?

    Yes .... ☐ 1
    No .... [SKIP TO Q96] ☐ 2
    Don't Know [SKIP TO Q96] ☐ 7
    Refused [SKIP TO Q96] ☐ 9

VOL69.   For about how many hours on average do you volunteer a month? ....

    TOTAL HOURS ☐☐☐

    Don't Know ☐ 777
    Refused ☐ 999

VOL70.   For how many organizations do you volunteer? .... **TOTAL NUMBER** ☐☐

    Don't Know ☐ 77
    Refused ☐ 99

VOL71.   What is the name of the organization **(you dedicate the most time to)**? [IWER: GET SPECIFIC NAME OF 1 ORGANIZATION ONLY] _______________________

____

    Don't Know ☐ 77
    Refused ☐ 99

VOL72.　What is the most important reason you volunteer for this organization? [IWER: ACCEPT ONLY 1]

Don't Know ☐ 77
Refused ☐ 99

Now I have a few questions on how you feel about the environment.

ENV73.　Are you concerned about environmental hazards in West Virginia?

Yes .... ☐ 1
No ... [SKIP TO Q108; IF NO CHILDREN 8-13, SKIP TO Q119 ON PAGE 17] ☐ 2
Don't Know [SKIP TO Q108; IF NO CHILDREN 8-13, SKIP TO Q119 ON PAGE 17] ☐ 7
Refused [SKIP TO Q108; IF NO CHILDREN 8-13, SKIP TO Q119 ON PAGE 17] ☐ 9

ENV74.　What environmental hazard or hazards would that be? [PROBE FOR 2] _______

Don't Know [SKIP TO Q108; IF NO CHILDREN 8-13, SKIP TO Q119 ON PAGE 17] ☐ 777
Refused [SKIP TO YTH85; IF NO CHILDREN 8-13, SKIP TO GUN96 ON PAGE 17] ☐ 999

[IWER: ASK THE FOLLOWING QUESTIONS FOR EACH HAZARD.]

ENV75.　Does your concern for [IWER: INSERT 1ST CONCERN] result from a personal experience?

Yes .... ☐ 1
No .... [SKIP TO Q100] ☐ 2
Don't Know [SKIP TO Q100] ☐ 7
Refused [SKIP TO Q100] ☐ 9

ENV76.　What did you experience?　[PROBE FOR 2] [SKIP TO ENV78] _______

Don't Know [SKIP TO Q101] ☐ 777
Refused [SKIP TO Q101] ☐ 999

ENV77.		What or who convinced you to be concerned about ______________?
		[PROBE FOR 2]

____

____

Don't Know ☐ 777
Refused ☐ 999

ENV78.		Are you actively involved in trying to address or do something about ____________ in West Virginia?

Yes . . . . ☐ 1
No . . . . [SKIP TO Q103] ☐ 2
Don't Know [SKIP TO Q103] ☐ 7
Refused [SKIP TO Q103] ☐ 9

ENV79.		How are you active? [PROBE FOR 2]_______________________________

____

____

Don't Know ☐ 777
Refused ☐ 999

[IWER: IF TWO HAZARDS MENTIONED, ASK THE FOLLOWING QUESTIONS ABOUT THE 2ND CONCERN] OTHERWISE, SKIP TO Q108.
IF NO CHILDREN 8-13, SKIP TO Q119.

ENV80.		Now thinking about _____________ , does your concern for this environmental hazard result from a personal experience?

Yes . . . . ☐ 1
No . . . . [SKIP TO Q105] ☐ 2
Don't Know [SKIP TO Q105] ☐ 7
Refused [SKIP TO Q105] ☐ 9

ENV81.		What did you experience? [PROBE FOR 2] [SKIP TO ENV83] ______________

____

____

Don't Know [SKIP TO Q106] ☐ 777
Refused [SKIP TO Q106] ☐ 999

ENV82.   What or who convinced you to be concerned about ______________?
          [PROBE FOR 2]

          ____

          ____

                                                              Don't Know ☐ 777
                                                                 Refused ☐ 999

ENV83.   Are you actively involved in trying to address or do something about ______________ in West
          Virginia?
                   Yes .... ☐ 1
                   No .... [SKIP TO Q108; IF NO CHILDREN 8-13, SKIP TO Q119] ☐ 2
                   Don't Know [SKIP TO Q108; IF NO CHILDREN 8-13, SKIP TO Q119] ☐ 7
                   Refused [SKIP TO Q108; IF NO CHILDREN 8-13, SKIP TO Q119] ☐ 9

ENV84.   How are you active? [PROBE FOR 2] _______________________________________

          ____

          ____

                                                              Don't Know ☐ 777
                                                                 Refused ☐ 999

[IWER: SKIP TO Q119 IF HOUSEHOLD HAS NO CHILDREN 8-13 YEARS OLD]

YTH85.   We would like to ask you some questions about groups and activities *for youths* between the
          ages of 8 and 13 in your community. What organized youth groups or after-school activities
          are available for youths in your community?
          [IWER: PROBE FOR 2]____

          ____

                                                              Don't Know ☐ 777
                                                                 Refused ☐ 999

YTH86.   What organized youth groups or after-school activities not available in your community
          would you like to have for the **child(ren)** in your household?
          [IWER: PROBE FOR 2]____

          ____

                                                              Don't Know ☐ 777
                                                                 Refused ☐ 999

[IWER: IF ONLY ONE CHILD 8-13, GO DIRECTLY TO Q110; IF MORE THAN ONE CHILD BETWEEN 8-13, FIRST ASK: Which of the children in your household between the age of 8 and 13 has had the most recent birthday? Now I would like to ask you some questions just about __________.

YTH87. Does __________ participate in any organized youth groups or after-school activities?

Yes . . . . [SKIP TO Q114] ☐ 1
No . . . . ☐ 2
Don't Know [SKIP TO Q114] ☐ 7
Refused [SKIP TO Q114] ☐ 9

YTH88. For what reasons does _______ not participate in available community youth groups and after-school activities? [IWER: PROBE FOR 2]____

____

____
Don't Know ☐ 77
Refused ☐ 99

YTH89. Is _______ encouraged at home to take part in organized youth groups or after-school . . . . . activities for children?

Yes . . . . ☐ 1
No . . . . ☐ 2
Don't Know ☐ 7
Refused ☐ 9

YTH90. What does *(s/he)* do in *(his/her)* free time? [IWER: PROBE FOR 2 ACTIVITIES]

____

____
Don't Know ☐ 77
Refused ☐ 99

YTH91. *Where* does __________ spend most of *(his/her)* free time?
[IWER: PROBE FOR 2 PLACES]____

____
Don't Know ☐ 77
Refused ☐ 99

YTH92. In what ways is ________ expected to be responsible? [IWER: PROBE FOR 2] ___________

____

Don't Know ☐ 77
Refused ☐ 99

YTH93. What was _______'s letter grade average in school last year?
[IWER: DO NOT READ CATEGORIES]

A .... ☐ 1
B .... ☐ 2
C .... ☐ 3
D .... ☐ 4
F .... ☐ 5

Don't Know ☐ 7
Refused ☐ 9

YTH94. How satisfied was your household with this grade? Would you say very satisfied, ...
satisfied, dissatisfied, or very dissatisfied?

Very satisfied .... ☐ 1
Satisfied .... ☐ 2
Dissatisfied .... ☐ 3
Very dissatisfied .... ☐ 4

Don't Know ☐ 7
Refused ☐ 9

YTH95. How many total years of education would your household like for __________
to complete? .... **TOTAL YEARS**

Don't Know ☐ 77
Refused ☐ 99

GUN96. Now we have some questions on a different topic.
Do you or does any member of your household participate in any archery or firearm shooting
activities?

Yes .... ☐ 1
No .... [SKIP TO Q122] ☐ 2
Don't Know [SKIP TO Q122] ☐ 7
Refused [SKIP TO Q122] ☐ 9

GUN97.   What type of shooting activity or activities would that be? [IWER: PROBE FOR 2]

____

____

Don't Know □ 77
Refused □ 99

GUN98.   Who in your household participates in a shooting activity? [IWER: RECORD
RELATION OF HOUSEHOLD MEMBER TO RESPONDENT; PROBE FOR 2] _______________

____

Don't Know □ 77
Refused □ 99

GUN99.   Do you or does any member of your household have some type of archery or shooting
equipment in your home?

Yes . . . . □ 1
No . . . . [SKIP TO Q126] □ 2
Don't Know [SKIP TO Q126] □ 7
Refused [SKIP TO Q126] □ 9

INJ100.   What kind of equipment is it? [PROBE FOR 2] _______________________________
[IWER: DON'T ACCEPT 'GUN' AS A RESPONSE.   Don't Know [SKIP TO Q126] □ 77
GET SPECIFIC TYPE OF GUN– RIFLE, SHOTGUN, PISTOL, ETC.]   Refused [SKIP TO Q126] □ 99

[IWER: IF NO GUN IN HOUSEHOLD, SKIP TO Q126]

INJ101.   What is the main reason you have (a gun/guns) in your home?
[DO NOT READ CATEGORIES]

Protection . . . . □ 1
Sport (Hunting, etc.) . . . . □ 2
Hobby (Gun collecting, etc.) . . . . □ 3
Other (Specify) ____

Don't Know □ 77
Refused □ 99

INJ102.   (Is/Are) the gun(s) usually loaded?

Yes . . . . □ 1
No . . . . □ 2
Don't Know □ 7
Refused □ 9

GUN103.   Have you or any member of your household had any formal training in the use of archery or firearms equipment?

Yes .... ☐ 1

No .... [SKIP TO Q128] ☐ 2

Don't Know [SKIP TO Q128] ☐ 7

Refused [SKIP TO Q128] ☐ 9

GUN104.   Who or what organization provided this training? [PROBE FOR 2] ___________________

____

Don't Know ☐ 77

Refused ☐ 99

GUN105.   Would you or any household member be interested in basic and/or advanced training in archery or firearm shooting equipment?

Yes .... ☐ 1

No .... [SKIP TO Q131] ☐ 2

Don't Know [SKIP TO Q130] ☐ 7

Refused [SKIP TO Q130] ☐ 9

GUN106.   What type of training would that be? [IWER: GET SPECIFIC EQUIPMENT OR ACTIVITY. PROBE FOR 2]

____

____

Don't Know ☐ 77

Refused ☐ 99

GUN107.   Would you or any member of your household be interested in a household- or family- oriented training and shooting program?

Yes .... ☐ 1

No .... ☐ 2

Don't Know ☐ 7

Refused ☐ 9

Now we have a number of health-related questions to ask you on topics ranging from health insurance and health care to injury, speech and hearing difficulties, and nutrition.

HTH108.   First of all, do you have health insurance?

Yes .... ☐ 1

No .... [SKIP TO Q133] ☐ 2

Don't Know ☐ 7

Refused ☐ 9

As I read a list of different kinds of health plans or health insurance, please tell me whether or not *you yourself* are covered by it [IWER: READ LIST AND GET RESPONSE FOR EACH]

		Yes	No	DK	Ref
HTH108A.	Health insurance through your work or union	☐ 1	☐ 2	☐ 7	☐ 9
HTH108B.	Health insurance through someone else's work or union	☐ 1	☐ 2	☐ 7	☐ 9
HTH108C.	Health insurance bought directly by yourself or your family	☐ 1	☐ 2	☐ 7	☐ 9
HTH108D.	Medicare	☐ 1	☐ 2	☐ 7	☐ 9
HTH108E.	Medicaid, or Public Aid	☐ 1	☐ 2	☐ 7	☐ 9
HTH108F.	Health insurance through some other group	☐ 1	☐ 2	☐ 7	☐ 9
HTH108G.	Other (Specify)_______________________				

HTH109.   Was there <u>any</u> time in the past two years when you were completely without any health plan or medical insurance coverage?

Yes .... ☐ 1
No .... [SKIP TO Q134] ☐ 2
Don't know [SKIP TO Q134] ☐ 7
Refused [SKIP TO Q134] ☐ 9

HTH109A.   Why were you without insurance? [ACCEPT ONLY 1] ____________________

____

Don't know ☐ 77
Refused ☐ 99

HTH109B.   For how long were you without any health insurance over the last two years? [IWER: SKIP TO Q134] .... MONTHS ☐☐   WEEKS ☐☐

TOTAL WEEKS ☐☐☐
Don't know ☐ 7777
Refused ☐ 9999

HTH110.   For how long has it been since you last had health insurance?________________

TOTAL WEEKS ☐☐☐☐

Never had insurance .... ☐ 8888
Don't Know ☐ 7777
Refused ☐ 9999

HTH111.   Overall, how do you feel about the health care services you or your household members have used in the last few years? Would you say you are very satisfied, satisfied, dissatisfied, or very dissatisfied?

Very satisfied .... □ 1
Satisfied .... □ 2
Dissatisfied .... □ 3
Very dissatisfied .... □ 4
Don't Know □ 7
Refused □ 9

HTH112.   How do you think the state government in WV is doing in addressing health care reform? Is it doing a good job, an adequate job, or a poor job.

Good job .... □ 1
Adequate job .... □ 2
Poor job .... □ 3
Don't Know □ 7
Refused □ 9

HTH113.   During the past 12 months was there a time when you or a household member needed medical care but did not get it?

Yes .... □ 1
No .... [SKIP TO Q138] □ 2
Don't Know [SKIP TO Q138] □ 7
Refused [SKIP TO Q138] □ 9

HTH113A. How many members didn't get medical care .... ⊔⊔
Don't Know □ 77
Refused □ 99

[IWER: IF MORE THAN ONE HOUSEHOLD MEMBER MENTIONED ASK: Which of these household members has had the most recent birthday? Now I would like to ask you some questions just about _____.

[ASK THE FOLLOWING Q ABOUT THE PERSON WITH MOST RECENT BIRTHDAY]

HTH114.   What was the main reason this person did not get the medical help needed?
             [ACCEPT ONLY 1]

____

____

____

Don't Know ☐ 77
Refused ☐ 99

MED115.   Do you have a household physician?
             Yes .... ☐ 1
             No .... ☐ 2
             Don't Know ☐ 7
             Refused ☐ 9

Each year, thousands of West Virginians are injured by falls, car crashes, fires, poisonings, drownings, assaults, and other kinds of unexpected incidents. I would like to ask you about any injuries that you or other members of your household may have experienced during the past year.

INJ116.   Has anyone who lives in your household experienced an accident or injury that required medical attention during the past year?
             Yes .... ☐ 1
             No .... **[SKIP TO Q140]** ☐ 2
             Don't Know [SKIP TO Q140] ☐ 7
             Refused [SKIP TO Q140] ☐ 9

INJ116A.   How many household members required medical attention due to an injury in the last year?

             ☐☐

             Don't Know ☐ 77
             Refused ☐ 99

[IF MORE THAN 1 ASK ABOUT MOST RECENT INJURY. IF ALL AT SAME TIME, ASK ABOUT MOST SERIOUS]

INJ116B.   How did the injury occur?
            [IWER: GET WHAT THE PERSON WAS *DOING* WHEN INJURED;
            PROBE FOR 2]

            ____

            ____

                                                         Don't Know ☐ 777
                                                           Refused ☐ 999

INJ116C.   What type of injury did <u>(you/the person)</u> experience? [IWER: PROBE, "WHAT BODY
            PART WAS INJURED?"; ACCEPT ONLY 1] _______________________________

            ____

                                                         Don't Know ☐ 777
                                                           Refused ☐ 999

INJ116D.   How old <u>(were/was)</u> <u>(you/the person)</u> at the time of the injury? . . . . ☐☐

                                                         Don't Know ☐ 777
                                                           Refused ☐ 999

[IWER: IF INJURED HOUSEHOLD MEMBER YOUNGER THAN 14, SKIP TO INJ116H]

INJ116E.   Did this injury happen while <u>(you/the person)</u> <u>(were/was)</u> at work?
                Yes . . . . ☐ 1
                No . . . . [SKIP TO Q139G] ☐ 2
                                                    Don't Know [SKIP TO Q139G] ☐ 7
                                                      Refused [SKIP TO Q139G] ☐ 9

INJ116F.   What work **activity** <u>(were/was)</u> <u>(you/this person)</u> doing? [IWER: ACCEPT ONLY 1]_______

            ____

                                                         Don't Know ☐ 777
                                                           Refused ☐ 999

INJ116G.   Had <u>(you/this person)</u> had any alcoholic beverages before being injured?
                Yes . . . . ☐ 1
                No . . . . ☐ 2
                                                             Don't Know ☐ 7
                                                               Refused ☐ 9

INJ116H.   [NOTE SEX OF INJURED PERSON. IF NOT SURE, ASK] . . . .
                                                  MALE ☐ 1 FEMALE ☐ 2

INJ116I.　　**(Were/was) (you/the injured person)** treated at a doctor's office, a hospital emergency room, or some other place?

      Doctor's office . . . . [SKIP TO Q139M] ☐ 1

      Emergency room . . . . ☐ 2

      Other (Specify)____[SKIP TO Q139M]

                           Don't Know ☐ 77

                           Refused ☐ 99

INJ116J.　　How **(were/was) (you/the person)** taken to the hospital?

      Private vehicle . . . . ☐ 1

      EMS/Ambulance . . . . ☐ 2

                         Don't Know ☐ 7

                           Refused ☐ 9

INJ116K.　　**(Were/Was) (you/this person)** admitted to the hospital? . . . . **Yes** ☐ 1

                       No [GO TO Q139M] ☐ 2

             Don't Know [GO TO Q139M] ☐ 7

                Refused [GO TO Q139M] ☐ 9

INJ116L.　　How many days did **(you/this person)** stay in the hospital? . . . . ☐☐☐

                       Don't Know ☐ 777

                         Refused ☐ 999

INJ116M.　　What was the final outcome of the injury? Did **(you/the person)** recover completely, are **(you/they)** temporarily disabled, permanently disabled, or what?

      Recover completely . . . . ☐ 1

      Temporarily disabled . . . . ☐ 2

      Permanently disabled . . . . ☐ 3

      Injured person died . . . . ☐ 4

                         Don't Know ☐ 7

                         Refused ☐ 9

How were the medical costs of the injury covered? Where they covered by....**[IWER: READ CATEGORIES AND RECORD AN ANSWER FOR EACH]**

		Yes	No	DK	Ref
INJ116N.	**Private funds?**	☐ 1	☐ 2	☐ 7	☐ 9
INJ116O	**Private insurance?**	☐ 1	☐ 2	☐ 7	☐ 9
INJ116P.	**Employer insurance?**	☐ 1	☐ 2	☐ 7	☐ 9
INJ116Q.	**Medicare/medicaid?**	☐ 1	☐ 2	☐ 7	☐ 9
INJ116R.	**Or some other way?**	☐ 1	☐ 2	☐ 7	☐ 9
INJ116S.	**Other (Specify)** _____________________________				

INJ116T.   In your opinion, how could this injury have been prevented?

[IWER: PROBE FOR 2]

                                                                            Don't Know ☐ 777
                                                                            Refused ☐ 999

INJ117.   During the past year, have you or has anyone in your household been physically hurt by
            another person (for example, during a fit of anger, in a fight or on purpose)?
            Yes .... ☐ 1
            No .... [SKIP TO Q141] ☐ 2
                                               Don't Know [SKIP TO Q141] ☐ 7
                                                 Refused [SKIP TO Q141] ☐ 9

INJ117A.   How was the injured person related to the person who hurt them? Were they strangers,
            acquaintances, or household members?
            Strangers .... ☐ 1
            Acquaintances .... ☐ 2
            Household members .... ☐ 2
                                                                            Don't Know ☐ 7
                                                                            Refused ☐ 9

INJ117B.   How did the injury occur?
            [IWER: GET WHAT THE PERSON WAS DOING WHEN INJURED;
            PROBE FOR 2]

                                                                            Don't Know ☐ 777
                                                                            Refused ☐ 999

INJ117C.   What type of injury did (you/the person) experience? [IWER: PROBE, "WHAT BODY
            PART WAS INJURED?"; ACCEPT ONLY 1] ________________________

                                                                            Don't Know ☐ 777
                                                                            Refused ☐ 999

INJ118.   Is any member of your household currently feeling the effects of an injury that occurred more than a year ago, to the extent that some activities are still difficult or impossible for them?

Yes . . . . ☐ 1
No . . . . [SKIP TO Q142] ☐ 2
Don't Know [SKIP TO Q142] ☐ 7
Refused [SKIP TO Q142] ☐ 9

INJ118A.   How did this injury occur?
[IWER: GET WHAT THE PERSON WAS DOING WHEN INJURED; PROBE FOR 2]

____

____

____

Don't Know ☐ 777
Refused ☐ 999

MED119.   If a member of your household was seriously injured, how difficult would it be to get to emergency medical assistance? Would you say it would be very difficult, somewhat difficult, or not at all difficult?

Very difficult . . . . ☐ 1
Somewhat difficult . . . . ☐ 2
Not at all difficult . . . . ☐ 3
Don't Know ☐ 7
Refused ☐ 9

MED120.   If a member of your household was seriously injured, how far would you have to travel to get emergency medical assistance?

[IWER: RECORD NUMBER OF MILES] . . . . TOTAL MILES ☐☐☐
Don't Know ☐ 777
Refused ☐ 999

MED121.   If a member of your household was seriously injured, how long would it take you to get to emergency medical assistance?

[IWER: RECORD HOURS AND MINUTES] _______________
TOTAL MINUTES ☐☐☐
Don't Know ☐ 777
Refused ☐ 999

INJ122.   If a member of your household was seriously injured, what phone number would you call for
                 an ambulance?   [IWER: DO NOT READ CATEGORIES]

                 911 .... ☐ 1
                 0 (operator) .... ☐ 2
                 Other (Specify)
                 [IWER: IF R GIVES ANOTHER PHONE NUMBER, RECORD NUMBER AND PROBE
                 FOR WHOSE NUMBER IT IS]____

                 ____

                                                                             Don't Know ☐ 77
                                                                               Refused ☐ 99

[IWER: IF CHILDREN 0-12 IN HOUSEHOLD, ASK Q146]
[IF CHILDREN 13-20 IN HOUSEHOLD, SKIP TO Q147]
[IF NO CHILDREN IN HOUSEHOLD, SKIP TO Q156]

Now I have two questions about children's exposure to injury.

INJ123.   Has a pediatrician or other doctor ever talked to you about ways to prevent injuries to the
                 children in your household?

                 Yes .... ☐ 1
                 No .... [SKIP TO Q147] ☐ 2
                 Does not apply (R never takes child to doctor) .... [SKIP TO Q147] ☐ 3
                                                           Don't Know [SKIP TO Q147] ☐ 7
                                                             Refused [SKIP TO Q147] ☐ 9

INJ123A.   What did the doctor suggest? [IWER: ACCEPT ONLY 1] __________________________

                 ____

                                                                             Don't Know ☐ 77
                                                                               Refused ☐ 99

                      [IWER: IF NO CHILDREN 12-20 IN HOUSEHOLD, SKIP TO Q156]

You mentioned earlier that there are {enter number} people between the ages of 12 and 20 living in your
household.

DRK124.   How likely is it that **(this teen/ any one of these teens)** in your household has consumed
                 alcoholic beverages? Would you say it is very likely, somewhat likely, or not at all likely?

                 Very likely .... ☐ 1
                 Somewhat likely .... ☐ 2
                 Not at all likely .... [SKIP TO Q150] ☐ 3
                                                           Don't Know [SKIP TO Q150] ☐ 7
                                                             Refused [SKIP TO Q150] ☐ 9

[IWER: IF ONLY ONE TEEN IN HOUSEHOLD, SKIP TO Q149]

[IWER: IF ONLY ONE TEEN IN HOUSEHOLD, SKIP TO Q149]

DRK125.   What are the ages of those teens who are likely to have consumed alcoholic
beverages?

_______   _______   _______   _______   _______

Don't Know ☐ 77
Refused ☐ 99

DRK126.   How likely is it that **(the teen/any one of the teens)** in your household has driven a vehicle
after consuming even a small amount of alcohol beverage? Would you say it is very likely,
somewhat likely, or not at all likely?

     Very likely . . . . ☐ 1
     Somewhat likely . . . . ☐ 2
     Not at all likely . . . . **[SKIP TO Q150]** ☐ 3
              Don't Know [SKIP TO Q150] ☐ 7
              Refused [SKIP TO Q150] ☐ 9

[IWER: IF ONLY ONE TEEN IN HOUSEHOLD, SKIP TO Q150]

DRK126A.   What are the ages of those teens who are likely to have driven after drinking alcoholic
beverages?

_______   _______   _______   _______   _______

Don't Know ☐ 77
Refused ☐ 99

DRK127.   How likely is it that the **teen/any one of teens** in your household has ridden in a vehicle with
a driver who has been drinking alcoholic beverages? Would you say it is very likely,
somewhat likely, or not at all likely?

     Very likely . . . . ☐ 1
     Somewhat likely . . . . ☐ 2
     Not at all likely . . . . **[SKIP TO Q151]** ☐ 3
              Don't Know [SKIP TO Q151] ☐ 7
              Refused [SKIP TO Q151] ☐ 9

[IWER: IF ONLY ONE TEEN IN HOUSEHOLD, SKIP TO Q151]

DRK127A.   What are the ages of those teens who are likely to have ridden with a driver who had an
alcoholic drink?

_______   _______   _______   _______   _______

Don't Know ☐ 77
Refused ☐ 99

DRK128. <u>(Is/are)</u> the teenager<u>(s)</u> in your household allowed to drink beer or other alcoholic beverages <u>in your home?</u>

Yes .... ☐ 1
No .... [SKIP TO Q153] ☐ 2
Don't Know [SKIP TO Q154] ☐ 7
Refused [SKIP TO Q154] ☐ 9

[IWER: IF ONLY ONE TEEN IN HOUSEHOLD, SKIP TO Q152]

DRK128A. What are the ages of the teens in your household who are allowed to drink alcoholic ....
beverages at home?

_______   _______   _______   _______   _______

Don't Know ☐ 77
Refused ☐ 99

DRK129. I will be reading some statements. Tell me which of the following statements best represents why the teen<u>(s)</u> in your household <u>(is/are)</u> allowed to drink alcoholic beverages at home:

The members of your household would rather have the teen<u>(s)</u> drink at home .....
than other places .... ☐ 1
Teens need to learn how to drink responsibly .... ☐ 2
Alcoholic beverages are a part of your household or religious celebrations .... ☐ 3
The members of your household are glad that the teen<u>(s)</u> is drinking alcoholic .....
beverages and is not involved in other drugs .... ☐ 4
Or is there some other reason? (Specify) _______________________________

Don't Know ☐ 77
Refused ☐ 99

[IWER: SKIP TO Q154]

DRK130.   I will be reading some statements. Tell me which of the following statements best represents why the teen(s) in your household (is/are) *not* allowed to drink alcohol beverages at your home:

It is illegal to give alcohol to anyone under the age of 21 .... ☐ 1
It is against your household's religion to use alcoholic beverages .... ☐ 2
It is not healthy for teens to drink alcohol .... ☐ 3
It increases the possibility of the teen(s) in your household
    becoming addicted to alcohol .... ☐ 4
Or is there some other reason? (Specify) _______________________________

Don't Know ☐ 77
Refused ☐ 99

DRK24.   Do you feel you could use more information on teen drinking and teen drinking and driving?

Yes .... ☐ 1
No .... [SKIP TO Q156] ☐ 2
Don't Know [SKIP TO Q156] ☐ 7
Refused [SKIP TO Q156] ☐ 9

DRK25.   Which of the following would be the *best* way for you to receive information on underage drinking (and/or) underage drinking and driving? [IWER: READ LIST AND ACCEPT ONLY 1]

Brochures/pamphlets/booklets .... ☐ 1
Videotapes .... ☐ 2
Attending group discussions/meetings .... ☐ 3
Or is there some other way? _______________________________

Don't Know ☐ 77
Refused ☐ 99

I have a few questions about underage drinking in general.

DRK26.   Some states have a law that teenagers arrested for driving after drinking alcohol must have
            their driver's license revoked or suspended, regardless of whether their blood alcohol content
            was above the legal limit. Do you strongly agree, agree, disagree or strongly disagree with
            such a law?

    Strongly agree .... ☐ 1

    Agree .... ☐ 2

    Disagree .... ☐ 3

    Strongly Disagree .... ☐ 4

                                                Don't Know [SKIP TO Q157] ☐ 7

                                                    Refused [SKIP TO Q157] ☐ 9

DRK26A.   Why do you say so? **[IWER: ACCEPT ONLY 1 REASON]**__________________________

            ____

            ____

                                                            Don't Know ☐ 77

                                                                Refused ☐ 99

DRK27.   Please tell me whether you strongly agree, agree, disagree or strongly disagree with the
            following statement: Underage drinking is a major societal problem.

    Strongly agree .... ☐ 1

    Agree .... ☐ 2

    Disagree .... ☐ 3

    Strongly Disagree .... ☐ 4

                                                            Don't Know ☐ 7

                                                                Refused ☐ 9

DRK28.   Again, please tell me whether you strongly agree, agree, disagree or strongly disagree with the
            following statement: Underage drinking *and driving* is a major societal problem.

    Strongly agree .... ☐ 1

    Agree .... ☐ 2

    Disagree .... **[SKIP TO Q160]** ☐ 3

    Strongly Disagree .... **[SKIP TO Q160]** ☐ 4

                                                Don't Know [SKIP TO Q160] ☐ 7

                                                    Refused [SKIP TO Q160] ☐ 9

DRK29. Who do you think should be responsible for dealing with underage drinking? [IWER: PROBE FOR 2]

____

____

____

Don't Know ☐ 77

Refused ☐ 99

Please answer the following questions with a yes or no.

DRK30. Based on what you know about laws concerning alcoholic beverages, is it illegal for people under the age of 21 to...

	YES	NO	DK	RF
DRK30A. **Buy alcoholic beverages**	☐ 1	☐ 2	☐ 7	☐ 9
DRK30B. **Possess alcoholic beverages**	☐ 1	☐ 2	☐ 7	☐ 9
DRK30C. **Drink alcoholic beverages**	☐ 1	☐ 2	☐ 7	☐ 9

DRK31. Based on what you know about laws concerning alcoholic beverages, is it illegal for an adult to give and sell alcoholic beverages to a person under the age of 21?

Yes ☐ 1

No ☐ 2

Don't Know ☐ 7

Refused ☐ 9

DRK32. Do you think the legal drinking age should be lowered to 18?

Yes ☐ 1

No ☐ 2

Don't Know [SKIP TO Q162] ☐ 7

Refused [SKIP TO Q162] ☐ 9

DRK32A. Why do you say so? [IWER: ACCEPT ONLY 1] _______________________________

____

Don't Know ☐ 77

Refused

Now we have some questions regarding tobacco products.

TOB33. Do you currently smoke cigarettes?

Yes ☐ 1

No ☐ 2

Don't Know ☐ 7

Refused ☐ 9

TOB34.   Do you currently use other tobacco products such as snuff, chewing tobacco, a pipe or cigars?

Yes .... ☐ 1

No .... ☐ 2

Don't Know ☐ 7

Refused ☐ 9

TOB35.   Currently there is no tax, other than a sales tax, on tobacco products such as snuff, chewing tobacco, pipes, or cigars in West Virginia. Would you support adding an extra tax on these products?

Yes .... ☐ 1

No .... ☐ 2

Don't Know ☐ 7

Refused ☐ 9

TOB36.   Besides a sales tax, currently there *is* an extra tax on cigarettes. This extra tax is 17 cents per pack and has not been increased since 1978. Would you support an increase in extra taxes on cigarettes?

Yes .... ☐ 1

No .... [SKIP TO Q165A] ☐ 2

Don't Know ☐ 7

Refused [SKIP TO Q165A] ☐ 9

TOB36A.   Would you support a cigarette tax going from 17 cents per pack to 25 cents per pack, 50 cents per pack, one dollar per pack, or more than a dollar per pack?

$0.25 per pack .... ☐ 1

$0.50 per pack .... ☐ 2

$1.00 per pack .... ☐ 3

$1.00+ per pack .... ☐ 4

Don't Know ☐ 7

Refused ☐ 9

TOB37.   Would you support an increase in taxes on cigarettes to pay for: [IWER: READ LIST AND GET RESPONSE FOR EACH ITEM]

	Yes	No	DK	Ref
Preventive health care	☐ 1	☐ 2	☐ 7	☐ 9
Education	☐ 1	☐ 2	☐ 7	☐ 9
Highways	☐ 1	☐ 2	☐ 7	☐ 9
Schools	☐ 1	☐ 2	☐ 7	☐ 9
Law enforcement of tobacco sales	☐ 1	☐ 2	☐ 7	☐ 9

TOB38.	Currently, retailers do not have to have a license to sell tobacco products. In order to prevent illegal tobacco sales to children under the age of 18, do you think retailers should be required to have a license to sell tobacco products?

Yes . . . . □ 1

No . . . . □ 2

Don't Know □ 7

Refused □ 9

TOB39.	Do you think cigarette vending machines should be allowed in locations that are accessible to children under the age of 18?

Yes . . . . □ 1

No . . . . □ 2

Don't Know □ 7

Refused □ 9

Our next set of health-related questions concerns West Virginia's public schools and the students attending these schools.

SCHL40.	Generally speaking, what do you think of the health status of the students attending kindergarten through 12th grade in West Virginia as compared to students attending kindergarten through 12th grade in other states? Would you say that the health status of West Virginia public school students is similar to, better than, or worse than the health status of students in other states?

Similar . . . . □ 1

Better . . . . □ 2

Worse . . . . □ 3

Don't Know □ 7

Refused □ 9

Please answer the following questions with a yes or no.

SCHL41.	Do you believe that sex education should be taught in public schools in West Virginia?

Yes . . . . □ 1

No . . . . □ 2

Don't Know □ 7

Refused □ 9

SCHL42.   Do you believe that public schools in West Virginia should be active in reducing the state's teenage pregnancy rate?

         Yes .... ☐ 1

         No .... ☐ 2

         Don't Know ☐ 7

         Refused ☐ 9

SCHL43.   Do you believe that public schools in West Virginia should provide social and psychological counseling services to students?

         Yes .... ☐ 1

         No .... ☐ 2

         Don't Know ☐ 7

         Refused ☐ 9

SCHL44.   Do you believe that *more* or *less* emphasis should be placed upon preventive health education in West Virginia's public schools?

         More .... ☐ 1

         Less .... ☐ 2

         Don't Know ☐ 7

         Refused ☐ 9

SCHL45.   Do you believe that public schools in West Virginia should deliver health care services to students and their families?

         Yes .... ☐ 1

         No .... ☐ 2

         Don't Know ☐ 7

         Refused ☐ 9

SCHL46.   Would you approve of (**children /the child/children in your household**) receiving primary health care services at school from a licensed, qualified care giver?

         Yes .... ☐ 1

         No .... ☐ 2

         Don't Know ☐ 7

         Refused ☐ 9

SCHL47.   Do you believe public education should assist children and youth in developing healthy behaviors and healthy life skills?

         Yes .... ☐ 1

         No .... ☐ 2

         Don't Know ☐ 7

         Refused ☐ 9

SCHL48.　　Some people believe that children who lack health care and/or do not engage in healthy behaviors are more likely to be absent from school due to health problems. Please tell me if you strongly agree, agree, disagree or strongly disagree with the following statements:

		SA	A	D	SD	DK	RF
SCHL48A.	**School health programs can help to improve academic performance of students in West Virginia**	☐1	☐2	☐3	☐4	☐7	☐9
SCHL48B.	**School health programs can help to reduce the public school dropout rate in West Virginia**	☐1	☐2	☐3	☐4	☐7	☐9

Another area of health we are interested in involves speech and hearing problems.

S&H131.　　Do you know anyone who has speech difficulty?

> **Yes** .... ☐1
> **No** .... [SKIP TO Q180] ☐2
> Don't Know [SKIP TO Q180] ☐7
> Refused [SKIP TO Q180] ☐9

[IWER: IF R INDICATES THAT S/HE HAS A SPEECH PROBLEM, SKIP TO Q155]

S&H131A.　　Is this person a member of your household?

> **Yes** .... ☐1
> **No** .... [SKIP TO Q180] ☐2
> Don't Know [SKIP TO Q180] ☐7
> Refused [SKIP TO Q180] ☐9

[IWER: IF R INDICATES MORE THAN ONE HOUSEHOLD MEMBER WITH SPEECH PROBLEM, GET FOLLOWING INFORMATION ON WHO HAS HAD THE MOST RECENT BIRTHDAY]

S&H132.　　**(Do/ Does) (you/ this person)** receive medical assistance for the speech difficulty?

> **Yes** .... ☐1
> **No** .... [SKIP TO Q180] ☐2
> Don't Know [SKIP TO Q180] ☐7
> Refused [SKIP TO Q180] ☐9

S&H132A.　　What kind of assistance **(do/ does) (you/ this person)** receive? [ACCEPT ONLY 1] ________

____

> Don't Know ☐77
> Refused ☐99

S&H133.　　Do you know anyone who has hearing difficulty?

Yes .... ☐ 1
No .... [SKIP TO Q184] ☐ 2
Don't Know [SKIP TO Q184] ☐ 7
Refused [SKIP TO Q184] ☐ 9

[IWER: IF R INDICATES THAT S/HE HAS A HEARING PROBLEM, SKIP TO Q157]

S&H133A.   Is this person a member of your household?

Yes .... ☐ 1
No .... [SKIP TO Q184] ☐ 2
Don't Know [SKIP TO Q184] ☐ 7
Refused [SKIP TO Q184] ☐ 9

[IWER: IF R INDICATES MORE THAN ONE HOUSEHOLD MEMBER WITH HEARING
PROBLEM, GET FOLLOWING INFORMATION ON WHO HAS HAD THE MOST RECENT
BIRTHDAY]

S&H134.   Does/do **(do/does)** **(you/ this person)** receive medical assistance for the hearing difficulty?

Yes .... ☐ 1
No .... [SKIP TO Q182] ☐ 2
Don't Know [SKIP TO Q182] ☐ 7
Refused [SKIP TO Q182] ☐ 9

S&H134A   What kind of assistance **(do/ does)** **(you/ this person)** receive? [ACCEPT ONLY 1] ________

____

Don't Know ☐ 77
Refused ☐ 99

Our next set of health-related questions concerns the foods you usually eat or drink either at home or away from home. First, a few questions about some general eating habits:

[IF 1 PERSON IN THE HOUSEHOLD, SKIP TO Q184]

DIET135.   In your household, who is primarily responsible for preparing food?
[IWER: DO NOT READ CATEGORIES. IF 2 HOUSEHOLD MEMBERS EQUALLY SHARE THE RESPONSIBILITY, INDICATE BOTH.]

Self .... ☐ 1

Spouse .... ☐ 2

Son/ Step .... ☐ 3

Daughter/ Step .... ☐ 4

Mother/ Step .... ☐ 5

Father / Step .... ☐ 6

Sister/ Step .... ☐ 7

Brother/ Step .... ☐ 8

Other (Specify)____

Don't Know ☐ 77

Refused ☐ 99

DIET136.   Primarily, who does the grocery shopping for your household?
[IWER: DO NOT READ CATEGORIES. IF 2 HOUSEHOLD MEMBERS EQUALLY SHARE THE RESPONSIBILITY, INDICATE BOTH.]

Self .... ☐ 1

Spouse .... ☐ 2

Son/ Step .... ☐ 3

Daughter/ Step .... ☐ 4

Mother/ Step .... ☐ 5

Father / Step .... ☐ 6

Sister/ Step .... ☐ 7

Brother/ Step .... ☐ 8

Other (Specify)____

Don't Know ☐ 77

Refused ☐ 99

DIET137.   When shopping for food, which of the following would you say is most important to
           you/your (spouse/father/mother/other)? [IWER: READ LIST AND ACCEPT ONE
           ANSWER]

                   Cost .... ☐ 1
                   Availability .... ☐ 2
                   Taste .... ☐ 3
                   Nutrition .... ☐ 4
           Or is there something else (Specify)____
                                                              Don't Know ☐ 77
                                                                 Refused ☐ 99

DIET138.   Are you on a special diet for a medical condition?

                   Yes .... ☐ 1
                   No .... [SKIP TO Q186] ☐ 2
                                          Don't Know [SKIP TO Q186] ☐ 7
                                             Refused [SKIP TO Q186] ☐ 9

DIET138A. What is the medical condition that requires a special diet?

           ____
                                                              Don't Know ☐ 77
                                                                 Refused ☐ 99

DIET139.   Do you want to lose weight?

                   Yes .... ☐ 1
                   No .... [SKIP TO Q188] ☐ 2
                                          Don't Know [SKIP TO Q188] ☐ 7
                                             Refused [SKIP TO Q188] ☐ 9

DIET140.   How are you planning or how would you plan to lose weight? Would you....   [IWER:
READ LIST AND GET RESPONSE FOR EACH]

		YES	NO	DK	Ref
DIET140A.	Reduce food intake	☐ 1	☐ 2	☐ 7	☐ 9
DIET140B.	Change the kinds of foods you eat	☐ 1	☐ 2	☐ 7	☐ 9
DIET140C.	Join a weight loss program	☐ 1	☐ 2	☐ 7	☐ 9
DIET140D.	Include advertised pills or food product(s) in your diet	☐ 1	☐ 2	☐ 7	☐ 9
DIET140E.	Increase physical activity	☐ 1	☐ 2	☐ 7	☐ 9
DIET140F.	Is there any other way?	☐ 1	☐ 2	☐ 7	☐ 9
DIET140G.	Other (Specify) ____________________________________				

DIET141. What time during a day do you typically eat the most– morning, noon, evening or does it vary?

     Morning .... ☐ 1

     Noon .... ☐ 2

     Evening .... ☐ 3

     It varies .... ☐ 4

     Don't Know ☐ 7

     Refused ☐ 9

DIET142. Do you snack between meals or late at night?

     Yes .... ☐ 1

     No .... **[SKIP TO Q190]** ☐ 2

     Don't Know [SKIP TO Q190] ☐ 7

     Refused [SKIP TO Q190] ☐ 9

DIET142A. What is the main reason you snack? **[ACCEPT ONLY 1]** _______________________

____

     Don't Know ☐ 77

     Refused ☐ 99

DIET143. Are you concerned about nutrition when selecting the food that you eat?

     Yes .... ☐ 1

     No .... ☐ 2

     Don't Know ☐ 7

     Refused ☐ 9

DIET144. Where do you get most of your information about what you should and should not eat?
     [IWER: PROBE FOR 2]____

____

     Don't Know ☐ 77

     Refused ☐ 99

DIET145. Do you ever read food labels?

     Yes .... ☐ 1

     No .... **[SKIP TO Q193]** ☐ 2

     Don't Know [SKIP TO Q193] ☐ 7

     Refused [SKIP TO Q193] ☐ 9

DIET145A. What do you look for when you read a food label? [PROBE FOR 2] _______________

____

                                                                              Don't Know ☐ 77
                                                                              Refused ☐ 99

DIET146. Which one of the following types of milk do you <u>usually</u> drink?
          [IWER: READ LIST AND ACCEPT ONE ANSWER]
                    Whole/Vitamin D .... ☐ 1
                    Low-fat or 2% .... ☐ 2
                    1% or 1/2% .... ☐ 3
                    Skim or Non-fat .... ☐ 4
                    Buttermilk .... ☐ 5
                    Powdered milk .... ☐ 6
                    Or do you not drink milk at all? .... ☐ 7
                                                                              Don't Know ☐ 77
                                                                              Refused ☐ 99

DIET147. Which one of the following do you <u>usually</u> use on bread, rolls, or other foods?
          [IWER: READ LIST AND ACCEPT ONE ANSWER]
                    Butter .... ☐ 1
                    Cream cheese .... ☐ 2
                    Regular margarine in a stick .... ☐ 3
                    Regular margarine in a tub .... ☐ 4
                    Diet margarine in a tub .... ☐ 5
                    Or do you not use any of these? .... ☐ 6
                                                                              Don't Know ☐ 77
                                                                              Refused ☐ 99

DIET148. Which one of the following types of salad dressings and/or mayonnaise do you use most often
          on salads and sandwiches? [IWER: READ LIST AND ACCEPT ONE ANSWER]
                    Regular .... ☐ 1
                    Low-fat .... ☐ 2
                    Nonfat .... ☐ 3
                    Or do you not use anything? .... ☐ 4
                                                                              Don't Know ☐ 7
                                                                              Refused ☐ 9

DIET149.   Which one of the following types of bread do you <u>usually</u> eat? [IWER: READ LIST AND ACCEPT ONE ANSWER. IF R SAYS 'WHEAT/GRAIN', PROBE "WOULD THAT BE 100% WHOLE ______?"; IF R NOT SURE, CHECK '2']

100% Whole Grain such as wheat, rye, pumpernickel or oatmeal . . . . □ 1

Grain bread which is not 100% whole . . . . □ 2

White bread . . . . □ 3

Or do you not eat bread? . . . . □ 4

Don't Know □ 7

Refused □ 9

DIET150.   Do you remove the skin before eating chicken or other poultry?

Yes . . . . □ 1

No . . . . □ 2

Don't eat chicken or other poultry . . . . □ 3

Don't Know □ 7

Refused □ 9

Now, we'd like to ask you some questions regarding the specific things that you ate last week.

DIET151.   How many times did you eat hot dogs, lunch meats such as bologna, bacon, sausage or pepperoni in the last week? . . . . □□

Don't Know □ 77

Refused □ 99

DIET152.   How many times did you eat red meat such as hamburgers, other ground beef dishes, steaks, or roasts in the last week? . . . . □□

Don't Know □ 77

Refused □ 99

DIET153.   How many times did you eat pork, such as chops, ribs or pork roasts in the last week? □□

Don't Know □ 77

Refused □ 99

DIET154.   How many times did you eat chicken or other poultry that was <u>not</u> fried in the last week?

□□

Don't Know □ 77

Refused □ 99

DIET155.   How many times did you eat fish or seafood that was **not** fried in the last

            week? .... ☐☐

                                                                    Don't Know ☐ 77
                                                                       Refused ☐ 99

DIET156.   How many times did you eat **fried** chicken or **fried** fish in the last week? .... ☐☐

                                                                    Don't Know ☐ 77
                                                                       Refused ☐ 99

DIET157.   Not counting fat-free cheese, how many times did you eat cheese in the last week including

            pizza, cheese slices on sandwiches or cheese as snacks? .... ☐☐

                                                                    Don't Know ☐ 77
                                                                       Refused ☐ 99

DIET158.   Not including green beans, how many times did you eat beans, spilt peas, or lentils such as
            baked beans, lima beans, kidney beans, chili beans, pintos, or other dishes with beans in the

            last week? .... ☐☐

                                                                    Don't Know ☐ 77
                                                                       Refused ☐ 99

DIET159.   During the past week, did you typically eat breakfast?
            Yes .... ☐ 1
            No .... [SKIP TO Q210] ☐ 2
                                                                    Don't Know ☐ 7
                                                                       Refused ☐ 9

DIET160.   During this past week, what did your breakfast <u>usually</u> consist of? [PROBE FOR 2]

            ____

            ____

                                                                    Don't Know ☐☐ 77
                                                                       Refused ☐☐ 99

DIET161.   How many times this past week did you eat at a fast food restaurant? .... ☐☐

                                                                    Don't Know ☐ 77
                                                                       Refused ☐ 99

DIET162.	If 1 serving is equal to 1 full cup of raw vegetables/salad or 1/2 cup cooked vegetable, thinking of all meals and snacks, how many servings of vegetables do you eat in an average day? . . . .

Don't Know ☐ 77
Refused ☐ 99

DIET163.	If 1 serving is equal to 1 full cup of cut fruit, 1 whole piece of fruit, or 1/2 cup fruit	juice, how many servings of fruit or fruit juice do you have in an average day? . . . .

Don't Know ☐ 77
Refused ☐ 99

DIET164.	Which of the following mostly determines your choice of fruits and vegetables you eat?

Cost . . . . ☐ 1
Availability . . . . ☐ 2
Taste . . . . ☐ 3
Nutrition . . . . ☐ 4
Or is there something else? ____

Don't Know ☐ 77
Refused ☐ 99

DIET165.	Excluding frozen yogurt, how many glasses or full cups of milk or yogurt do you <u>usually</u> have in an average day? . . . .

Don't Know ☐ 77
Refused ☐ 99

DIET166.	Do you see yourself as more concerned about health and nutrition now as opposed to one year ago?

Yes . . . . ☐ 1
No . . . . ☐ 2

Don't Know ☐ 7
Refused ☐ 9

DIET167.   In the past year, have you made any major changes in what you eat or drink?

Yes .... ☐ 1

No .... [SKIP TO Q215] ☐ 2

Don't Know [SKIP TO Q215] ☐ 7

Refused [SKIP TO Q215] ☐ 9

DIET167A.   What was your main reason for changing your eating pattern? [ACCEPT ONLY 1]

____

Don't Know ☐ 77

Refused ☐ 99

DIET168.   The United States Department of Agriculture and the Department of Health and Human
            Services have established Dietary guidelines in a education tool called the "Food Pyramid".
            Have you heard of the Food Pyramid?

Yes .... ☐ 1

No .... ☐ 2

Don't Know ☐ 7

Refused ☐ 9

DIET169.   The Food Pyramid divides foods into 6 food groups each having a recommended number of
            daily servings. Could you tell me how many servings the USDA recommends for: [IWER:
            READ LIST AND GET ANSWER FOR EACH. EITHER A RANGE OR A SPECIFIC
            NUMBER IS ACCEPTABLE.]

OF SERVINGS

D169A.   **Meat, Fish, Poultry, and Beans**____

Don't Know ☐ 77

Refused ☐ 99

D169B.   **Fruit**____

Don't Know ☐ 77

Refused ☐ 99

D169C.   **Milk, Yogurt, and Cheese**____

Don't Know ☐ 77

Refused ☐ 99

D169D.   **Fats and Sweets**____

Don't Know ☐ 77

Refused ☐ 99

D169E. **Grains (including breads, pasta, rice, and cereal)**______________________

Don't Know ☐ 77

Refused ☐ 99

D169F. **Vegetables**______________________________________

Don't Know ☐ 77

Refused ☐ 99

Before we close, I have just a few remaining questions:

DIET170. What is your approximate height?______________ **TOTAL INCHES** (CODER) ☐☐

Don't Know ☐ 777

Refused ☐ 999

DIET171. What is your approximate weight?______________ **TOTAL POUNDS** (CODER) ☐☐☐

Don't Know ☐ 777

Refused ☐ 999

CRACE. Of what race do you consider yourself? **[DO NOT READ CATEGORIES]**

White/Caucasian . . . . ☐ 1

Chicano/Mexican/Hispanic . . . . ☐ 2

Black/African American . . . . ☐ 3

American Indian/Native American . . . . ☐ 4

Asian . . . . ☐ 5

Other race (Specify) ________________________________

Don't Know ☐ 77

Refused ☐ 99

CINC1. Is your total household income more than $30,000 or less than $30,000 a year?

$30,000 or more .... [GO TO CINC2] ☐ 1

Less than $30,000 .... [GO TO CINC3] ☐ 2

Don't Know [SKIP TO CLOSING STATEMENT] ☐ 7

Refused [SKIP TO CLOSING STATEMENT] ☐ 9

CINC2. Lastly, I am going to mention a number of income categories. When I mention the category which describes your total household income in the last 12 months, please stop me.

$30,000 to less than $40,000 .... ☐ 1

$40,000 to less than $50,000 .... ☐ 2

$50,000 to less than $60,000 .... ☐ 3

$60,000 to less than $70,000 .... ☐ 4

$70,000 to less than $80,000 .... ☐ 5

$80,000 or more .... ☐ 6

Don't Know ☐ 7

Refused ☐ 9

[SKIP TO CLOSING STATEMENT]

CINC3. Lastly, I am going to mention a number of income categories. When I mention the category which describes your total household income in the last 12 months, please stop me.

Less than $5,000 .... ☐ 1

$5,000 to less than $10,000 .... ☐ 2

$10,000 to less than $15,000 .... ☐ 3

$15,000 to less than $20,000 .... ☐ 4

$20,000 to less than $25,000 .... ☐ 5

$25,000 to less than $30,000 .... ☐ 6

Don't Know ☐ 7

Refused ☐ 9

That's all the questions I have for you. Thank you very much for your time and cooperation.

Have a good _____________.

Name Index

Subject Index